The New Sartre

THE NEW SARTRE

Explorations in Postmodernism

NIK FARRELL FOX

continuum
NEW YORK • LONDON

Continuum

The Tower Building, 11 York Road, London SE1 7NX
370 Lexington Avenue, New York, NY 10017-6503

First published 2003

British Library Cataloguing-in-Publication Data

A catalogue record for this book is available from the British Library

ISBN 0-8264-6183-2 (hardback)
  0-8264-6184-0 (paperback)

Typeset by Aarontype Limited, Easton, Bristol
Printed and bound in Great Britain by The Bath Press, Bath

Contents

Preface

This book emerged gradually over a number of years and sprang from a deep fascination with the work of Sartre and Foucault. As I steeped myself in the nuances, concerns, evolutions and intricacies of each, it struck me more and more that there was a great deal in common between them in spite of the polemic between structuralism and humanism that conscripted them into opposing warring camps in France in the 1960s. This soon led me to broaden my enquiry to other post-structuralist philosophers such as Derrida and Deleuze where again I found significant areas of overlap that unite them with Sartre alongside the oft-repeated differences that separate them. As the French post-structuralists are all linked so closely to the postmodern ethos, it seemed like a natural extension to somehow bring Sartre into the 'postmodern equation' in a move that would recast his traditional image and bring attention to the contemporary resonance of his philosophical project and critical spirit.

Although I endeavour in this book to provide a systematic and comprehensive overview of Sartre's philosophical work, particular emphasis is given to his two main theoretical texts, *Being and Nothingness* and *The Critique of Dialectical Reason* (vol. 1), as they contain the fullest and most explicit expression of his philosophical viewpoint. However, I also refer to Sartre's other key theoretical texts, such as *Anti-Semite and Jew*, *Words*, the *Cahiers* and *Transcendence of the Ego*, as well as to his political essays, existential biographies and interviews he gave in the 1970s, in an attempt to trace the full trajectory and evolution of his thought from the 1930s to his death in 1980.

Similarly, although I will refer to some elements of structuralism, my main focus is on the French post-structuralists (Foucault, Derrida, Deleuze and Guattari, Baudrillard, Lyotard) as postmodernism is much more ostensibly and directly linked to these thinkers than to their structuralist counterparts (Lévi-Strauss, Lacan, Althusser) whose theoretical quest for objectivity and scientific truth places them much closer to the modernist paradigm. Among the post-structuralists, greater emphasis is given to Foucault and Baudrillard as their work can generally be seen as paradigmatic of the distinction between Affirmative postmodernism (Foucault) and Sceptical postmodernism (Baudrillard) which this book employs throughout.

Inevitably, in a project of this scope, there are certain omissions that may disappoint the reader. One may notice, for instance, that there is only scant reference to Sartre's early work on the imagination or to his novels and plays. Although his famous literary texts such as *No Exit* and *Nausea* are bursting with philosophical themes, ascertaining how the views of his characters actually represent his own, is not straightforward. Similarly, I make only passing reference to those who had an important influence on the evolution of Sartre's thought, such as Simone de Beauvoir, Maurice Merleau-Ponty and Martin Heidegger. Extensive and scholarly studies that examine Sartre's relation to these thinkers have already been undertaken and including them in detail would inevitably have meant sacrificing depth on the French post-structuralists.

Acknowledgements

I would like to acknowledge and extend my gratitude especially to Mike Scriven for his initial support and enthusiasm, but also to Christina Howells, Colin Davis, Ben O'Donohoe, William McBride and all others who have made valuable comments on some version of the text. Thanks also to Tristan Palmer at Continuum for all his efforts and support.

Finally, my deepest gratitude goes to my family, young and old, whose patience, warmth and love nourished my spirit throughout and made this possible.

Notes on the Text

The following abbreviations are used in the text to designate those works by Sartre most frequently cited or referred to:

BN   *Being and Nothingness: An Essay in Phenomenological Ontology*, tran. H. Barnes, New York: Philosophical Library, 1956.

CDR   *Critique of Dialectical Reason*, Volume 1 *Theory of Practical Ensembles*, tran. A. Sheridan-Smith, London: New Left Books, 1976.

SM   *Search for a Method*, tran. H. Barnes, London: Vintage Books, 1968.

Au renardeau

Introduction

> Even after death our acts pursuè us. We survive ourselves in them, even when they develop in opposite directions that we would not have wanted. (Sartre in Contat and Rybalka 1970, 256)

> for every thought one must expect a strange tomorrow. (Baudrillard, 1987, 99)

In the eyes of many, Jean-Paul Sartre was the foremost intellectual of the twentieth century, a master thinker of freedom whose diverse literary talents earned him notoriety as a philosopher, playwright, novelist and polemicist. And yet, Sartre is often seen as a philosopher of a world that has passed, a child and relic of modernity whose voice rang out amidst the alienations and horrors of the twentieth century but which is now scarcely detectable in the soundwaves of our contemporary postmodern condition. After all, history has it that the Sartrean corpse was laid to rest not only in the cemetery at Montparnasse upon his death in April 1980, but also twenty years or so earlier when a (post-)structuralist revolt organized by Foucault, Derrida and others overthrew the monarchical Sartrean regime and buried its humanist entrails in the ground.

In some respects, it is not altogether unsurprising that standard interpretations have cited Sartrean existentialism as the principal target for the (post-)structuralist revolution of the 1960s and 1970s. An initial sense of hostility between Sartre and the (post-)structuralists found expression in a series of polemical exchanges that took place in the 1960s between Sartre and Lévi-Strauss, Foucault and others in which Sartre was criticized for relying on a humanist and idealist theory of the subject and, in turn, criticized (post-)structuralism for dissolving human freedom by holding history hostage to the play of impersonal forces. As Foucault describes it, the (post-)structuralist attack on Sartre arose 'from a dissatisfaction with the phenomenological theory of the subject' and 'involved different escapades, subterfuges, breakthroughs . . . in the direction of linguistics, psychoanalysis or Nietzsche' (in Raulet, 1983, 199). It was a matter, as he states elsewhere, 'of calling this theme of the subject into question once again, that great fundamental postulate which French philosophy, from Descartes until our own time, had never abandoned' (Foucault, 1991, 56).

This polemic between Sartre and Foucault perhaps reached its greatest point of intensity in 1966 when, in an article in *La Quinzaine Littéraire*, Foucault identified Sartre's philosophy with a bygone era, cursorily dismissing Sartre and Merleau-Ponty as 'courageous and generous men' who were animated by a spirit that had passed from the intellectual scene. In response, Sartre acknowledged the importance of *Les Mots et les choses* but criticized Foucault for avoiding the question of history (i.e. how one episteme is supplanted by another), arguing that Foucault effectively 'replace[s] movies with a magic lantern, movement with a sequence of immobile images'.[1]

Since Sartre's death in 1980, however, interpretations of his work have begun to probe the underbelly of this standard account. In recent years the phenomenon of 'the new Sartre' has gradually been emerging out of the ashes of his philosophical *œuvre* which points to a fundamental reappraisal of Sartre's work in its relation to post-structuralism and, in a wider sense, to postmodernism.[2] In Christina Howells' words, this idea of 'the new Sartre' presents him

> as a figure whose diversity was far from being mastered, who could not, without distortion or impoverishment, be identified with the 'classical existentialism' of the 1940s, and whose relationship to Structuralism and Post-Structuralism, as well as to psychoanalysis, Marxism, and literary theory, was far more complex than ha[s] generally been supposed. (1992, 1)

In this respect, traditional accounts of post-war intellectual history in France can be said to have pitted Sartre as a theoretical adversary to (post-)structuralists[3] such as Foucault, Lacan, Deleuze and Derrida far too readily. Moreover, standard interpretations of Sartre's work can be seen to rely too heavily on certain themes or on particular passages in his 'classical existentialist' works of the 1940s to the serious neglect of other elements in his work of this period, and indeed, in the wider trajectory of his work as a whole. Howells makes the further claim that since Sartre's two main works of philosophy, BN and CDR, pre-date the main wave of (post-)structuralist texts in the 1960s, 1970s and 1980s, they can be seen in effect to prefigure many key (post-)structuralist themes such as

> the decentred subject, the rejection of a metaphysics of presence, the critique of bourgeois humanism and individualism, the concept of the reader as producer of the text's multiple meanings, the recognition of language and thought structures as masters rather than mastered in most acts of discourse and thinking, [and] a materialist philosophy of history as detotalized and fragmented. (1992, 2)

These themes, she argues, are not 'the inventions of Lacan, Foucault, Lévi-Strauss and Derrida', but can 'be found in Sartre's later works' and are 'present from the outset' in even his early work which dates from *Transcendence of the Ego* in 1936 (1992, 2). Taken together, they serve to contradict the simple identification of Sartre with his usual image of a classical intellectual steeped in a Cartesian tradition of modern philosophy which is, by implication, a form of philosophy diametrically opposed to the postmodernizing strategies of the post-structuralists.

Until now, Sartre has been a marginal and mainly absent figure in discussions of postmodernism which have tended to focus upon critiques of modernism put forward by the French post-structuralists such as Michel Foucault, Gilles Deleuze, Félix Guattari, Jean-François Lyotard, Jacques Derrida and Jean Baudrillard. When he is included, it is usually as no more than the target for these critiques. My aim in this book is to bring Sartre in from the margins and, for the first time, to place him at the focal centre of the postmodern debate through a *systematic* analysis which will trace the strands of opposition and convergence between Sartre's work and post-structuralist theory across a broad range of study. This will involve piecing together suggestions made by others in essays and articles into an integrated and comprehensive overview that will attempt to assemble a full and faithful picture of Sartre's philosophy from the 1930s to his death in 1980. In the process, I endeavour to expand the idea of 'the new Sartre' into one that recasts his popular image from an archetypal and classical modernist thinker to one who shares a complex and multifaceted relationship to the postmodern ethos. This will, I hope, have the further effect of highlighting the contemporary relevance and value of Sartre's work as a kind of critical searchlight that helps to cut through the mist of our present postmodern condition. Much of this value, I argue, derives from the way in which Sartre's work occupies a transitional space between modernist and postmodernist categories, integrating elements of each into a constellated and synthetic whole. Sometimes this has the effect of catapulting the Sartrean system into contradiction and antinomy but for the most part it serves to form it as a window through which we are better placed to view and to reflect upon the inadequacies and the revelations of postmodernist theory and its trenchant critique of modernity.

In this respect, one can cite Roland Barthes who has located the special value of Sartre's work in its 'divided' or 'transitional' nature.[4] In an interview in 1976 with Jacques Chancel, Barthes put forward the view that Sartre can be seen as the exemplary intellectual of his period due to the fact that he was situated at the crossroads of two cultures — at the point of division between the disintegration of the old and the birth of the new. This was evident in the way that Sartre managed to straddle both pre-war and post-war ideological and political currents in France, thus marking him out, according to Barthes, as a uniquely important transitional figure. As we will see throughout this book, Sartre's philosophy can be situated in a transitional space that straddles the divide and creates a sometimes uneasy tension between a postmodern sense of despair, plurality, fragmentation and indeterminacy and a modernist longing for comprehension, meaning, constructivism and totality.

In recent years, the idea of postmodernism has dominated academic dialogue in the humanities and the social sciences. Although the term 'postmodernism' has long been in use in one form or another to describe developments in literary theory, architecture and art which attack the dominant modernist paradigm, it has become associated more recently with theories of cultural, political, economic and philosophical change, taking its inspiration from critiques of modernist theory found in the work of the French post-structuralists.[5] As we will see, however, the identification of postmodernism with post-structuralism is not always straightforward or precise. In the work of some postmodernists like Foucault and Deleuze, for example, it is possible to find a complex blend of pre-modern, modern and postmodern perspectives and thus it is misleading to describe them as postmodernists *tout court*. Added to these difficulties is the fact that postmodernists tend to retreat from the label 'postmodern' since they sense it promotes a singular view of reality that encourages closure and denies complexity. Moreover, some postmodernists like Foucault and Lyotard shift their focus and theoretical approach quite considerably during the course of their work and move away from postmodernist concerns to more overtly modernist ones like the status of the subject and the Enlightenment (Foucault) or the concept of justice (Lyotard) in their later work. This means that, in general, most post-structuralists have been anxious to avoid any description of their work as 'postmodernist'. This is particularly apposite in the case of Baudrillard who by the end of the 1980s was heralded as 'the high priest of postmodernism' and yet who stated openly 'I have nothing to do with postmodernism' (in Gane, 1991, 46–7). To complicate matters further, the terms 'modern' and 'postmodern' have been so widely applied that their meaning, as Bernstein notes, has become 'vague, ambiguous, and slippery'. This is particularly so with 'postmodernism' which signifies a prevailing mood that is 'amorphous, elusive, protean ... difficult to pin down and characterise', but which 'nevertheless exerts a powerful influence ... that radically calls into question entrenched ways of thinking, acting, and feeling' (1993, 205, 204).

In spite of these considerations, however, it is possible to draw definite parallels between post-structuralism and postmodernism as well as to identify general determinate features that demarcate the modern from the postmodern. Although post-structuralism and postmodernism are not identical, in so much as postmodernists are orientated more towards cultural critique whereas post-structuralists focus on method and epistemological matters, they do overlap considerably, the major difference being one of emphasis more than substance. To help distinguish between a variety of attitudes towards modernity found in the works of the post-structuralists, in this book I make use of a general distinction between 'Affirmative' and 'Sceptical' forms of postmodernism.[6] Although this distinction is not always clear-cut (some thinkers, like Foucault, can be interpreted either as 'Affirmative' or

'Sceptical' according to the emphasis of a particular text), it does help us to distinguish between postmodernists who generally seek to refashion or to reconstruct affirmative modernist notions such as individual agency and political progress and those, like Baudrillard, who view affirmative projects such as Guattari's model of 'molecular revolution' or Foucault's idea of 'resistance to power' as 'archaic, regressive or nostalgic' (Baudrillard, 1983a, 60). As we will see, Sartre is significantly closer to Affirmative forms of postmodernism like Foucault's than he is to the Sceptical form practised by Baudrillard.

In general terms, it is the radical questioning or 'unmaking' of modern assumptions and modes of understanding that, as Ihab Hassan points out, can be said to define the postmodern movement:

> It is an antinomian moment that assumes a vast unmasking of the Western mind – what Michel Foucault might call the postmodern *episteme*. I say 'unmasking', though other terms are now *de rigueur*: for instance, deconstruction, decentering, disappearance, demystification, discontinuity, *différance*, dispersion etc. Such terms express an ontological rejection of the traditional full subject, the *Cogito* of Western philosophy. They express, too, an epistemological obsession with fragments, and a corresponding commitment to minorities in politics, sex and language. To think well, to feel well, to act well, to read well according to the *episteme* of unmasking, is to refuse the tyranny of wholes: totalization in human endeavour is potentially totalitarian. (1987, 37)

For the purposes of this book, I identify three main areas of inquiry in which it is possible to discern points of difference that separate modernist and postmodernist approaches:

1. Against the modernist idea of a rational, humanist, unified and autonomous *subject*, postmodernists call for a conception of the subject as socially and linguistically decentred, fragmented and multiple.
2. In reaction to modernist assumptions of *social* and *historical* coherence, linearity and causality, as well as to its macro-theoretical, universalizing and totalizing claims, postmodernists stress 'microtheory', relativism, indeterminacy, detotalization and multiplicity.

3. In opposition to modernist forms of *political* understanding and organization (i.e. Marxism and liberalism), postmodernists call for new
   forms of political life which stress plurality, locality and difference.
   Where modern political strategies focus centrally upon (macro)
   issues of political economy and the state, postmodernists concentrate
   instead on 'superstructural' concerns relating to identity, culture and
   the realm of everyday life.

Throughout this book I examine these three general areas of difference
between modernist theory and postmodernist critique as they relate to
Sartre's philosophy and to the work of the French post-structuralists.

In Chapter 1 I begin by looking at Sartre's approach to the subject,
tracing the development from the radically free consciousness of *BN* to
the more 'encumbered' subject of his later work, before considering the
deconstruction of the subject undertaken by (post-)structuralists in the
1960s and 1970s. Then I compare Sartre's theory of the subject with
post-structuralist approaches to the subject (put forward by Foucault
and Deleuze and Guattari) and examine the common features and similarities between the two. In particular, I argue that Sartre's idea of a
contingent, non-essential subject (which he argues for consistently
throughout his work) has much in common with, and indeed prefigures,
the decentred subject theorized by post-structuralists and postmodernists. In the final section I consider the critical implications of Sartrean
and postmodernist theories of the subject, assessing both their positive critical value as well as their theoretical limitations and closures.
In regard to the former, I highlight the ways in which the Sartrean and
postmodernist subject improves upon the praxis-centric or instrumental
view of the subject that dominates the modernist outlook. On a less
positive note, I criticize Sartrean and postmodernist theorizations of
the subject for failing to give sufficient recognition to the importance
of social contexts and other people in projects of self-development. As a
result both tend, I argue, to provide only a 'thin' and rather monadic
conception of individuality.

In Chapter 2 I begin by looking at Sartre's social theory in *BN* and how
he set about revising it subsequently in the *CDR*. After examining the key
elements of Sartre's conceptual apparatus in the *CDR* (praxis/inertia, the
practico-inert, the fused/serial group, totalization, dialectical reason,

the progressive-regressive method), I outline the social theory of post-modernism by looking in particular at the genealogical approach of Foucault and the semiological theory of Baudrillard. Then I compare Sartrean and postmodernist socio-historical theory, focusing mainly on their respective critiques of Marxist economism and teleology. These critiques, I argue, give us a view of history based on the notion of *contingency* that rallies against Enlightenment conceptions of history as a process of linearity and progress. Moreover, both extend critical analysis beyond narrow reductionisms of the social field to uncover sources of alienation and domination that exist beyond the sphere of political economy. In the final section I critically assess Sartrean and postmodernist approaches, highlighting both the ways in which they expand our understanding of society and history as well as some of the difficulties that arise from within their general theoretical frameworks.

Political theory and practice are the focus of Chapter 3 where I begin by tracing the development of Sartre's political outlook from the detached, individualist form of anarchism which characterized his political thinking in the 1930s to his committed 'gauchiste' perspective of the 1970s. This development is seen through the varying attitudes Sartre adopts towards Marxism and the French Communist Party (PCF) through the course of his life which change from early indifference in the 1930s to uncritical support in the early 1950s and finally to disillusionment and apostasy in the 1970s. Then I examine this revolt against traditional Marxist theory and political practice by looking at the politics of postmodernism through the events of May 1968 in France which, I argue, represent an important transition point in the formation of a new political practice which contrasts markedly with the labour-centric, centralizing, Party-based strategies of modern (Marxo-liberal) politics. In the final section I critically examine Sartrean and postmodern political theory using criticisms made of Foucault's postmodern political search for self-invention by Alex Callinicos (1989) as a means of assessing the opposition between modern macro-politics and postmodern micro-politics. I go on to examine the ways in which Sartre's political theory reproduces some of the difficulties in both modern and postmodern perspectives as well as the more positive ways in which it helps to resolve this critical opposition.

Finally, in Chapter 4 I draw together the conclusions and critical observations of the previous three chapters into a systematic overview that assesses the interplay and relative influence of the modern and the postmodern in Sartre's work and how this impacts upon the growing phenomenon of 'the new Sartre'. Beyond this, I outline the contemporary relevance and value of Sartre's work as a critical resource through which to clarify and to evaluate the current discourse of postmodernism.

1

The Question of the Subject

Our entire science still lies under the misleading influence of
language and has not disposed of that little changeling, the
'subject'. (Nietzsche, 1967, 179)

I don't want to be integrated, nor do I want my lovely red
blood to fatten up that lymphatic beast: I won't be so silly as
to call myself an 'antihumanist'. I am not a humanist, that's
all. (Roquentin in Sartre, 1966a, 118)

If, as Alfred North Whitehead famously remarked, the history of western
philosophy can be read as a footnote to Plato, then much the same can be
said of modern French philosophy and René Descartes. The Cartesian
subject founded on the certainty of the cogito is the main reference point
and critical target for Sartrean and post-structuralist theorizations of
the subject.

In his famous 'method of doubt' that he outlines in *Meditations on First
Philosophy*, Descartes argues for a disjunctive or dualistic picture of self
and world. In doubting the existence of the outside world which,
Descartes imagines, might be the product of the sleight-of-hand of an evil
demon (*malin génie*), one thing alone is certain – that is, my own
existence. My most sceptical doubt, he argues, is itself an act of thinking
that proves my existence – *cogito ergo sum* (I think therefore I am). From
this basic starting point of an indubitable thinking subject, Descartes
proceeds to sketch a dualistic philosophy that founds a binarist logic
which lies at the heart of the antinomies of modern western philosophy
(subject/object, reason/emotion, body/soul, self/world, freedom/neces-
sity). All the French post-structuralists without exception direct their
critical venom towards this binarist system of reasoning that emerges
from the thinking and disengaged Cartesian subject. As we will see,

Sartre's relation to the Cartesian cogito is a complex one, veering in his early work between repudiation and repetition.

The Sartrean subject

The existential pour-soi

Sartre's early phenomenological and existentialist work (dating from *The Transcendence of the Ego* (1936) to *Being and Nothingness* (1943)) is commonly seen as a prime example of the (modern) humanist tradition in French philosophy which (post-)structuralists relentlessly attacked in the 1960s, putting forward their own form of theoretical anti-humanism as a corrective. Sartre's theory of the subject (as *pour-soi*) in *BN* has been interpreted in this light as an essentially Cartesian construct divorced from material, social, historical and linguistic configuration. In particular, it was Sartre's popular conception of absolute freedom in *BN* which his detractors criticized most of all, arguing that he effectively committed the cardinal sin of idealism by reducing the impact of circumstance and situation to no more than a function of individual freedom. As Sartre states:

> What we call freedom is impossible to distinguish from the being of 'human reality'. Man does not exist first in order to be free subsequently; there is no difference between the being of a man and his being free. (*BN*, 30)

> Man cannot be sometimes a slave and sometimes free; he is wholly and forever free or he is not free at all. (*BN*, 516)

In *BN* Sartre insists that all situations are equally transcendable by the individual; however much they impact upon us, we are always free, by dissolving their significance, to sidestep or 'nihilate' the force of this impact:

> There is no privileged situation. We mean by this that there is no situation in which the given would crush beneath its weight the freedom which constitutes it as such – and that conversely there is no situation in which the for-itself would be more free than others. (*BN*, 549)

Even in the deepest, darkest abysses of human impotence and suffering, Sartre maintains, 'the executioner's tools cannot dispense us from being free' (*BN*, 587). Whether I am in the grip of torture or in a state of complete and abject servitude, this impacts on me only to the extent that I 'embrace' this within my project and attach significance to it. In the case of the slave, for instance, 'if . . . he chooses to revolt, slavery, far from being first an obstacle to this revolt, takes its meaning and its coefficient of adversity only from this revolt' (*BN*, 635). Thus, for Sartre, the weight of circumstance and objective conditions that situations bring to bear on consciousness do not dissolve its freedom but form the very basis of that freedom: 'There can be a for-itself only as engaged in a resisting world. Outside of this engagement the notions of freedom, of determinism, of necessity lose all meaning' (*BN*, 621).

Whatever situation I am born or thrust into, this simply defines the particular terrain in which I am free to determine the meaning of my life (*BN*, 245–6). According to Sartre, it is only the constitutive power of the individual project which causes there to be 'an organization of things in situation' (*BN*, 509). One example he uses to illustrate this is the prospect of being faced with a steep mountain slope. The 'brute given' of the mountain face (its slipperiness, inaccessibility, the severity of its contours, etc.) constitutes what Sartre calls the 'coefficient of adversity in things' (*BN*, 482). This we cannot change of course (in the immediate term at least), but, he insists, this forms a precondition rather than a limit on freedom since freedom consists in transcending the 'given'. If I am an artist contemplating the aesthetic form of the mountain instead of a climber practically orientated towards it, my project would screen its unscalability and effectively put this aspect 'out of circulation': 'the crag is not revealed as scalable or unscalable; it is manifested as beautiful or ugly' (*BN*, 488).

The general term Sartre uses to describe the weight of our social and material configuration is what he calls *facticity*. This involves our being thrown into a world that pre-exists us and into a web of situations that are not all of our choosing. As he makes clear in *BN*, however, facticity encroaches upon us only to the extent that we integrate it into our personal project – I am always able to 'disengage myself from the world where I had been engaged' (*BN*, 39). The language that I speak, the historical situation of my race and culture, my gender, my childhood experiences are viewed in this light as no more than transient surface aspects of me which I can choose to exclude from my personal project and thus can withdraw from. Even the existence of a rigid class structure in which one class is systematically oppressed by the other has, says Sartre, merely 'significative value' for the individual class member (*BN*, 421).

Not surprisingly, Sartre's attachment to the 'hegemony of the project' in *BN* drew strong criticism from (neo-)Marxist quarters. In his essay on Sartre's existentialism first published in 1948, Herbert Marcuse criticizes Sartre's conception of the *pour-soi* as a nihilating consciousness for sharing a deep affinity with the egoic individual of classical liberalism since they both appear, he argues, 'with all the attributes of absolute autonomy' (1983, 174). This gives rise ultimately to a form of political quietism since, as we are inviolably and ubiquitously free, there seems little need or point in acting to change or to improve the social conditions in which we live. As Sartre himself states: 'It is therefore senseless to think of complaining since nothing foreign has decided what we feel, what we live, or what we are' (*BN*, 617).

The Sartrean *pour-soi* is viewed in this light by Marcuse as a Cartesian and Lutheran construct whose freedom 'remains the same before, during, and after the totalitarian enslavement of man' (1983, 162). Like Descartes' ghostly individual, the *pour-soi* remains untouched by its material immersion in a cruel, desperate, oppressive or pressing world:

> 'To be free' does not mean, 'to obtain what one has wished', but rather, 'by oneself to determine to wish' (in the broad sense of choosing). In other words success is not at all important to freedom. (*BN*, 483)

It was this form of Cartesian logic underpinning Sartre's conception of absolute freedom that prompted Claude Lévi-Strauss to declare in *La Pensée sauvage* that the Sartrean subject is essentially 'the prisoner of the Cogito' (1966, 249). Impermeable and fully autonomous, the *pour-soi* secretes a Cartesian resin that acts to seal it off from the world outside, cocoon-like in the inner recesses of the individual cogito from which it builds its own meanings and constructs its reality. Indeed, Sartre himself confirms this characterization in *BN* when he argues for the theoretical primacy of the cogito, describing it unequivocally as 'the sole secure point of departure' (*BN*, 244).

Beneath this Cartesian surface of *BN* there were, however, significant undercurrents which distanced this work from a simple idealism and which foreshadowed a more encumbered conception of the subject that Sartre later sketched out in the *CDR*. Sartre's attachment to the Cartesian cogito in his early work is never a complete or exhaustive one. To begin with, his stated theoretical aim in *BN* was not to reiterate Cartesianism but instead to 'provide a philosophical foundation for realism . . . In other words, how to give man both his autonomy and his reality among real objects, avoiding idealism without lapsing into mechanistic materialism' (1969, 46). Although Sartre clearly gives undue theoretical weight to the side of the subject in his early work, the emphasis of radical separation between subject and object is generally overridden by the notion of co-dependence. Consciousness is seen in this way by Sartre as essentially *relative* – 'from the start it refers to the thing' (*BN*, 618) and is 'born supported by a being which is not itself' (*BN*, lxi): 'the for-itself without the in-itself is a kind of abstraction; it could not exist any more than a color could exist without form or sound without a pitch and timbre' (*BN*, 621).

Unlike Husserl, for instance, who 'shut himself up inside the Cogito' (*BN*, 734), Sartre sets out in *BN* to liberate intentionality from the confines of the cogito and to release it into the world in order to explore the concrete, that is 'man within the world in that specific union of man with the world' (*BN*, 3). Furthermore, there are instances in *BN* where Sartre begins to consider more deeply the force of circumstance and raise the possibility that the *pour-soi* is not the impermeable sanctum of freedom that he characterizes it as elsewhere. This is evident, for instance, on page 435 of *BN* where, describing the case of the factory workers in Lyon in 1830, Sartre declares a state of affairs for them in which facticity had encroached upon and effectively paralysed their freedom to such a degree that, for the individual worker, '[to] suffer and to be are one and the same for him':

> Their misfortunes do not appear to them habitual but rather *natural*: they *are*, that is all, and they constitute the workers' condition. They are not detached, they are not seen in a clear light, and consequently they are integrated by the worker with his being. (*BN*, 435)

The impermeability of the *pour-soi* is also cast into doubt by Sartre in *BN* when he considers the existence of others. To live in the world, he maintains, is to be 'haunted by my fellowman' and 'to find myself engaged in a world in which instrumental complexes can have a meaning which my free project has not first given them' (*BN*, 509–10). He concedes in this respect that the qualities others ascribe to us can constitute a determinant, factitious character:

> if my race or my physical appearance were only an image in the Other or the Other's appearance of me, we should soon have done with it; but we have seen that we are dealing with objective characteristics which define me. (*BN*, 581)

However, perhaps most significant of all in distancing Sartre from a simplified Cartesianism in *BN* are his concept of Bad Faith and the radical theory of subjectivity he advances that underpins it. Although Sartre's point of departure remains tied to certain Cartesian categories in *BN* – he confessed many years later in an interview that 'I consider myself a Cartesian philosopher, at least in *L'Être et le néant*' (1981b, 8) his idea of the *pour-soi* in many ways constituted a radical break from traditional French Idealism and its abstract view of the individual as a spiritual or immaterial essence divorced from concrete determinations.

Contra Husserl, Sartre argues that the 'I' of selfhood cannot be a substantial entity that sits behind my acts and thoughts, unifying them, but is itself the result of the synthetic unification of a pattern of actions: 'the ego is not the owner of consciousness, it is the object of consciousness' (1957, 97). Since the 'I' does not correspond to any kind of inner sanctum or to an original, pre-given subject, it must be *created* – we do this, according to Sartre, either by describing past acts under a certain description to which we impart the 'characteristics of identity, of purity, of permanence', or by reference to a particular, non-existing state of affairs, a future 'I' or 'ideal self' or original project – 'consciousness confronts its past and its future as facing a self which it is in the mode of not-being' (*BN*, 34). In this way, the 'I' can refer ambiguously to the past (character) or to the future (ideal self) – it is, as such, a *temporal construct*, a particular 'relation to being' (*BN*, 216) which is impermanent and fluid.

It is only when consciousness 'nihilates' itself, that is, takes a thetic, positional awareness of itself as an object, that the unity of the 'I' is constructed: 'negation is the cement which realizes this unity' (BN, 21).

In his lecture *Existentialism and Humanism* delivered at the Club Maintenant in Paris in October 1945, Sartre emphasizes that his philosophy in BN is at heart a 'humanist philosophy of action, of effort, of combat, of solidarity' and not, contrary to popular opinion, an invitation to people to dwell in 'the quietism of despair' (1966b, 39). Since we are 'nothing else but the sum of [our] actions', we are thus defined by and through our acts and cannot hide behind 'inwardness or potentia' (1966b, 41). Since consciousness is, he maintains, pure activity, it is a form of agency without substantiality which has nothing to be and everything to do. Sartre makes it clear in this respect that self-understanding arises not from private introspection, the deciphering of a self that stands behind or prior to the act (as in the Cartesian model), but by observing how we are reflected in the 'world of tasks' which constitutes 'the image of myself' (BN, 200). In this way, Sartre's existentialist subject diverges from the Cartesian subject in that it is constituted *outwardly* by its engagement and actions in the concrete world rather than *inwardly* within the private sanctum of the soul.

Sartre's general tendency to paint the subject in Cartesian colours is also obscured elsewhere in BN where he turns his attention to the ways in which freedom becomes alienated. This is most evident in his celebrated concept of *Bad Faith* (*mauvaise foi*) which plays a significant role in Sartre's existentialist narrative. As a synthetic construct of consciousness, the 'I' possesses for Sartre none of the noumenal certainty it had in the Idealist philosophies of Kant and Husserl. Since there is no essential character or eidetic pattern which the self conforms to, the apprehension that one must choose and create this self gives rise, he argues, to the 'anguish' of responsibility and the tendency to seek to dissolve the weight of this responsibility through Bad Faith – 'Anguish as the manifestation of freedom in the face of self means that man is always separated by a nothingness from his essence' (BN, 35).

Sartre's concept of Bad Faith can be seen to represent in general a movement away from a purely static and oppositional account of *pour-soi*/*en-soi* to a more dialectical or conjunctive approach in which he views human reality as *both* body and consciousness, materiality and transcendence. Bad Faith, Sartre argues, lies in the attempt to cancel out completely one of these dimensions through a form of self-deception or lying to oneself. Thus, to think of ourselves as pure transcendence in the Sartrean system is a prime act of Bad Faith.[1] This is illustrated in *BN* where Sartre presents a situation in which a woman is faced with the amorous advances of a man who takes her hand. According to Sartre:

> [s]he is profoundly aware of the desire which she inspires, but the desire cruel and naked would humiliate and horrify her ... We know what happens next; the young woman leaves her hand there but she *does not notice* because it happens by chance that she is at this moment all intellect. (*BN*, 55–6)

She is in Bad Faith, Sartre argues, because she tries to effect a counterfeit, Stoical flight to the realm of mere thoughts and pure consciousness by attempting to disown her body and to exist as 'all intellect'. Consciousness, Sartre insists, 'exists its body' (*BN*, 329) and is 'wholly body' (*BN*, 305) since the body is its 'center of reference' (*BN*, 326) in the material world of experience, action and engagement. Human reality is accordingly 'a useless passion' (*une passion inutile*), vacillating between *pour-soi* and *en-soi* (*BN*, 615), unable to fix itself completely to one of these dimensions which, in the throes of Bad Faith, is exactly what we attempt to do.

Thus, as Ronald Aronson notes, it is possible to discern 'two contrary impulses' in Sartre's early philosophy – 'one leading towards the world and the other away from it' (1980, 89). In popular images of Sartre's existentialism it is this latter impulse which is emphasized where the *pour-soi* is seen as absolutely free and able at any time to escape its facticity. However, as we have seen, Sartre breaks away from this in other places and moves towards a more dialectical understanding of subject and object in which the subject is engaged, immersed and permeable to the world, both transcendent and material. As we will see in the next section, this dialectical view of the subject as 'encumbered' through its factitious immersion in the world is steadily extended in Sartre's work subsequent to *BN* as he moves towards a more ostensibly Marxist and Freudian frame of reference.

The Encumbered Subject: the CDR *and beyond*

As Sartre states in his *War Diaries*, it was his mobilization in the war when he was seized by forces beyond his control that led initially to profound changes in his outlook: 'as for the little well-scrubbed atom I believed myself to be, powerful forces seized him, and sent him to the front with others without asking his opinion' (1974b, 24).

By the end of the war Sartre confessed that, in writing *BN*, he had not yet 'learned history' (in Archard, 1980, 33). The experience of Nazi occupation had inevitably alerted him to some of the shortcomings of his early conception of freedom. Remaining firmly embedded within individualist categories, his existentialist perspective could not explain how the inalienable freedom he had celebrated in *BN* had been eroded by the collective experience of Occupation. Sartre's so-called 'conversion' to Marxism in the *CDR* was his attempt to go beyond the limitations of his early philosophy in *BN* which, he later admitted, had resulted 'in the clear affirmation of the autonomy of thought' grounded in 'a rationalist philosophy of consciousness' (1969, 41–2).

In the post-war years before the publication of the *CDR* in 1961, Sartre began to modify his earlier conceptual foundations in *BN* in order to take account of the social and historical context of a freedom that was no longer absolute and inviolable, but now 'situated' and contextual. In *Anti-Semite and Jew*, published in 1946, for instance, he offers a distinction between 'freedom-in-consciousness' and 'freedom-in-situation', the latter requiring, according to Sartre, the freedom of others and a change in the 'social bases and structures of choice' (1965, 148–9). By 1952, the 'obscure constraints' of situation had hardened into determinants of historical necessity:

> The historical whole determines our powers at any given moment, it prescribes their limits in our field of action and our real future; it conditions our attitude toward the possible and the impossible, the real and the imaginary, what is and what should be, space and time . . . it is history which shows some exits and makes others cool their heels before closed doors. (1968, 80)

Sartre's philosophical conversion to Marxism in the *CDR* is regarded by some as marking a clear invalidation of his early philosophy of freedom in *BN*. In Warnock's view, for instance, his work in the *CDR* involves 'a deliberate rejection of the individual' (1965, 135), while for Levi the *CDR* is a treatise of 'crude materialism', guilty of 'the dogma of the serious' (1967, 243) which Sartre had earlier levelled at Marx in *BN*. Contrary to Warnock's criticism of Sartre, it will become clear throughout this study that the individual remains an integral foundation stone in his Marxist edifice. The vertiginously free subject of *BN* does lose its abstract sovereignty as Sartre inscribes it into the determinations of the material (practico-inert) field and into the network of collective groupings, but its essential capacity to go beyond immediate circumstances and, whatever its limitations are, to 'make something out of what is made of [it]' (1974a, 35) remains. Sartre's commitment to the individual is reflected, as we will see in Chapters 2 and 3, in his analysis of group life and in his theory of *Dialectical Nominalism*, as well as in the kind of political strategy his libertarian form of socialism points towards. We will see that, if anything, Sartre's commitment to individualism is too strong as it leads him (like many postmodernists) to restrict the positive scope of community in his work.

Moreover, although the force of materiality assumes a greater priority in the *CDR* than it does in *BN*, it was never Sartre's intention to simply dissolve subject into object in the form of a 'crude materialism'. His whole Marxist project was in fact aimed at restoring the 'subjective pole' of a Marxist theory which had become rigid and moribund in the hands of Stalinist orthodoxy, abandoning its true starting point of 'real, living men'. Sartre was not prepared to abandon his own voluntarist existentialist philosophy until the 'subjective dimension' it analysed had been incorporated into the Marxist explanatory framework: 'from the day that Marxist thought will have taken on the human dimension (that is, the existential project) as the foundation of anthropological knowledge, existentialism will no longer have any reason for being' (*SM*, 181).

In the *CDR* Sartre sets about reinterpreting his philosophical categories in *BN* by connecting them much more firmly to the material and social field. Thus, 'consciousness' in *BN* is reinterpreted as 'praxis' in the *CDR* while the idea of 'lack' is replaced by the notion of 'need' – where consciousness was seen in *BN* as propelled by its own lack,[2] in the *CDR* need is seen as the starting point of individual praxis: 'Everything is to be explained through need; need is the first totalising relation between the material being, man, and the material ensemble of which he is a part' (*CDR*, 80). This can be seen to mark an important transition in Sartre's work since it begins to explain how the actual state of the world can provide motivation for action. In *BN* consciousness is intentionally co-constituted with the world but able to integrate that world within any hermeneutical purview it chooses to encompass – in other words, consciousness is able to determine its own projected relation to the world. The category of need overcomes the difficulties which stem from the hegemony of the individual project in *BN* since it denotes a material relation with the world that is given independently of the rationalizing project. In this way, Sartre goes on to replace the idea of the individual project with that of totalization, defined as a conscious attempt 'to grasp the world from the front in a practical unveiling' (1977(8), 441) which now includes the socio-material field as a necessary aspect of its intelligibility – like the project it involves mapping a particular meaning onto the world but a meaning now constrained by the demands of material need and the exigencies of situation.

For Sartre, praxis is the human activity through which the individual overcomes need. Faced with hunger, for instance, he totalizes the material field before him as an opening onto a complex reality. His praxis involves unifying and reorganizing the transcendence of existing circumstances towards the practical field (see *CDR*, 310n.). It is only by working on and transforming matter that he can go beyond existing circumstances and overcome need. Like Marx, Sartre identifies praxis as a distinctly human activity involving purposeful, rational action towards a proposed solution of satisfying need. Since, Sartre maintains, it is a conscious, intentional activity, praxis involves a definite project, a 'movement of temporalization' in which action orientated towards the future totalizes a given field (*CDR*, 60–1).

In contrast to the concept of nihilation which Sartre employs in *BN*, however, praxis preserves what it totalizes and becomes itself an embodiment of the inert quality of the material world. In order to transform the material field the individual must introduce into himself features of that field and make of his body a tool. Thus in the course of praxis he undergoes a profound interior alteration taking on the qualities of an object. The living act of his praxis is in turn absorbed into matter and transformed into an inert material fact. Sartre describes praxis in this way as 'a passage from objective to objective through internalisation' (*SM*, 97). At the heart of praxis lies the totalizing project which,

> as the subjective surpassing of objectivity towards objectivity, and stretched between the objective conditions of the environment and the objective structures of the field of possibles, represents in itself the moving unity of subjectivity and objectivity, those cardinal determinants of activity. (*SM*, 97)

Materiality is viewed by Sartre in the *CDR* as the primary bond between the organism and its environment, but one that can be understood only in conjunction with human praxis. The concept of negation, so prominent in *BN*, is preserved in the *CDR* – 'it is through man that negation comes to man and to matter' (*CDR*, 83) – but is no longer detached from matter, eventually becoming absorbed into it and so in turn negated by matter. In the *CDR* materiality and praxis are dialectical co-ordinates, each contiguous to, and dependent on, the other. It is the presence of inorganic matter which makes praxis possible and in satisfying organic need, praxis finds itself subject to the laws of inorganic matter even as it negates and totalizes it (see *CDR*, 82). For Sartre, this circularity of praxis and matter always reveals a double element at work – 'objectification (or man working upon matter) and objectivity (or totalized matter working upon man)' (*CDR*, 284). A true dialectical understanding of the subject, Sartre states, involves 'the perpetually resolved and perpetually renewed contradiction between man-as-producer and man-as-product' (*CDR*, 158).

It is not, however, just the material world which circumscribes and in turn determines the individual but also the social and historical world in which he or she lives with others. In this respect, Sartre turns his attention elsewhere in the *CDR* to the importance of language in the formation of the subject. Where in *BN* language is viewed as a purely creative and expressive tool for voicing one's inner thoughts which does not precede the use which is made of it (see *BN*, 515–16), in the *CDR* Sartre stresses our essential situatedness in language which he now describes as the 'objectification of a class, the reflection of conflicts, latent or declared, and the particular manifestation of alienation' (*SM*, 113).

As with other aspects of Sartre's thought, his theorization of self and language undergoes a considerable change as we move from his early writings to his later work.[3] Sartre's early work (*The Transcendence of the Ego*, *Nausea*, *Being and Nothingness*) theorizes the subject in isolation from language and presupposes that any particular linguistic determination of the self will not affect it in any substantive way. This can be seen in *Nausea*, for instance, when Roquentin becomes aware that his self is not identifiable with the referent 'historian', giving rise eventually to the experience of nausea itself. In Sartre's middle stage, however (which includes *What is Literature?* and *Saint Genet*), language assumes much more importance in the constitution of self and world. In *Saint Genet*, for example, language is said to become Genet's 'most inward reality and the most rigorous expression of his exile' (1963, 276) while in *What is Literature?*, writing and words are seen as the essential medium for the expression of freedom in communication with others. By the time of Sartre's later period (which includes the *Critique* and *Words*), self and language have become deeply and irrevocably intertwined:

> significations come from man and from his project, but they are inscribed everywhere in things and in the order of things. Everything at every instant is signifying and significations reveal to us men and relations among men across the structures of our society. But these significations appear to us only insofar as we ourselves are signifying. (*SM*, 156)

Sartre's autobiography *Words* can be seen in this respect as a deliberate attempt on his part to theorize this dialectical interdependence of the subject and language by showing how identity is formed through its expression in words. Along with *The Family Idiot* (his biography of Flaubert), *Words* reveals just how much the subject progressively becomes more and more encumbered as his work evolves. In these texts he no longer conceives self-determination as something we sculpt from the ground up (as in *BN*), but as a process of reworking and integrating an already sculpted material. Agency is found in this sense only *within* the limits of our given psychological, biological and historical influences and not *in spite* of them.[4]

Indeed, what is perhaps most striking about *Words* and *The Family Idiot* are Sartre's numerous concessions to Freudianism, a theory he had criticized so trenchantly in *BN*. This conversion to Freudian categories can also be glimpsed in *SM* where Sartre speaks of psychoanalysis as 'the one privileged mediation' in understanding how a child lives his family relations inside a given society (*SM*, 61). The examination of the individual within the family which psychoanalysis undertakes alone enables us, according to Sartre, 'to study the process by which a child, groping in the dark, is going to attempt to play, without understanding it, the social roles which adults impose on him' (*SM*, 60). Commenting on his own self-formation in *Words*, Sartre gives great weight to the determining influence of childhood:

> One gets rid of a neurosis, one doesn't get cured of one's self. Though they are worn out, blurred, humiliated, thrust aside, ignored, all of the child's traits are still to be found in the quinquagenarian. (1964a, 254)

In *The Family Idiot* Sartre reiterates this Freudian emphasis and sets out to show how, in the case of Flaubert, 'the structures of [this] family are internalized in attitudes and re-externalized in practices by which the child makes himself be what others have made of him' (1971, 3). Tracing this back to the very earliest stages of childhood, Sartre emphasizes the way in which the infant Gustave is structured by the loving attention or by the indifference of his mother: 'To begin with, the baby internalizes the maternal rhythms and tasks as the lived qualities of his own body . . . His own mother, engulfed in the depths of his body, becomes the pathetic structure of his affectivity' (1981a, 57–8). The lack of love shown by Gustave's mother who, Sartre maintains, was only a 'mother out of duty', formed a deep frustration which 'penetrates him and becomes within him an impoverishment of his life – an organic misery and a kind of ingratitude at the core of experience' (1981a, 129–30). Inevitably, Sartre argues, Flaubert is pathologically impelled towards art by damage inflicted by his bourgeois upbringing (where the imaginary was prioritized above the real and words above things): '[t]he prehistoric past comes back to the child like Destiny' (1981a, 55). Even his individual preferences, talents and interests are the result of societal and familial forces that inhibit or develop his potentiality: 'the dunce and the prodigy are both monsters, two victims of the family institution and institutionalized education' (1974c, 24). He concludes to this end in *Words* that '[e]very man has his natural place; its altitude is determined neither by pride nor value: childhood decides' (1964a, 60).

Thus, in his later period Sartre conceives the subject as formed predominantly by the opaque forces of history and family destiny. Indeed, by the time of *The Family Idiot*, he has almost entirely abandoned his notion of the freely chosen project which dominated his early philosophy, no longer conceiving of the subject as a 'nihilating consciousness' but rather as

> a function of the society in which he lives, of the mode of production, of the technical knowledge available at the time, of the structure of the family, of antecedent circumstances, of the historic *future* which reveals itself as his destiny, but also of the singularity of his own previous history and of his biological characteristics, inherited or acquired. (1974c, 442)

Sartre's later philosophy moves further beyond his early conception of consciousness as he introduces the concept of *le vécu* (lived experience). As 'the equivalent of unconscious-conscious', *le vécu* no longer shares the self-transparency of consciousness, Sartre maintains, but involves forgetting, opacity, unself-consciousness and a lack of self-knowledge:

> What I call *le vécu* is precisely the whole of the dialectical process of psychic life, a process that remains opaque to itself for it is a constant totalization, and a totalization *that cannot be conscious of what it is*. (1977 (10), 108)

This of course represents a significant shift away from the Cartesian roots of his existential subject for whom the idea of self-transparency was seen as essential to its autonomy. In the *CDR* the self-transparency of the *pour-soi* is transformed into a pre-reflective comprehension of 'the translucidity of praxis to itself' (*CDR*, 74), but Sartre's emphasis is now much more practical than theoretical and thus less prone to the forms of Cartesian mystification that were evident in his early work. By the time of *The Family Idiot*, however, transparency has been practically blotted out by opacity as even Sartre's previous sanctuary of infallible self-awareness, the pre-reflective cogito, is now opened up to external influence – 'presence to self for each of us possesses a rudimentary structure of praxis . . . At the very level of nonthetic consciousness, intuition is conditioned by individual history' (1981a, 148).

Later in this chapter I will look at the ways in which this new opaque, encumbered Sartrean subject compares and contrasts with the *decentred subject* theorized by Foucault, Deleuze, Guattari and Derrida.

Postmodernism and the death of the subject

One of the principal targets for postmodernist critique has been the modernist conception of the subject as rational, unified, foundational and autonomous. This conception of the subject, inaugurated by Descartes and then continued most notably by Kant and Husserl, had dominated modern European philosophy until the structuralist revolt against humanism in France in the 1960s. Following Lévi-Strauss's rallying call (1966) that the aim of the human sciences was 'not to constitute but to dissolve man', structuralism embarked upon a concerted critique of humanism and anthropocentrism, inverting humanist premises by prioritizing structure over the subject, the unconscious over the conscious, and the objective analyses of scientific laws over ego-based epistemologies. Although structuralism was eclipsed in the 1970s by a new wave of poststructuralism which fulminated against the search for 'invariant universals' and objective scientific laws, all thinkers, whether structuralist or post-structuralist, sought to desubjectify or decentre the self. Within this decentring, the 'I' is seen essentially as a synthetic construct, a crossing-point of public interpretation where waves of cultural and linguistic meanings intersect. Culler well describes the effect of this theoretical deconstruction:

> As it is deconstructed, broken down into component systems that are all trans-subjective, the self or subject comes to appear more and more as a construct: the result of systems of convention. When man speaks, he heartfully 'complies with language'; language speaks through him, as does desire and society . . . The 'I' is not something given; it comes to exist – as that which is seen and addressed by others. (1976, 82)

This deconstructive attack on the subject brought with it a new theoretical standpoint from which to address the questions of individual subjectivity, collective agency and political action. The 'I' is displaced from its sovereign role in modernist theory as a basis for epistemological, moral and political claims and becomes instead a mere effect or epi-phenomenon of systems of acculturation. As the subject is displaced further and further from the constitution of the socio-historical field, humans steadily become more redundant and ineffectual in determining their conditions of existence. In Lacan's work, for example, the power of the unconscious (in which the 'discourse of the Other' is lodged) is such that 'Man is, from before his birth and beyond his death, taken up in the symbolic chain . . . he is a pawn in the play of the Signifier' (1977, 468).

In Lacan's psychology, the object of study is not taken to be that of an already existing human nature, but the ways in which the self 'becomes human' by learning to see itself as a particular kind of subject. In *Ecrits* Lacan argues that this perception of the 'I' comes about through two stages. The first of these involves the perception of individual physical embodiment when children first become aware of their own image in the mirror – an image of a unified and coherent self clearly separated off from the rest of the world. The second stage of 'selfhood' occurs when the child enters into society and society's language enters into the child. Since language belongs to society, the child must surrender some of itself and learn to speak from the position of the 'Other'. However, Lacan argues, this serves only to reinforce the sense of self since to speak the language of society is at the same time to enter into a language of subject and predicate – to speak in terms of 'I', 'me', and 'myself' and to enter into a personal name. The individual, Lacan argues, derives in this way entirely from outside, from the Other, and not from some real inner sense of self. Selfhood is thus seen not as a natural outgrowth or onto-logical datum, but as a *méconnaissance*, imposed and extraneous, always preceded by the unconscious 'discourse of the Other'.

Lacan's view of the self as a 'misrecognition' was integrated within the structural Marxism of Louis Althusser (and Etienne Balibar) which can be seen as a paradigmatic expression of this diminution of the active subject in the socio-historical process. Like Lacan, Althusser views the 'I' as a purely social effect, which 'has no "centre" . . . except in the imaginary misrecognition of the "ego" i.e. in the ideological formations in which it "recognizes" itself' (1971, 218). Individuals are seen in this way as simple 'effects', 'supports' or 'ideological constructs' of the social process rather than as constitutive of it. Consequently, Althusser and Balibar argue that the subject of history is not the individual nor collective groups of individuals, but the structural relations of production:

> the structure of the relations of production determines the place and functions occupied and adopted by the agents of production, who are never anything more than the occupants of these places, insofar as they are the supports of these functions ... The true 'subjects' are those definers and distributors: the relations of production (and political and ideological social relations). (1970, 180)

The French Nietzscheans: Foucault, Deleuze and Guattari
Where structuralists like Althusser and Lacan took their inspiration from a certain reading of Marx and Freud, post-structuralists like Foucault, Derrida, Deleuze and Lyotard turned to Nietzsche. In *Beyond Good and Evil* Nietzsche criticizes the form of binary logic that pervades western thought. The 'typical prejudice' and 'fundamental faith' of this logic is, Nietzsche argues, 'the faith in opposite values' (1966, 2). Among the 'opposite values' which most distort our thinking is the opposition of subject and object. According to Nietzsche, it is only 'the seduction of language' which causes us to think of a subject. The subject is simply an illusion of our grammar for 'there is no substratum; there is no "being" behind doing, effecting, becoming; "the doer" is merely a fiction added to the deed – the deed is everything' (1967, 13).

Echoing this view of Nietzsche, Deleuze argues in *Difference and Repetition* that the self-consciousness of human subjects is no more than a simulated product of language. The 'I' expressed in language is simply a 'syntactical marker' (1994, 17) and does not designate any unified centre or inner sanctum – 'we speak of our "self" ', he comments, 'only in virtue of these thousands of little witnesses which contemplate within us: it is always a third party who says "me" ' (1994, 75). For the French post-structuralists in general, Nietzsche's genealogical deconstruction of the subject emerges as the first break from modernity – 'What Nietzsche's thought heralds', according to Foucault, is not so much the 'Death of God', but 'the end of his murderer' (1970, 385).[5]

In Nietzsche's rejection of the rational modernist subject, he makes use of three related concepts that explode the idea of stability and unity these are, the concept of *becoming*, the idea of the subject as *multiple*, and the notion of self-cultivation as an essentially *aesthetic* exercise. As mentioned, there is no essential or inner self that stands behind one's actions in Nietzsche's view – 'no substratum . . . behind . . . doing, effecting, becoming' (1967, 13). Within what he calls 'the innocent play of becoming', one must refrain, he warns, from conceiving the subject as something static or enduring. The French Nietzscheans develop this idea of a contingent, non-essential self and, like Nietzsche, examine the ways in which the individual is produced through the influence of social, historical and linguistic forces.

In *Discipline and Punish* Foucault attempts to show, following on from Nietzsche, how the constitution of 'psyche, subjectivity, personality, consciousness' is the result of definite 'methods of punishment, supervision and constraint' (1977a, 29). His analysis of Bentham's Panopticon explores the way in which the production of subjectivity occurs in the confined and incarcerated body of the prisoner and how the techniques of power deployed in the prison produced a definite kind of individual, 'the hardened criminal'. In the Panopticon (where prisoners are kept visibly and physically apart from one another, each unable to see who watches them and supervises their every movement) definite effects are produced in those observed and subjected to the prison regime of normalization. The prisoner is produced within the prison system by means of individualizing disciplines (in which he is isolated and his behaviour fragmented) which signify him in his specificity and throw him back into a self-conscious remorse:

> He who is subjected to a field of visibility, and who knows it, assumes responsibility for the constraints of power; he makes them play spontaneously upon himself, he inscribes himself in a power-relation in which he simultaneously plays both roles; he becomes the principle of his own subjection. (1977a, 202–3)

In their co-authored texts, Deleuze and Guattari set about turning the Cartesian cogito inside out by reconfiguring it as a new assemblage shot through with social categories. Where Kant added the component of time to the cogito by situating it in the phenomenal world of sense and experience, Deleuze and Guattari add the dimension of the Other and prepare the way for Rimbaud's formula 'Je est un autre' by situating the appearance of the subject in the discourse of the Other which produces and sustains it (1994, 31–2). In *Anti-Oedipus* the subject is viewed in this way as constituted by social assemblages of 'desiring-production'. 'Territorialization' is the name they give to this process whereby subject-positions are produced and individual and collective desire is tamed, channelled and repressed under capitalism – 'To code desire', they argue, 'is the business of the Socius' (1983, 139). Like Nietzsche, Deleuze and Guattari use this as a starting point for articulating an affirmative project of agency aimed at freeing identity from the territorializing processes of 'the Socius'. This project is conceived in terms of 'bodies without organs' which, they argue, involves a form of somatic existence that is free from social organization and no longer articulated, disciplined, semioticized and subjectified, but disarticulated, dismantled and deterritorialised.[6] It is a matter, as Deleuze states elsewhere, of people undergoing 'the harshest exercises in depersonalization, by opening themselves up to the multiplicities everywhere within them, to the intensities running through them' (1987, 6).

In *A Thousand Plateaus* Deleuze and Guattari liken the subject to a *hand* which, they argue, is structured like a network of multiple lines of which there are three essential types made up of 'molar' and 'molecular' features. Molarity, they point out, denotes structure, hierarchy and organization in which desire becomes congealed and serves to obstruct the flow of meaning. The molecular, by contrast, entails 'unstructured and rhizomatic libidinal energies' based on multiplicity, possibility and becoming. According to Deleuze and Guattari, molarity functions most of all within 'rigid segmentary lines' that construct fixed and normalized identities within a range of social institutions by means of binary oppositions (e.g. boss/worker, man/woman, etc.). These correspond to and are the result of repressive, closed structures of territorializing desire that prevail under capitalism. Second, there are 'supple segmentary lines' which involve a molecular movement away from molar rigidity that disturbs its normalcy and organization – these might be described as 'cracks' in one's identity where we become consciously aware of and begin to reflect on the contingent and repressive nature of these institutional identities. Finally, Deleuze and Guattari point to 'lines of flight' which they see in a positive light as full, deterritorializing movements away from molar identity where 'cracks' grow into 'ruptures' and the subject is 'shattered' in a process of *becoming-multiple*. Lines of flight, they argue, constitute full expressions of molecularity and take place on the plane of creativity, desire, possibility, experiment, death and destruction (1987, 26–38).

This affirmation of becoming-multiple in Deleuze and Guattari's work can be seen most of all in their normative ideal of the Schizophrenic (in *Anti-Oedipus*) and of the Nomad (in *A Thousand Plateaus*). Schizophrenia, they argue, is a potentially liberatory condition insofar as it involves a 'decoding' process where individuals escape the bourgeois reality principle that represses desire and creativity in place of needs, interests and material production. The 'Schizo-Subject' embodies their conception of the subject as multiple, decentred and fragmented since they do not see their behaviour as belonging to a conscious, encompassing 'I', often referring to themself in the third person and refusing to speak the word 'I'. Their ideal of the Nomad is similarly one who is never static, enduring or fixed, but who must 'keep moving, even in place, never stop moving' (1987, 159). In *What is Philosophy?* they reiterate this idea of multiplicity and becoming, calling for the creation of forms of desubjectification that involve the exploration of different forms of consciousness beyond the confines of molar normality. To this end, they celebrate the death of the majoritarian individual subject by invoking experimental modes of consciousness which are excluded from normalizing reason such as those esoteric and Dionysian practices which involve rapture, excess and intoxication (1994, 44). These are fully fledged lines of flight which, they observe in *A Thousand Plateaus*, combine 'travel, hallucination, madness, the Indians, perceptive and mental experimentation, the shifting of frontiers, the rhizome' (1987, 520).

For Foucault, the Nietzschean ideal of becoming-multiple is attained through what he calls 'transgressive practice' (1984, 48). This involves particular practices (e.g. sexual, narcotic, aesthetic) that deliver us to the limit of our (normalized) identities without attempting to live securely beyond it. According to Foucault, we should look for 'limit experiences' within experimental practices which tear the subject apart from itself in an attempt to 'reach the point of life which lies as close as possible to the impossibility of living' (1991, 31). In this way, Foucault, like Deleuze and Guattari, points to the Dionysian realm as a potential repository for somatic freedom in which we can escape the psychological training of the body and effect 'the destruction of the subject as pseudo-sovereign' (1977b, 222).

In his later 'ethical' period, Foucault gives particular primacy to aesthetic forms of self-cultivation as a means of 'refusing the type of individuality that has been imposed on us for several centuries' (1984, 308). According to Foucault, since there is no essential subject, no self grounded in biological or ontological necessity, 'there is only one practical consequence: we have to create ourselves as a work of art' (1984, 321).[7] It is through art that the imagination is nurtured in a realm of possibility, difference, sense-experience and renewal. It is only when we begin to give ourselves style through self-reflective forms of aesthetic and experimental practice that we are able, he argues, to withstand the impact of historical, objectifying forces. If we see ourselves as a 'work of art', continually being made and unmade, we become constant activists for whom it is necessary to prevent enabling limits from congealing into constraining limitations, and to generate new limits and new forms of subjectivity which constitute selves. Transgressive and aesthetic practice is vital for the creation of new forms of subjectivity, Foucault argues, because it shakes us out of our usual categories, enabling us to think in different ways by unifying and differentiating experience in unusual ways (1977b, 190–1). This makes possible a form of self-understanding through self-expression that takes us beyond the 'given' of our historical, social and linguistic conditioning which, as he so effectively shows throughout his work, penetrates us to the very core of our being.

The postmodern subject

As several commentators have noted, the *aestheticization* of the subject is the dominant trend in postmodern thought.[8] Drawing on the 'aestheticist sensibility'of the French post-structuralists, postmodernists present the subject as fragmented, decentred and multiple, dispersed throughout different subject-positions or identities that are constituted by modern mass consumer and media-dominated societies. In the postmodern world, identities are no longer maintained primarily in one's role as a producer (as an agent of praxis), but in the consumer choices and 'sign-values' (to use Baudrillard's term) one subscribes to. For both Affirmative and Sceptical postmodernists, the subject, as a site of positive agency, is held to be inherently objectionable as an ideological construct of modernity, the source of an unacceptable subject—object dichotomy where it assumes a dominating and oppressive role – 'man as master of the universe, dominating, controlling, deciding' (Vattimo, 1988). As Foucault states emphatically, this instrumental conception of the subject in which the individual is given 'an exact and serene mastery of nature' does not give rise 'to the constitution and affirmation of a free subject', but is tied instead to 'a progressive enslavement to its own instinctive violence' (1977b, 163).

In Sceptical forms of postmodernism, however, there is generally little attempt to offer a positive account of the subject or to formulate alternative conceptions of subjectivity that contrast with the instrumental modernist subject. This is evident in Baudrillard's work where he is keen to criticize in depth Marx's humanist subject (*homo faber*), but offers no positive sense of agency in its place, preferring instead to renounce altogether subjective strategies to control or to determine the world. Ultimately, Baudrillard dissolves agency into a form of individual passivity and collective disability – the mass, he argues in *In the Shadow of the Silent Majorities*, is no more than 'an opaque nebula whose growing density absorbs all the surrounding energy' (1983a, 3–4): 'Messages are given to them, they only want some sign, they idolize the play of signs and stereotypes, they idolize any content so long as it resolves itself into a spectacular sequence' (1983a, 10).

In *Fatal Strategies* this abandonment of agency is taken a step further where Baudrillard adopts the idea of a 'postmodern metaphysics' in which the subject has lost its battle completely to dominate the object (social) world. The subject remains as little more than the passive ground upon which networks of cultural, semioticized meanings and codes are imprinted. The responses individuals make to coded signals inscribe them into the simulated order of postmodern society through a structured binary system of affirmation or negation (e.g. opinion polls, elections, consumer surveys) – they are thus mobilized into a coded system of similarities and dissimilarities, of identities and programmed differences. 'Individuals', he insists, 'exist only as undifferentiated particles within the mass', which itself 'only exists as the point of convergence of all the media waves that depict it' (1983a, 39). In *The Postmodern Condition* Lyotard takes much the same view:

> A *self* does not amount to much, but no self is an island; each exists in a fabric of relations that is now more complex and mobile than ever before. Young or old, man or woman, rich or poor, a person is always located at 'nodal points' of specific communication circuits, however tiny these may be. Or better, one is always located at a post through which various kinds of messages pass. (1984a, 15)

In Baudrillard's work this gives rise to a resounding feeling of nihilism and despair that hangs like a dark pall over his postmodern narrative. Unlike the 'active nihilism' of Nietzsche which aims at the dissolution of apathy and passivity, Baudrillard's nihilism is joyless, devoid of energy and without hope:

> melancholy is the fundamental tonality of functional systems, of the present systems of simulation, programming and information. Melancholy is the quality inherent in the mode of disappearance of meaning, in the mode of volatisation of meaning in operational systems. (1984, 39)

> If being nihilist is to privilege this point of inertia and the analysis of this irreversibility of systems to the point of no return, then I am a nihilist. (1984, 39)

Thus, the postmodern subject, as depicted in the more 'Sceptical' versions of postmodernism like Baudrillard's, takes to the extreme the view of the subject as fragmented and decentred. Its lack of unity culminates ultimately in a distinct lack of agency, dispersed totally in the linguistic, semiotic and cultural codes that constitute and determine it.

In assessing this conception of the fragmented postmodern subject, it has been argued that this model of selfhood as constant change and fragmentation serves to validate the idea of the consumerist self which lacks any real sense of unity, hungrily acquiring new commodities in which its identity becomes dispersed and configured. This connects to further criticisms of what is perceived as the narrowly 'individualist' nature of the postmodern subject — although postmodernism set out to deepen the attack on the individual subject initiated by (post-)structuralism, the postmodern era has come to represent, to use Lipovetsky's phrase, the 'Golden Age of the Individual'. This is particularly evident in Baudrillard's Sceptical postmodernism where all sense of collective political agency has disappeared in a privatized and atomistic postmodern landscape. Indeed, as Corlett points out, the postmodern subject shies away from communal affiliation and collective responsibility, seeing them as a threat to personal development and privacy. If postmodern community is possible, then it is so only on the condition of 'community without unity' (Corlett, 1989, 6–7). It is, however, not just the Sceptical postmodernists who have come under criticism for the restrictive, individualist way in which they conceive the subject. As we will see in the final section of this chapter, Affirmative postmodernist projects of 'aesthetic self-cultivation' put forward by Foucault and others can be similarly criticized for conceiving the idea of self-development in separation from other people and thus lacking any real basis for an inter-subjective ethic or project.

Sartre and the decentred subject

As we saw in the Introduction, Sartre's existentialist subject has been commonly viewed as antithetical to the decentring strategies of the post-structuralists. Discussing Foucault's project to 'create new subjectivities' and to style an 'aesthetics of existence', Schrift argues along these lines:

> In displacing the question of the 'free subject's' endowing things with meaning, it is clear ... Foucault was distancing himself from the phenomenological-existential and, in particular, the Sartrean subject. By returning to a Nietzschean account of the subject, Foucault replaces the Sartrean project of an authentic self with the Nietzschean project of creatively constructing oneself. In so doing, he displaces both the valorized, free, existential subject and retrieves a more ambivalent subject whose constitution takes place within the constraints of institutional forces that extend its grasp and even at times its recognition. (1995, 47)

With regard to the first difference Schrift cites – between Sartrean and Foucauldian perceptions of the subject as a centre and endower of meaning – it can be argued that this difference is not always significant or large enough to override similarities that exist between the two. To begin with, as we have seen, the Sartrean subject is not just a thinking, rationalizing consciousness which gives meaning to things, but is also engaged – an actor immersed in the world of things. In this sense it incorporates both freedom and necessity, transcendence and facticity. Similarly, Foucault's conception of the subject is not always uniform or consistent but oscillates between poles of 'unbearable Lightness and Heaviness'.[9] Whereas, for example, Foucault characterizes thought in his early 'archaeological phase' as constrained by linguistic conditions to the extent that we cannot even render an account of the limits a particular thought is constrained in, he suggests later (in language strongly reminiscent of BN) that the practices of philosophy in reflection are themselves ways to free our thoughts – 'Thought is a freedom in relation to what one does, the motion by which one detaches oneself from it, establishes it as an object, and reflects on it as a problem' (1984, 388). In a later interview Foucault goes on to reinstate philosophy as a privileged discourse, arguing that the role of the philosopher is 'to make oneself permanently capable of detaching oneself from oneself [while] altering one's thought and that of others' (1988, 263–4).

However, it is not just Foucault's later 'ethical' subject who bears some similarity to the Sartrean subject in this respect, but also the more encumbered genealogical subject which Foucault describes in *Discipline and Punish*. In *Power/Knowledge* Foucault emphasizes how 'power is co-extensive with the social body' (1980, 141), permeating all discourse and practice. His main interest in this respect is to show how power plays upon the individual to produce specific effects in him. The power relations of modern society are seen by Foucault to have produced a subject who is the carrier of prevailing norms trained through regimes of 'insidious leniencies, petty cruelties, small acts of cunning, calculated methods, techniques, "sciences"' (1977a, 308). In the place of the old 'body politic', modern society now revolves around a 'politics of the body' under which individuals 'are gradually, progressively, really and materially constituted' (1980, 97). Once the body has been trained through techniques of discipline and surveillance, however, Foucault is keen to emphasize that the subject himself becomes the carrier of norms by which he measures himself:

> there is no need for arms, physical violence, material constraints. Just a gaze. An inspecting gaze, a gaze which each individual under its weight will end by interiorising to the point that he is his own overseer, each individual thus exercising the surveillance over, and against himself. (1980, 155)

What Foucault illustrates here is that power is not just exercised by the law of repression, but operates by producing psychological and social conformity. In this sense, individuals themselves are complicit in their own subjection – they are not just empty skeins which power pours itself into, but conscious, psychological beings who interpret themselves according to the context and relations of power within which they are situated. For Foucault, experiences of subjectivity are self-interpretations based on concrete interactions with the world. In modern carceral society these concrete interactions are enmeshed in networks of power that validate certain self-interpretations and obstruct others. A certain kind of subject is produced as it comes to know itself by means of stable, identifiable points of reference conditioned through intersubjective practice. The production of the subject is, however, by no means automatic or entirely uniform for Foucault since, as Hoy points out, the network of power relations is more like a 'structural grammar' than a 'causal process' for it conditions action but does not determine which specific actions will take place (1986, 142). Although we are the products of power in the sense that our self-interpretations are conditioned by it, it is through self-interpretation that we come to regard ourselves as originators of our own actions.

The difference between the Sartrean and Foucauldian subject is not so much about the existence of a meaningful centre (as Schrift contends), but the way this meaning is produced by the Sartrean subject in ontological-individual rather than in socio-linguistic terms. A clear example of this can be found in Sartre's and Foucault's conception of the gaze (in *BN* and *Discipline and Punish*) where both thinkers ruminate at length on the subjectifying force of observation in which the subject is thrown into an objective apprehension of itself. Working from abstract ontological assumptions in *BN*, Sartre chooses only negative examples of the gaze (most famously of the voyeur at the keyhole whose overriding apprehension of himself is dominated by shame) and draws individualist and universal conclusions from it. In the Sartrean system, the gaze is essentially alienating and conflictual – the observation of a nameless, unknown other who casts objective judgement on me. Foucault's account of the normalizing gaze in *Discipline and Punish* avoids ontological conclusions, by contrast, but relates the significance of the gaze to its social and historical context. In the Panopticon the prison guard and the self-conscious prisoner are positioned in a network of relations in which they are not equal participants. A fundamental asymmetry flows between them due to the arrangements of the social field in which they find themselves – first, because observation is a one-way process (due to the architecture of the prison) and, second, because the guard stands in a relation of authority to the prisoner upon whom he passes punitive judgement according to pre-defined norms. The gaze is in this sense an institutional gaze anchored in definite power relations within a specific social and historical milieu.

Thus, although Sartre and Foucault theorize the gaze in different terms, both are agreed on its importance in the formation and constitution of the subject. Sartre's emphasis on the gaze also bears similarity to the work of Lacan who, as Dews notes, is often closer to Sartre (by analysing the dialectic between self and other, seer and seen) than he is to Freud (who adopts a biological theory of drives) (Dews, 1987, 58).[10]

This leads on to the second difference Schrift cites – between 'the Sartrean project of an authentic self' and the Foucauldian project of 'creatively constructing oneself'. Although Sartre's *pour-soi* was judged initially by post-structuralist critics to be a repetition of the Cartesian subject, this judgement ignored other emphases in Sartre's work which, as we have seen, placed his existential subject at a distance from the disengaged, abstract and immaterial Cartesian subject. In later years Foucault came to recognize this and applauded Sartre for moving beyond the entrenched Cartesianism of his time and, in particular, for avoiding 'the idea of the self as something which is given to us' (1983, 64). In this respect (contrary to what Schrift suggests), the notion of a non-essential contingent subject intrinsic to Sartre's existentialism is what perhaps unites his work most clearly with post-structuralist approaches adopted by Foucault, Lacan, Deleuze, Guattari and Derrida.

In common with post-structuralist theories of the subject, Sartre takes the 'I' to be no more than a synthetic construct of consciousness which is impermanent and fluid. In the same way that, for Lacan, 'the true "I" is not the ego' (in Ferry and Renaut, 1990, 191), for Sartre, 'the intuition of the Ego is a perpetually deceptive mirage' (1957, 69). Sartre continues this theme in *BN* where he argues at length against the idea of an authentic or 'deep' self which is pre-given or original, insisting instead that the *pour-soi* is fundamentally a *relation* (*BN*, 121), a 'perpetual deferring' (*BN*, 713) and '*diasporique*' (*BN*, 182). In *The Family Idiot* this is re-emphasized once more where Flaubert's self is theorized throughout as an imaginary construct rather than an original source. In this respect, the authentic self which Sartre hints at in *BN* and Foucault's later ethical subject bear close similarity in that they both revolve around the idea that the self must be *created* through action and self-interpretation rather than *discovered* through introspection and withdrawal as in the Cartesian model (which Schrift attributes to Sartre).

With regard to Schrift's third difference — between a 'valorized, free' Sartrean subject and an 'ambivalent', opaque Foucauldian subject — once again it might be said that this conveys only a partial glimpse of what is a much more complex and variable Sartrean subject. Although certain elements of Sartre's existential subject do conform to this interpretation, this is offset, as we have seen, by the emergence and steady growth of a much more encumbered and opaque Sartrean subject who, like the post-structuralist subject, originates not from a transcendental subject, but who is instead non-essential, non-identical, historical, decentred, impermanent and contingent. In general, the Sartrean subject is not the autonomous, self-sufficient foundation as it has often been portrayed, but is divided, non-egoic and never self-identical and, as such, can be seen to prefigure 'the decentred subject' and the rejection of a 'metaphysics of presence' taken up in later years by post-structuralists like Foucault and Derrida.

This idea of a non-identical, relational subject is intrinsic to both Sartre's theory of consciousness and Derrida's theory of *différance*. Like the Derridean sign, for instance, Sartrean consciousness differs from itself through a temporal movement of 'deferral' (*BN*, 713) whereby the present can be what it is only through the mediation of the future. This gives the clue to Sartre's famous description of consciousness as 'a being which is what it is not and not what it is' (*BN*, 100). According to Sartre, since all consciousness is intentional (consciousness *of* something), it is nothing other than this activity of directing awareness towards an object. This awareness comes about by consciousness transcending the immediate appearance of the object and projecting towards the 'horizon' of other possible appearances of the object, the sum of which define it and which constitute the future consciousnesses of that object. The present of consciousness (awareness of an object) is defined by Sartre on the basis of a future and irreal totality of consciousness which is *not yet*:

> The nature of consciousness implies . . . that it project itself in front of itself in the future; one can understand what it is only through what it will be, it is determined in its actual being by its own possibilities. (1977 (1), 96)

And yet, Sartre maintains, consciousness is unable to fix itself to this future totality which defines it since consciousness cannot be anything other than consciousness *of* its object. The totality that consciousness seeks is something '*irréalisable*': it will never find it since such a totality would involve the impossible synthesis of *pour-soi* and *en-soi*, openness and completion, transcendence and determinacy (*BN*, 140). Consequently, consciousness both *is* and *is not* the totality of future consciousnesses through which it defines itself and suffers the absence of that totality as a 'lack' of its own being (*BN*, 138). This lack must necessarily remain unsatisfied for Sartre since this totality could only become closed and completed if consciousness ceased to be intentional and transcendent. He argues as such that human reality

> is *perpetually haunted* by a totality which it is without being able to be it, precisely because it cannot attain the in-itself (closure, identity) without losing itself as for-itself. It is thus by nature an unhappy consciousness, with no possible transcendence of its unhappy state. (*BN*, 140)

The Sartrean subject is constituted in *BN* by a temporal deferral which means that it 'has its being outside it, before it and behind' (*BN*, 179), always caught between a future which is not yet and a 'never present past' or 'original contingency' (*BN*, 408) that coincides with its facticity and thrownness: 'There is never an instant at which we can assert that the for-itself *is* precisely because the for-itself never is. Temporality, on the contrary, constitutes itself as the refusal of the instant' (*BN*, 211). The temporality of consciousness means for Sartre that the subject is non-identical and non-contemporaneous with its present, a relation to self grounded in self-difference and self-otherness that is inadequate to itself. Thus, as Baugh notes, there is no 'simple present' in Sartrean consciousness as 'the present of consciousness is always double, always duplicitous, always the folding-back of a never-present future upon what consciousness has transcended towards that future' (1999, 72). As Sartre himself states:

> The self . . . indicates a relation of the subject to itself and this relation is precisely a duality . . . In fact, the self cannot be grasped as a real existent: the self cannot *be* self because, as we have seen, coincidence with self causes the self to disappear . . . The for-itself's law of being, as the ontological foundation of consciousness, is to be itself in the form of presence-to-self . . . All 'presence to' implies duality, and thus an at least virtual separation. (*BN*, 123–4)

Viewed in this light, Sartrean consciousness can be seen to fit closely Derrida's description in *Of Grammatology* of 'a self presence that has never been given but only dreamed of and always split, incapable of appearing to itself except as its own disappearance' (1976, 112). In the same way that Sartrean consciousness is separated from itself by a temporal deferral, in Derrida's analysis of signification 'an interval must separate the present from what it is not in order for the present to be itself' and hence 'this interval that constitutes [the present] as present must . . . divide the present in and of itself' (1982, 13). In *Margins of Philosophy* and *Writing and Difference* Derrida draws the conclusion from Saussure's linguistics that, as a 'duality-in-unity' of a material signifier and a conceptual signified, the linguistic sign 'is never present in itself' since it is 'essentially inscribed in a chain or system within which it refers to . . . other concepts by the systematic play of differences' (1982, 140). According to Derrida, each term is caught up in 'infinite implication, the indefinite referral of signifier to signifier' in which each signified concept 'always signifies again' (1978, 25). In this way, a concept never is what it is since it is constituted by its difference with other concepts so that what it lacks is constitutive of what it is — it is what it is not.

Like Sartrean consciousness, Derridean *différance* is constituted by 'the temporal and temporalising mediation of a detour that suspends the accomplishment or fulfillment of a "desire" or "will" ' (1973, 136). To constitute its object in a living present consciousness must, in Derrida's view, take up past consciousnesses (retention) and synthesize these along with the projected future consciousnesses (protention) into a unity that constitutes the same object (1978, 132). The consequence of this for Derrida is that consciousness and its object are never fully present since temporality 'fissures and retards presence, submitting it simultaneously to primordial division and delay' (1973, 88).

Thus, rather than being an obvious or natural target for Derrida's critique of a 'metaphysics of presence', Sartre's early theory of consciousness can be seen to prefigure it in several respects. Although denounced by Derrida in *Glas* as 'the onto-phenomenologist of freedom' who is oblivious to the interminability and undecidability of signification (1986, 28), Sartre fulfils in *BN* and elsewhere the Derridean project of deconstructing the self-identical and self-present metaphysical subject. His ethical theory of authenticity, like Derrida's theory of *différance*, valorizes an acceptance of 'distance from self', openness, incompletion and contingency, pointing towards an ideal of a subject which 'chooses not to *reappropriate* itself, but to flee itself, not to coincide with itself, but to be always at a distance from itself' (*BN*, 798).

As we have seen above, it is possible, both in Sartre's early phenomenological texts and in his later existential–Marxist work, to discern many of the themes which were taken up, extended, developed or modified by post-structuralists. Although certain aspects of Sartre's early work fixed themselves firmly to the 'pole of Lightness',[11] while that of post-structuralists, like Foucault, focused on the 'Heaviness' of the subject, in later years this situation would be reversed, with Sartre's emphasis becoming much more *deconstructive* and that of the post-structuralists more *reconstructive*. Sartrean and post-structuralist conceptions of the subject start out in this sense from different positions but eventually converge, both resting upon a conception of the subject as decentred, opaque, material and historical and yet able, through praxis, reflection, transgression or aesthetic practice, to escape its conditioning. In this respect the Sartrean subject can be recast as a spurious target for the deconstructive critiques of Foucault, Derrida and others. Indeed, Sartre's existential epithet – 'existence precedes essence' – captures well the anti-essentialist emphasis of the decentred postmodern subject.

In the next section, I assess some of the main critical considerations that arise from Sartrean and postmodernist conceptions of the subject as well as examining some of the differences which, in spite of the general commonality argued for above, persist between the two.

Critical considerations

A common theme linking the work of Sartre and the French post-structuralists is the rejection of the bourgeois humanist subject, charac-terized by what Sartre calls 'the spirit of seriousness' (l'ésprit de sérieux). For Sartre, the spirit of seriousness that lies at the heart of the humanist subject is characterized by the following actions – 'to deny the radical contingency of the world', 'to depend upon objective considerations', 'to seek determinateness instead of fluidity', 'to seek in attitude the solidity of a rock' and 'to believe in the illusion of a permanent self'.[12] Throughout his writings, Sartre argued consistently against a closed picture of the subject which post-structuralists would later follow, taking their inspiration from Nietzsche rather than Sartre himself. His later texts in particular (that still pre-date the main wave of post-structuralist texts in the 1960s and 1970s) in which he argues for a more encumbered subject can be seen in this way to directly anticipate the decentred subject popularized by post-structuralists and postmodernists. Like the post-modernist subject, the later Sartrean subject is shot through with codes of linguistic and historical inscription. In *Situations*, for example, Sartre even drops his earlier antipathy to Lacan and accepts his interpretation of the Unconscious as the 'discourse of the Other':

As far as I'm concerned, Lacan has clarified the unconscious as a discourse which separates through language or, if you prefer, as a coun-terfinality of speech: Verbal structures are organized as a structure of the practico-inert through the act of speaking. These structures express or constitute intentions that determine me without being mine. (1977 (10), 97)

In *Search for a Method* Sartre reiterates this Lacanian emphasis by showing the ways in which language (as a constituent feature of the practico-inert) precedes, constitutes, determines and ultimately alienates us:

Language and culture are not inside the individual like stamps registered by his nervous system. It is the individual who is inside culture and inside language. (*SM*, 113)

Man is for himself and for others a *signifying* being ... a creator of signs. (*SM*, 52)

Sartre develops this deconstructive impetus further still in the *CDR*, stating for instance, that '[t]he concept of Man is an abstraction' (*CDR*, 183) and, in language which could easily be found in the anti-humanist discourses of Derrida or the early Foucault, writing openly of 'acts without an author' (*CDR*, 152) and 'constructions without a constructor' (*CDR*, 754).

Despite rejecting the bourgeois humanist subject, however, Sartre endeavoured to retain some coherent sense of agency and not to fall into an easy or complacent anti-humanism. Although the margin of freedom steadily contracted in his work as it progressed after the Second World War, his guiding existential principle that a 'man can always make something out of what is made of him' (1974a, 35) remained. As Christina Howells rightly observes, although the subject in Sartre's later works is 'deferred, dissolved, and deconstructed', it 'is not relinquished' (1992, 342):

Totally conditioned by his class, his salary, the nature of his work, conditioned in his very feelings and thoughts, it is he [the proletarian] who freely gives to the proletariat a future of relentless humiliation or one of conquest and victory, according as he chooses to be resigned or revolutionary. And it's for this choice that he is responsible. (Sartre, 1977 (2), 27–8)

Thus, although Sartre agrees with (post-)structuralists like Lacan that 'structure produces behaviour' he maintains that we should not pass over 'the reverse side of the dialectic in silence' (1977 (9), 86): 'Man can only "be spoken" to the extent that he speaks' (1971, 1977). In this respect, Sartre's consistent attachment to some form of agency can be seen to contrast with some of the earlier excesses of (post-)structuralist thought and some of the contemporary excesses of postmodernists who dissolve the subject in an acid bath of anti-humanism. Commenting on the rising tide of anti-humanism in an interview in 1966, Sartre observes that the subject as 'a sort of substantial I, or central category, always more or less given . . . has been dead for a long time'. What is missing in the anti-humanist discourse, however, is how 'the subject . . . constitutes itself from a basis anterior to itself by a continual process of interiorisation and re-exteriorisation' (1966c, 91).

The works of Foucault and Derrida in particular provide two good examples of a need to re-think earlier dismissals of the subject and to work towards a more affirmative conception of agency. Despite their exorcism of the Sartrean ghost in the 1960s, both Foucault and Derrida return in their later writings to the Sartrean project of reconfiguring the subject as a possible site for freedom:

> there are revolts and that is a fact. It is through revolt that subjectivity (not that of great men but that of whomever) introduces itself into history and gives it the breath of life. (Foucault, 1981, 8)

> I believe that at a certain level both of experience and of philosophical and scientific discourse, one cannot get along without the notion of a subject. It is a question of knowing where it comes from and how it functions. (Derrida, in Schrift, 1995, 27)

Similarly, despite their attack on the sovereign individual, Deleuze and Guattari warn against dissolving the subject completely in *A Thousand Plateaus* and, like Sartre, theorize the lines of escape that detach us from the heaviness of our social and historical conditioning:

> You have to keep enough of the organism for it to reform each dawn; and you have to keep small supplies of significance and subjectification, if only to turn them against their own systems when the circumstances

demand it, when things, persons, even situations, force you to; and you have to keep small rations of subjectivity in sufficient quantity to enable you to respond to the dominant reality. (1987, 160)

In Deleuze's own work, as Constantin Boundas points out, it is also possible to discern 'a timid retrieval of the subject' and a theoretical progression towards a more Sartrean viewpoint. Although Deleuze's early texts of the 1960s follow Foucault's and Derrida's in their interest in the 'structure-Subject', the influence of May 1968 led Deleuze, in Boundas's view, to first of all dismantle subjectivity and finally, in his texts of the 1970s, to retrieve the subject as 'folded interiority' (1991, 12).

Beneath the elements of convergence, however, there are certain aspects of the Sartrean subject which stand at odds with postmodernist theory. This is particularly apparent in the *CDR* where Sartre largely adopts a Marxist model of the subject (as primarily an agent of praxis) and reinforces the binary logic of *pour-soi/en-soi* which dominated his work previously in *BN*. In posing a duality of being in this way, Sartre can be seen to conform to what Derrida pejoratively refers to in *Margins of Philosophy* as 'binarism' — that is, the incipient tendency of modernist theory to operate *disjunctively* (either . . . or) rather than *conjunctively* (both . . . and). In Derrida's view, traditional binary oppositions rarely exist together equally — rather, one side is privileged and the other devalued, thus establishing a hierarchical 'order of subordination' within the opposite terms (1982, 329). In *BN* Sartre clearly establishes an order of this kind, valorizing and separating the free, creative *pour-soi* from the raw, homogenous, passive and inert realm of the *en-soi*.

It is true that in the *CDR* Sartre goes a long way to redress this previous imbalance and offers a much more dialectical, 'mediated' approach to the *pour-soi/en-soi* opposition in which both poles now interpenetrate in a process of what he calls 'trans-substantiation' (*CDR*, 178). However, although Sartre theorizes the *pour-soi/en-soi* distinction dialectically in the *CDR*, he continues to view the realm of the *en-soi* in uniform, negative terms.[13] This is reflected most of all in the way in which Sartre continues to theorize matter in the *CDR* as an undifferentiated *en-soi*. By homogenizing all the various features of the natural world into a simple inorganic and passive externality, he fails to distinguish between the more active elements of that world, such as plants and animals, and the more passive, inorganic ones, such as rocks and sand — nor does he make any such distinction between naturally occurring forms (animals, rivers, etc.) and synthetic human constructions (chairs, machines, dams, buildings, etc.).

Sartre's insistence on the *pour-soi* (active)/*en-soi* (passive) distinction has led some critics to associate his work with the logic of instrumentality intrinsic to the modern humanist project of control and domination. According to Kirsner, for instance:

> In his personal and philosophical refusal of surrender, Sartre wants consciously directed activity to dominate the body and nature. Sartre is echoing the view of the body and the world that has enshrined the project of Western civilisation for many centuries. This is the logic of domination which views the world as there to be subdued and controlled and uses an instrumental, managerial form of rationality that regards oneself, others and the environment as objects to be quantified and manipulated. (1985, 225)

This can be seen in the *CDR,* for example, where Sartre insists that dialectical reason is applicable only to human life since it is, he argues, only humans who can have projects. In this regard, Sartre clearly valorizes the human realm above that of the rest of nature, reserving his existentialist ideals of freedom, creativity and transcendence for humans and denying any notion of autonomy to animals and other life forms which presumably, as they cannot be understood dialectically, must be so analytically, 'from the outside with a total scientific objectivity and like an inert object' (1968, 90). Like Marx, Sartre insists on the valuative distinction between man 'who makes his life activity an object of his will and consciousness' and the animal who 'is immediately at one with its life activity' (Marx, 1975, 328). Sartre's view of nature conforms in this respect to a modernist logic of instrumentality which seeks to demythologize the world and to dissolve the transcendent and magical into the measurable and rational, reflecting a mythical fear of the unknown and the different, and reducing the qualitative variety of nature celebrated in magic to the homogenous and quantitative.[14]

In contrast to this Marxo-Sartrean view of nature, however, it is possible to juxtapose a different, less anthropocentric rationality common to less instrumental, symbolic societies which postmodernists like Baudrillard use in order to criticize modernity. Within communities (ancient and contemporary) whose lifeworld is based on a spiritual, mythological and harmonious symbiotic relation to nature, animals are not seen as empty, quantitative machines devoid of purpose, intelligence or emotion, but as living parts of a mystical and organic whole − they are dynamic, practical, resourceful and sacred ciphers of nature's complex secrets, patterns and rhythms. The Aboriginals, for example, observe the practical guile and understanding of animals in order to learn about their environment. They find water by following birds, learn about the medicinal properties of plants and herbs by watching the actions of animals in pain (as modern scientists do but in a very different, altogether more sinister way) and sense danger or climatic change by their sudden, nervous behaviour. This form of symbolic rationality posits an organic, dialectical relation between humans and the natural world which respects what is different and strange, aiming not to control and to dominate but to decipher, to learn and to be a part of something beyond itself.[15] Despite his stated preference for dialectical rationality in the *CDR*, Sartre fails to implement this fully enough in relation to his theorization of nature and generally falls back upon a form of analytical reason that he attacks so fervently elsewhere in this text.

However, this conveys only a singular, albeit a very important, aspect of Sartre's theorization of nature for although Kirsner's criticisms identify a very discernible humanist and anthropocentric bias in Sartre's work, they do not take account of other, more postmodernist emphases in his philosophy that work against this humanist impulse. In his later years, for instance, Sartre distanced himself from a simplified, instrumental and reductive view of nature:

nature is not exclusively the in-itself. A plant that is growing is no longer altogether in-itself. It is more complex. It is alive. (1981b, 40)

I think animals have consciousness. In fact I have always thought so. (1981b, 28)

Furthermore, some commentators have discerned a nascent ecological rationality in the *CDR* which, they argue, warns against a purely instrumental or dominating approach towards nature.[16] This is evident most of all, as we will see in the next chapter, in Sartre's emphasis on the 'counterfinality' of matter and in his analysis of the practico-inert which, I argue, both call into question a purely exploitative relation to the natural world.

Although Sartre adopts a strong praxis-based conception of agency in the *CDR* which bears a close resemblance to the Marxist model, he does recognize elsewhere in the *CDR* and, particularly in *Words*, the importance of wider codes of signification (e.g. language) that extend beyond the model of labour in the constitution of the subject. This can be seen also in Sartre's early existential subject which, like the postmodernist subject, is marked most of all by the feature of *contingency*. Since Sartre and postmodernists both envisage the subject as something which must be *created*, they tend as a result to *aestheticize* the subject and the project of authentic self-determination. In *What is Literature?*, for instance, Sartre ventures to suggest that it is only through art that we are able to overcome the separation of subject (*pour-soi*) and object (*en-soi*), the aesthetic object (e.g. the novel) representing an end product and grand fusion that is 'fully myself and fully beyond myself' (1978, 53). Unlike the psychological freedom (of *BN* and *Nausea*) which torments what it lacks (i.e. being), the freedom of art uplifts: '[t]he recognition of freedom by itself is joy' (1978, 52). Although this aestheticized subject goes a long way in providing a positive and important alternative to the calculating and instrumental modernist subject, it is not, however, without difficulties of its own. In the process of aestheticizing the subject, for instance, it has been noted how both Sartre and post-structuralists and postmodernists, like Foucault and Baudrillard, tend to conceive self-determination in restrictive, individualist terms.[17]

According to Terry Eagleton, for instance, by equating the subject with the body and substituting the aesthetic for the ethical, Foucault's subject can be seen essentially as 'a matter, very scrupulously, of surface, art, technique, sensation' (1990, 391). Since Foucault fails to acknowledge the ethical relevance of the subject as a centre of affections, impulses and emotional resistances

> [he] still cannot bring himself to address the subject as such. What we have here, rather than the subject and its desires, is the body and

pleasures – a half-way, crab-wise, aestheticising move towards the subject which leaves love as technique and conduct rather than as tenderness and affection, as praxis rather than interiority. (1990, 391)

Despite Foucault's dislike of techniques of modern power, there is, Eagleton notes, a certain kind of 'aesthetic gratification at its productivity' in his conception of 'bodies and pleasures'. By reducing the emotional core of the subject to the 'thinness' of somatic surface and technique, Foucault resurrects the 'sexual subject' of popular discourse (found in sex manuals, magazines, etc.) for whom sexuality is conceived precisely as a matter of surface, sensation and technique.[18] In the realm of ascetic sexual practice we are not, as Eagleton notes, 'permitted to enter into the tabooed realms of affection, emotional intimacy' (1990, 395).

This reveals, as Eagleton makes clear, a very discernible 'thinness' in Foucault's conception of the subject that arises from a failure to consider the emotional and mutual context of sexuality. This can be seen too in Sartre's treatment of sexuality in *BN* where the sexual act is seen to involve simply the objectification and appropriation of the other. Within this context the other becomes a featureless, anonymous other, a sexual instrument whose interiority is insignificant in the heat of bodily sensation and appropriation. There is accordingly no affective or emotional context that underpins and nourishes the act of sexual union as Sartre describes it in *BN* – the *ecstasis* of flesh takes place in an absence of other forms of communication or contact that are non-appropriative or carnal.

As mentioned previously, the postmodernist subject has been similarly criticized for its 'thinness' and lack of substance. Ferry and Renaut pose the question in this context, whether the 'scattered', 'pulverised' and 'exploded' subject popularized by postmodernists can 'really make a person?' (1990, 65). This 'exploded' and fragmented subject, they argue, mirrors the rise of individualism and egoism under contemporary capitalism as its identity is essentially located in the aesthetic (consumer) choices and styles it adopts rather than in the affective ties or emotional impulses it has towards others. Since the postmodernist subject is isolated and atomized, they have no real sense of continuity or stable, identifiable points of self-reference (gained through the ongoing narrative of our relations with others) and thus have nothing substantial to hold them together. This can be seen most of all in Baudrillard's postmodern individual who, anonymous and disconnected from others, is pulled in all directions by media forces and by networks of cultural codes that totally overhang them and prevent them from organizing themselves as a unified, meaningful or effective centre of agency. Lacking a proper account of intersubjectivity and any sense of an 'emotional core' to the subject, postmodernism ultimately restricts and strips down the subject to a thin aesthetic surface underneath which there is seemingly nothing but a chaotic process of change and fragmentation. One can conclude in this respect that the postmodern discourse of the subject – despite desperate protests to the contrary – has failed to break out of an individualist framework and is thus caught within the aporias of (what Habermas refers to as) a 'philosophy of subjectivity' that closes off possibilities for reciprocal action and for more dialogical modes of self-understanding.

To a certain extent, Sartre's theorization of the project in *BN* provides some way out of these difficulties associated with the postmodern subject. Through the notion of the project, for instance, Sartre provides some sense of an ongoing narrative that unifies the subject and makes possible a determinate self-reference. This is developed further in the *CDR* where the 'totalizing project' now includes the socio-historical (intersubjective) milieu as a necessary matrix for its realization. Similarly, Sartre's idea of authenticity involves accepting one's dual nature as both freedom (change) and facticity (stability),[19] thus avoiding the simple valorization of change sometimes found in postmodernist idealizations such as Deleuze and Guattari's 'Schizo-subject' and 'Nomad'.

In spite of this, however, the underlying basis of the Sartrean subject is strongly individualist and in this respect confirms and mirrors the anomic postmodern individual. This is reflected in Sartre's treatment of the other in *BN* (who is seen to represent a necessary threat to my freedom and identity rather than as a possible means of extending and confirming it) and in his tendency to view authenticity as a purely personal rather than collective overcoming. I will investigate Sartre's individualism further (and his attempts to overcome it in the *CDR* and in his later work) in Chapter 3 where I consider the political implications and logic of his work.

In conclusion, it is possible to discern a number of common features between the Sartrean subject and the decentred post-structuralist and postmodernist subject. As Sartre's work evolves from the early phenomenological–existential subject to his later 'encumbered' subject, this commonality becomes more apparent, but, as we have seen, there is still much in Sartre's earlier conception of the subject that prefigures later post-structuralist approaches despite his underlying Cartesian emphasis. Even Sartre's residual attachment to some form of binarism (which he maintains throughout *BN* and the *CDR* by means of the *pour-soi/en-soi* distinction) is not always posed in terms of strict separation or opposition and might not be interpreted as necessarily invalidating the possibility of convergence with some post-structuralists like Deleuze and Foucault. In the case of Deleuze and Guattari, for instance, it can be seen that, like Sartre, they are generally content to work within the framework of a certain kind of binarism and generally multiply dualistic concepts (e.g. paranoia/schizophrenia, molar/molecular, arborescent/rhizomatic, State apparatus/nomad war machine, smooth/striated) rather than dissolve them. Similarly, Foucault's work can be located within a certain binarist logic that revolves around the generation of dualities. As Bannet points out, for instance:

> Dualities are not merely the object of Foucault's historical studies; they are also an essential dimension of his method. Foucault's histories are written at the point of division between dualities, at the point where opposites mutually define and determine each other while remaining absolutely distinct. (1989, 99)

Bannet's description above could be applied equally to Sartre's dialectical method in the *CDR*. As we will see in the next chapter, Sartre's guiding concept of dialectical reason incorporates a form of analysis that uncovers the indissoluble unity of the organic and inorganic, criticizing 'binarist' forms of exploration that are static between entities (subject/object). Thus, although Sartre continues to rely on dualistic distinctions in the *CDR*, he forces us (as Henri Lefebvre observed shortly after its publication in 1961) 'to reconsider the classical philosophical categories dialectically' (1961, 61) and so, like Foucault, locates his analysis 'at the point where opposites mutually define and determine each other'. Unlike the Hegelian dialectic, Sartre's dialectic does not collapse one term into the other but explores the ground that lies between them – the space of the con-juictive and . . . and the 'intermezzo', which, as Deleuze and Guattari state in *A Thousand Plateaus*, allows us 'to pass between the traditional dualisms' (1987, 277).

Despite this commonality between Sartre and the post-structuralists, their approaches to the subject do move along reverse trajectories. Although Sartre deconstructs the subject and works against a metaphysics of presence, he refrains from abandoning agency or effacing the subject completely, consistently preserving a space for the freedom 'which makes of a totally conditioned social being someone who does not render back completely what his conditioning has given him' (1974a, 35). In the 1970s Foucault, Derrida and others dropped their outright hostility to the subject and moved on to the project of articulating an affirmative conception of agency guided, as Foucault acknowledged, by Sartre's 'theoretical insight to the practice of creativity' (1983, 64).

While Sartre's consistent commitment to preserving a space for freedom contrasts favourably with post-structuralist excesses that embraced an extreme form of anti-humanism in the 1960s, it is also the case that the decentred postmodernist subject inspired by Deleuze and others can help guide us beyond some of the problems connected with Sartre's theorization of the subject, particularly in the *CDR*, where Sartre generally conceives the subject primarily as an agent of instrumental praxis. In place of this instrumental conception of the subject based on the notion of purposeful, redirective and instrumental activity, postmodernists focus instead on more experiential, aesthetic and discursive modes of self-understanding which are based less on a notion of 'doing' than on a sensation of 'being' and relate not so much to the development of the subject's practical powers as to the enhancement of his or her conceptual and sensual powers. These involve, in Marcuse's words, 'an acceptance of becoming' rather than those, like labour, which reveal 'an imposition of being', and imply a much more receptive and less possessive or domineering conception of selfhood, based on a 'being-with' rather than a 'being-against' nature (1955, Chapter 4). Indeed, Sartre's general tendency to reduce the qualitative variety of nature to the homogenous and quantitative in the *CDR* stands in direct contrast to the postmodernist project to re-enchant nature and so reverse the dry, analytical, utilitarian and instrumental logic of modern science.

Although the Sartrean and postmodernist subject can critically gain from each other in this respect, it is also possible to find problems common to both which stem, as we have seen, from what Eagleton calls the 'thinness' of the aesthetic subject and from the general lack of intersubjectivity or collectivity in Sartrean and postmodernist theory. In the next two chapters, I will examine these considerations further as they relate to Sartre's social, historical and political theory.

2

Social Theory and History

Is it not necessary to draw a line between those who believe that we can continue to situate our present discontinuities within the historical and transcendental tradition of the nineteenth century and those who are making a great effort to liberate themselves, once and for all, from this conceptual framework? (Foucault, 1977b, 120)

The most important discovery of dialectical experience is that man is mediated by things to the extent that things are mediated by man. (*CDR*, 82)

Sartre's social theory

'Hell is other people' (Being and Nothingness)
Alongside his conception of absolute freedom, perhaps the best-known feature of Sartre's existentialism in *BN* is his idea that conflict lies at the centre of our relations with other people. This dimension of Sartre's existentialism is illustrated most famously, of course, in his play *Huis Clos* which revolves around the central dramatic idea that 'hell is other people'.[1]

Responding to Heidegger, Sartre insists that '[t]he essence of relations between consciousnesses is not Mitsein, it is conflict' (*BN*, 429). According to Sartre, my actions do not just take place in the world of inert matter, but are equally actions in a human world – that is to say, other people constitute a fundamental structure of my situation. Since, in Sartre's view, situations are essentially individual in the sense that they are 'subjectively constituted', when another person enters my situation they bring with them an individual perspective of their own (in which I am an element) and represent for me a focal point of 'counter-organization': 'Thus, the appearance among the objects of my universe of an element of disintegration in that universe is what I mean by the appearance of one man in my universe' (BN, 255). Unlike a simple object such as a knife, the other is not an inert en-soi easily integrated into my situation, but has an alternative individual perspective within which they organize and constitute their own situation. According to Sartre, this gives rise to an essential conflict of interests since I seek to make the situation 'mine' and they organize it as 'theirs'. This conflict is fought on the level of 'the gaze', where I am either subject (pour-soi), directing it, or object (en-soi), constituted by it:

> It is in relation to every living man that every human reality is present or absent on the basis of an original presence. This original presence can have meaning only as a being-looked-at; that is, according to whether the other is an object for me or whether I myself am an object-for-the-other. (BN, 279–80)

Since, Sartre maintains, I can never be how the other objectifies me (all I am is the activity of consciousness, a 'perpetual surpassing towards a coincidence with [myself] which is never given' (BN, 139)), and equally, they are not how I objectify them, our meeting is catapulted into a circular conflict where I 'steal' the freedom of the other or lose my own to their objectifying glance: 'Thus being seen constitutes me as a defenceless being for a freedom which is not my freedom. It is in this sense that we can consider ourselves as slaves in so far as we appear to the Other' (BN, 358).

My image in the eyes of the other constitutes a fundamental shackle on my free consciousness in Sartre's view since the effect of being-looked-at is that 'I cause myself to learn from outside what I must be' (BN, 263). Relations with others are founded in this way on conflict and objectification (domination and counter-domination): 'All of men's complex patterns of conduct towards one another are only enrichments of these two original attitudes' (BN, 407). Even love in the social universe of BN is a scene of appropriation and struggle, precluding synthesis or equilibrium – 'a battle', as Iris Murdoch (1953) describes, 'between two hypnotists in a closed room'. Sartre concludes that a state of unity among individuals is impossible, for such an assimilation 'would necessarily involve the disappearance of Otherness in the Other' (BN, 366). The possibility of community or common transcendence is thus seen at the outset to be antithetical to individuality and subjective freedom: 'We are always . . . in a state of instability in relation to the Other. We pursue the impossible ideal of the simultaneous apprehension of his freedom and of his objectivity' (BN, 408). Clearly, Sartre's metaphysical narrative of the gaze runs against the grain of any sense of collective overcoming and solidarity. The Hobbesian struggle between individuals is always fought in BN on the level of the singular possessive pronoun, whether it be 'mine' or 'theirs', thus precluding any sense of collective responsibility for the situation as 'ours'. Indeed, as the term suggests, the pour-soi is concerned primarily for-itself and is present to itself before being present to the other. Consequently, the other is cast in an entirely negative light by Sartre – he represents for me only the assassin of my identity whom I apprehend in cold exteriority and is, as such, but a pale imitation of the concrete other whom I meet in everyday life. In Sartre's early philosophical scheme we are always pour-autrui and only in a secondary, derivative sense are we ever avec-autrui as reciprocal subjects: 'The being-for-others precedes and founds the being-with-others' (BN, 44). Thus, there exists an ontological asymmetry between 'us' and 'we' in BN since the former is said to be real whereas the latter is 'a purely subjective experience' (BN, 429).

In this respect, Sartre's social theory in BN remains abstract and incomplete since he does not go beyond a dyadic account of self and other, which, as he realized later in the CDR, is insufficient for the explanation of 'macro-phenomena', such as institutions, languages and collective structures. Although Sartre does begin to probe the dynamic of class structure and collectivity in BN through his concept of 'the Third' (he illustrates, for instance, how the experience of a unified, common 'we' can arise when imposed on me and an other by the objectifying glance of the Third, thus forming a basis for class unity when workers experience the 'we' of solidarity by being characterized as a common group of 'them' by the capitalist Third), he does this by extrapolating from dyadic structures and so yields only an abstract account of the interpersonal rather than a proper account of the social.

By reducing the social to the level of the interpersonal, Sartre effectively reinforces some basic assumptions of liberalism in *BN* in spite of the obvious vitriol he directs towards bourgeois humanist values in his early work. In Marcuse's view for instance, '[b]ehind the nihilistic language [of *BN*] lurks the ideology of free competition, free initiative and equal opportunity' (1983, 174). This is revealed most clearly in Sartre's concept of the gaze where, according to Marcuse, the other is glimpsed as directly hostile and 'appears as the one who usurps, appropriates and appraises my world, as the "thief" of my possibilities'. Indeed, the methodological framework Sartre generally employs in *BN* is one which he later repudiates in the *CDR* and elsewhere for generating an analytic spirit of social atomism which 'resolves collectivities into individual elements' and fails to see 'synthetic realities' (1965, 55–6). This kind of analytical reason which constitutes bonds between individuals only 'in the milieu of exteriority' (*CDR*, 285) forms the basis of capitalist hegemony by reinforcing the 'absolute separation between people which is so crucial to the continuing domination of the individualistic bourgeoisie' (*CDR*, 97).

As we will see in the rest of this chapter, Sartre's social theory of 'practical ensembles' adumbrated in the *CDR* is an explicit attempt to overcome the deficiencies of this atomistic methodology which plagues his philosophy in *BN*.

Fusion and Seriality (Critique of Dialectical Reason)
Sartre's work between *BN* and the *CDR* can be seen as a transitional phase in which his focus shifts steadily from individualistic to more overtly social categories, precipitated for the most part by criticisms levelled at the abstract and individualistic nature of his early work by his companions, Simone de Beauvoir (in *Force of Circumstance*) and Maurice Merleau-Ponty (in *Phenomenology of Perception*), who both stressed the conditional, situational and social nature of freedom. In *Existentialism and Humanism*, for instance, Sartre begins to consider the importance of the intersubjective realm (public life) as a necessary condition for individual freedom:

> The man who discovers himself directly in the Cogito recognizes that he cannot be anything . . . unless others recognize him as such . . . Thus

we discover a world which we shall call intersubjectivity. It is in this world that a man decides what he is and what others are. (1966b, 303)

In *What is Literature?* he anticipates his denunciation of bourgeois analytical reason in the *CDR* by attacking the bourgeois denial of pro-letarian solidarity — 'the bourgeois . . . sees only psychological relations among the individuals whom his analytic propaganda has seduced and separated' (1977(2), 159–60).

In the *CDR* Sartre turns his attention first of all to the impact of materiality, arguing that the structure of relations between individuals is underdetermined and abstract until 'the ensemble of material circum-stances' on which it is established has been defined (*CDR*, 255). As we have seen, Sartre's methodology in the *CDR* revolves around the dia-lectical circularity of praxis and matter. It is the presence of inorganic matter that makes praxis possible and, in satisfying need, praxis finds itself subject to the laws of inorganic matter even as it negates and totalizes it. Conversely, it is the inertness of matter which holds the imprint of praxis after it has ceased (*CDR*, 82).

Throughout the *CDR*, Sartre gives numerous examples to illustrate the intimate bond between the two. In describing a system of deforestation in China, for example, he shows how '[t]he positive system of cultivation was transformed into an infernal machine' (*CDR*, 162). In this situation, each peasant sought to increase and ameliorate his own plot of land by tearing down trees, the aggregated effect of which led to a radical loss of soil protection and poor soil quality for all. In each case, Sartre argues, '[t]he worker becomes his own material fatality; he produces the inundations which will ruin him' (*CDR*, 234).

In the numerous examples Sartre gives, he demonstrates how matter 'reacts' to human praxis with an anti-praxis of its own, distorting it in the process into an oppressive force which obstructs and demands further praxis. For Sartre, throughout everyday life praxis spawns 'vampire objects' (*CDR*, 169) that demand further praxis — a machine, for instance, once created, requires a constant regime of reconditioning and maintenance as well as other machines and people to work them. In the case of bourgeois property owners, Sartre describes how matter becomes alienated in the process of working it and how praxis turns back upon its originators to demand further action which was not part of the original project. The dialectical relation between praxis and its material object becomes inverted so that praxis is now determined by matter:

> To preserve its reality as a dwelling, a house must be inhabited, that is to say, looked after, heated, swept, repainted, etc.; otherwise it deteriorates. This vampire object constantly absorbs human action, lives on the blood taken from man and finally lives in symbiosis with him. (*CDR*, 169)

In this way, Sartre maintains, the circularity of praxis and matter always reveals a double element at work: 'objectification (or man working upon matter) and objectivity (or totalized matter working upon man)' (*CDR*, 284). It is a form of osmosis in which each, through interaction, becomes imbued with the features of the other.

The practico-inert

Sartre's concept of the practico-inert transposes the dialectical circularity of praxis and matter onto a collective, societal level in which human praxis gives rise to contingent social arrangements and relations that, once fixed, serve to limit and circumscribe the very freedom from which they originate. These relations, according to Sartre, form the practico-inert and represent the accretions and the sedimentations of past action in the form of a network of meanings and demands to be interiorized by totalizing individuals and groups. The practico-inert thus refers to the role of human action in the constitution of an inert social reality which in turn comes to dominate further action. Sartre describes this process in the following way:

> in dissolving the inherited practico-inert, the sovereign and, through him, the society, interiorize the social structures it conditioned; and the transcendence of this interiorization, that is, its practical re-exteriorization, has as its outcome, in a slightly different context, the constitution of another practico-inert that reconditions men, into personal structures and finally praxis itself. (*CDR*(2), 288)

In the *CDR* Sartre puts forward a theory of 'practical ensembles' to reveal exactly how individual and multiple praxes condition and modify each other to give rise in turn to a further series of totalizations and praxis. Individuals encounter each other in this context no longer as 'looks' (as in *BN*), but primarily as practical organisms competing for scarce resources in order to satisfy need. Thus, Sartre tells us, investigation must

> set out from the immediate, that is to say from the individual fulfilling himself in his abstract praxis so as to rediscover, through deeper and deeper conditioning, the totality of his practical bonds with others and, thereby, the structures of the various practical multiplicities and, through their contradictions and struggles, the absolute concrete: historical man. (*CDR*, 52)

'Historical man' is, for Sartre, no longer the isolated individual of *BN* for whom the social realm comprises but a single aspect of his factitious situation, but is now an irreducibly 'social being' whose actions unfold in the same material milieu as the actions of others and are in turn conditioned by them. To illustrate the determining power of the material world in structuring definite relations between individuals, Sartre introduces the notion of scarcity which, he argues, constitutes a determining historical project that implicates everyone, arising not just from the individual totalizing the field as need but as the entire society totalizing the field as one in which there is not enough.

In conditions of scarcity, the gratification of one individual's need is at the same time a threat to everyone else. Conflict becomes inevitable in this way as the result of material scarcity which casts each as the potential enemy and thief of the possibilities of the other: 'scarcity realizes the passive totality of the individuals within a collectivity as an impossibility of co-existence' (*CDR*, 129). In such conditions it is inevitable that some people are designated in some way as 'expendables' and as 'non-human' in relation to the provision of scarce resources: 'as long as the reign of scarcity continues, each and every man will contain an inert structure of non-humanity which is in fact no more than material negation which has been interiorized' (*CDR*, 130).

Sartre's analysis of scarcity demonstrates that social relations cannot be properly understood without considering the determining role of matter and the mediation of the material field. He shows in this respect how scarcity can stamp human relations with the hallmark of matter and, in doing so, transforms reciprocity between individuals into a state of imminent violence. However, it is not just in circumstances of scarcity that the practico-inertia of reified matter impinges upon the structure of human relations. The practico-inert manifests its influence in all spheres of social life – in the range of objects we use (e.g. computers, machines), in the buildings we live and work in, in the range of conventions that we appeal to, and, of course, in the languages we communicate through. In the case of language, for instance, Sartre points in his later work to its practico-inert character and to the influence of linguistic structures in constituting thought:

> On [this] level, language presents itself, in effect as an autonomous system which reflects social unification . . . This is the stage of structure, in which the totality appears as a thing without man, a network of oppositions in which each element is defined in terms of another, where there is no fixed point, but only relations, only differences. (1966c, 88)

Since all social forms, including language, have their basis in the practico-inert, the practico-inert is said to constitute 'fundamental sociality' (CDR, 318): 'it is at the practico-inert level that sociality is produced in men by things as a bond of materiality which transcends and alters simple human relations' (CDR, 304).

In places, Sartre's analysis of the practico-inert does seem to signify a descent into a form of determinism where the fragile, exteriorized freedom of human beings inevitably congeals into imperious, crystalline structures which control all subsequent action. In this respect, Sartre makes it clear that practico-inert existence represents a definite curtailment of the freedom he popularized in BN:

> It would be quite wrong to interpret me as saying that man is free in all situations, as the Stoics claimed. I mean the exact opposite: all men are slaves in so far as their life unfolds in the practico-inert field and in so far as this field is conditioned by scarcity. (CDR, 331)

> History, taken at this level, presents a terrible and hopeless meaning; it appears, in effect, that men are united by this inert and demoniacal

negation which takes their substance (that is to say their labour) away from them in order to return it against all of them in the form of *active inertness* and of totalization through extermination. (*CDR*, 123)

However, despite odd moments in the *CDR* where Sartre edges towards a fatalistic analysis of the practico-inert, he makes it clear elsewhere in this text that free praxis must form an essential element in the explanation of all 'impersonal processes':

> The practico-inert can be treated as a process . . . but this process in so far as it is already passive action, presupposes the entire praxis . . . which it reabsorbs and transforms in the object, while still being based on its real, abstract pullulation. (*CDR*, 713)

Since the practico-inert is 'simply the activity of others in so far as it is sustained and diverted by inorganic inertia' (*CDR*, 556), it always remains possible to invert its structures through common praxis. With regard to language, for instance, Sartre states that:

> this thing without man is at the same time matter worked by man, bearing the trace of man . . . If you admit the existence [of structure], you must also admit that language exists only as spoken, in other words, in act. Each element of this system refers to a whole, but this whole is dead if nobody takes it up for his own purposes, makes it work . . . In the system of language there is something that the inert cannot provide by itself, the trace of a practice. Structure imposes itself upon us only to the extent that it is made by others. (1966c, 88)

In contrast to *BN* where Sartre dealt with structure only in the metaphysical sense of elucidating the ontological structures of individual experience (such as death and temporality), in the *CDR*, structure forms a constituent part of social life. The constitution of a practico-inert field of structure precipitates a process in which humans become a product of their own product, only to reorientate themselves and their activity to become producers again. The practico-inert reveals the dynamic relation between 'action as the negation of matter (in its present organization and on the basis of a future re-organization), and matter . . . as the negation of action' (*CDR*, 159).

Serialities, groups and institutions

One of the most original aspects of Sartre's work in the *CDR* is the way in which he transposes his basic ontological couplet of praxis and inertia onto the realm of individual–group relations to reveal definite domains of social life. This move is effected by Sartre through the separation of distinct, but abstract 'social wholes' onto which are juxtaposed the features of praxis and inertia.[2]

The inert structure of social life, according to Sartre, can be found in the *serial* group. Seriality involves a certain ordering of people which 'becomes a negative principle of unity and of determining everyone's fate as other by every Other as Other' (*CDR*, 261). The series constitutes a negative unity of inertia, a reified totalization maintained by what Sartre calls 'hexis' (habit) in which, rather than transforming a situation, individuals instead merely endure it. In this serial group they are bound together from without by an object which they do not control – 'The series represents the use of alterity as a bond among men under the passive action of an object' (*CDR*, 266).

Examples Sartre gives of serial processes include a radio broadcast, elections and bus queues. In a bus queue, for instance, commuters are both united and separated by the collective object, the bus. It unites them by assembling them together in a demarcated space and by introducing a common interest between them – 'improvement of public transportation, freezing of fares etc.' (*CDR*, 259) – but separates them by making each one an interchangeable and anonymous ordinal unit. Relations between commuters, he insists, are not defined by a positive sense of reciprocity but by otherness and numerical equivalence since each is determined and defined by others in relation to the position to the collective object. It is this sense of anonymity and interchangeability among members of a series which leads Sartre to conclude that '[e]veryone is the same as the Others in so far as he is Other than himself' (*CDR*, 256). My individual characteristics are inessential in the series since, as just 'one other' to the others, I am instantly replaceable by anyone else who might come along: 'In the series everyone becomes himself (as Other than self) in so far as he is Other than the Others, and in so far as the Others are Other than him' (*CDR*, 262).

Serial existence is, for Sartre, a common feature of social life that can be found wherever individuals are brought together 'horizontally' in alterity under the directing force of the practico-inert, through which their relations become structured. It is in the 'otherness' of the serial collective (where relations are unauthored and anonymous) that Sartre finds an enhancement of the relation between persons and things and a decomposition of organicity in social life.

After describing the alienating experience of the series, Sartre proceeds in the *CDR* to counterbalance the negative gravity of serial existence with his analysis of the *groupe-en-fusion*. Where inertia forms the basis of the serial group, *praxis* is the constituent feature of the fused group: 'Praxis is the only real unity of the fused groups: it is praxis which creates the group, and which maintains it and introduces its first internal changes into it' (*CDR*, 418). Fusing groups emerge, according to Sartre, when the practico-inert presents itself both as a negative threat and as a positive occasion for unity. To illustrate this, he describes a situation during the French Revolution where Parisians in the Quartier Saint-Antoine found themselves hemmed in and encircled by the army. It soon became apparent to the people that their survival depended upon breaking out from the narrow streets and storming the Bastille to seize the cache of arms with which the army would make their attack. In this situation, the cache of arms in the Bastille became the practico-inert object and condition of negative threat and of positive unity.

To meet the needs of their situation, Sartre tells us, a group of individuals gathered on the streets united under the common purpose of removing the menace of the army by storming the Bastille. The essential features of this group, Sartre points out, were its spontaneity and its egalitarian structure in which were engendered relations of positive reciprocity. Realizing the full gravity of their situation, each joins together collectively with the others and, once united, each individual act serves to enlarge and to reinforce the collective project. Since each individual praxis is directed towards a common objective, the other becomes for me an embodiment of my own possibilities – 'In the group-in-fusion, the third party is my objectivity interiorised. I do not see it in him as Other, but as mine' (*CDR*, 377).

By joining together, *power* is the first common quality that the group possesses – each individual, according to Sartre, 'receives the power he gives, and . . . sees the other (third party) approaching him as his power' (*CDR*, 376). In the eruptive collective struggle, each individual seizes spontaneously upon the situation and takes upon himself a sphere of responsibility (to act as 'look-out' or as a front-line fighter, to distribute the arms, etc.) within the parameters of the common objective. In the fused group, however, this remains a provisional and contingent activity: X, for instance, assumes the role of watchman because he happens to be standing in an elevated position at the time. No feature of this group is in this sense stratified or structured from without – each responds to the vitality of his own free project in a network of organic solidarity.

In the fused group no individual sacrifices his freedom to the social whole – individual will coincides with the general will of the group and, as in a Rousseauian dream, each finds a confirmation of his own act in the actions of others. As a result, all signs of alterity between individuals dissolve – 'everyone continued to see himself in the Other, but saw himself there as himself . . . everyone sees his own future in the Other' (*CDR*, 354). The fused group represents a state of genuine organic community, in Sartre's view, since it encompasses 'the individual discovery of common action as the sole means of reaching the common objective' (*CDR*, 387). Since no praxis in the group serves to violate or to obstruct any other, but only to enrich it, 'the essential character of the group-in-fusion is the abrupt resurrection of liberty' (*CDR*, 401).

The dialectical movement of group transition does not, however, end with the fused group. From the moment of its inception, the free praxis of the group 'carries a destiny of seriality' (*CDR*, 679) – it is, Sartre maintains, essentially unstable and constantly liable to congeal into seriality. Since the group emerges as a defensive reaction against fear and imminent threat, once this is removed, the fused group falls into dissipation since the practical basis of its unity no longer exists. In order to stop this process of fragmentation the group must impose stability by other means – this happens, Sartre points out, through the introduction of organization, function and the division of labour into the group in addition to a pledge taken by the group for reciprocal protection against the relapse into seriality, alterity and indifference: '[my] pledge becomes my surety for myself in that it is in offering myself, in every third party, as everyone's guarantee of not relapsing, in my person or through my conduct, into social alterity' (*CDR*, 422).

Once the group has achieved the common objective that brought it together, the series of free individual praxes which constituted it becomes an internal threat to its continued existence. To meet this threat, the group tries to achieve what Sartre says it is unable to – ontological status – and thus consolidates itself through the imposition of the pledge and the stratification of function. This serves as a concrete limit to the activity of each individual since, by differentiating tasks, hierarchy is introduced among types of praxis and among members in the group. Alterity returns to the group and, as in the serial group, internal relations between individuals become determined by external relations to objects. In this process the inner qualities of each cease to be relevant and serve only to threaten destabilization and obstruction to the prescribed function. Each member is no longer seen as an initiator of free praxis but, 'through the Other and through all, as an inorganic tool by means of which action is realized' (CDR, 599).

As it develops, the organized, pledged group crystallizes into its final and most solid and inert form – the institution. In the institution, Sartre points out, the individual is no more than a (quasi) inorganic entity whose inertia carries and executes the orders of the sovereign; she must empty herself of herself and submit mechanically to this: 'there is only one freedom for all members of the group; that of the sovereign' (CDR, 620). In order to strengthen its power, the governing group within the institution implements a system of authority (headed by the sovereign) which is designed to guarantee the permanent powerlessness of others by keeping them in serialities. These serialities, manipulated from above, share no common purpose and must be prevented from acquiring one, else they threaten to become 'fused' and thus jeopardize the regulated order of the institution. The vertical structure of the institution ensures that, by means of each level of the totality, the level beneath it is transformed into a 'manipulated thing' (CDR, 657).

According to Sartre, the 'otherness' of the institution differs from that of the serial collective in two important respects. First, the *passive seriality* of the institution differs from the *social inertia* of the series in that it is the result of a collective operation, 'a systematic self-domestication of man by man' (CDR, 606) in favour of a common regulative practice. Second, the *vertical* otherness of the institution differs from the *horizontal* otherness of the serial group in that, in the latter, each is united to the others from without via a collective object, whereas in the former, each is united to the others primarily through a bond of interiority, the command-obedience relation. This relation is founded upon a network of *authority*, the acceptance of which involves the 'interiorization of the impossibility of resisting it' (*CDR*, 630). The sanctions of this authority can range from minor rebuke to physical torture, but in each case, Sartre points out, the authoritarian structure will inevitably produce 'internal anxieties' for those who wish to resist it. If an individual does rebel through radical conscience or through the demand for creative praxis, their acts are treated as the acts of 'the alien, the suspect, the trouble-maker' (*CDR*, 656). The vertical otherness of the institution is in this way founded on 'the mineralization of man at every level, except the highest' (*CDR*, 658).

Perhaps the most important feature of Sartre's analysis of group life in the *CDR* is that relations between individuals can either be antagonistic or cooperative, 'either positive or negative' (*CDR*, 113). This of course marks a significant advance over earlier conclusions in *BN* where relations are seen as *a priori* hostile. The objectifying other, who represents only an 'alienating third' in *BN*, is no longer the sole basis for all social existence — the fused group revolves, in contrast, around the 'mediating third' who constitutes a potential regulatory third without becoming a transcendent other to the group. In the fused group all are seen as co-sovereigns and as organizers of a common project. It represents the archetype of a genuinely free, egalitarian and reciprocal community which has managed to overcome alienation and serial existence and effect 'a transition from the Other to the same' (*CDR*, 612). Within the reciprocal exchanges of the group, the other no longer signifies the one who objectifies and steals my world but one who enables, confirms, reflects and enlarges my possibilities as a partner in common action.

The progressive–regressive method

Marx's famous observation in *The Eighteenth Brumaire* that 'men make history . . . but not in conditions directly chosen' has often split Marxists down opposing paths of historical explanation. The result of this, according to Perry Anderson, is

> the permanent oscillation, the potential disjuncture in Marx . . . between his ascription of the primary motor of historical change to the contradiction between the forces of production and the relations

of production on the one hand ... and to the class struggle on the other hand'. (1983, 34)

The problem for Marxists has been to find the means to reconcile these two distinct types of causality in which the first 'refers essentially to a structural ... reality' and the second 'to the subjective forces contending and colliding for mastery over social forms and historical processes'. Sartre's progressive–regressive method and his social theory of Dialectical Nominalism which he sketches out in the CDR can be seen as his attempt to overcome and to reconcile this 'disjuncture' in Marx's philosophy.

Throughout the CDR, Sartre argues for the indissoluble unity of the organic and the inorganic, characterizing dialectical exchange as a kind of 'osmosis', and thus criticizing philosophical exploration that is static between entities (subject/object) and which covers over the essential fluidity within multiple human situations. In order to make human history and society intelligible, it is thus essential to uncover in precise detail the movement in which individual projects and the generality of the social interpenetrate – to find, in Sartre's words, 'none other than the fundamental identity between an individual life and human history' (CDR, 70). To this end, Sartre's study of Flaubert in The Family Idiot attempts to illuminate the dialectical movement which made of Flaubert a 'Universal Singular' – that is, an individual who was an authentic expression of his historical time, but one with his own unique situation. By means of the progressive–regressive method, Sartre sets out to demonstrate exactly how Flaubert's original choice of being was at the same time a totalization of the French society he lived in.

As Sartre makes clear in the CDR, social life throws us into specific situations (objective) which we interpret and act upon (subjective) and which then place us into new situations (objective). In order to understand this fully, it is essential to analyse each stage of this dialectical transition from objective to subjective to objective. To this end, Sartre's method begins with the social structure and traces its markings in the individual before going back to the individual to follow their actions in the social field: 'The movement of comprehension is simultaneously progressive (towards the objective result) and regressive (I go back towards the original condition)' (SM, 154).

Orthodox Marxism has curtailed analysis by stopping at the objective result and failing to examine the intermediate subjective dimension which, in Sartre's view, must appear 'as a necessary moment in the objective process' (*SM*, 97). It has accordingly left untheorized the space of individual agency which encompasses 'the internalisation of the external and the externalisation of the internal' (*SM*, 97). In doing so, Marxism has abandoned its theoretical legitimacy in regard to revolution which, according to Sartre, is possible only 'if we restore to the individual man his power to go beyond his situation by means of work and action' (*SM*, 99).

If we conceptualize the socio-historical field from the vantage point of revolution, the question of class consciousness (or the lack of it) becomes paramount for Marxist theory. Since each individual project has the quality of totalization, it contains an interpretation and valorization of the world which is connected to living in that world in a determinate place at a given time. The project of going to work each day, for instance, involves an individual recognition that the existing order of production and the socio-political systems which support it cannot at that moment be overturned. It is thus in the realm of subjective, lived experience that revolution is negated or actively encouraged according to whether we choose 'to be resigned or revolutionary' (1977(2), 28). In order to understand the nature of resignation and revolutionary consciousness, Marxism needs to look, in Sartre's view, not just at the objective totality, but must regress back to the individual and see how this totality is sustained in their consciousness and activity. As Sartre makes clear, the socio-historical field comprises moments of objectivity *and* subjectivity and is thus constituted not just by the objective totality of things but also by the multiplicity of human totalizations and the countless interlocked meanings which interpret this totality in various ways.

The progressive–regressive method would make available to Marxism, Sartre hoped, the concrete living experience of human life. In the living experience of the worker, for instance, there exists a whole range of mediations and social contexts that precede or correspond indirectly to their consciousness as a worker and member of an oppressed proletariat. Sartre points out that the worker was not born and does not live their entire life in the workplace, but lives in the context of a family, residential group, community and nation. Many of their basic projects are shaped accordingly through the influence of family, ethnic tradition and community before they even enter the workplace. These influences impinge upon us from the moment we spring from the womb and, Sartre maintains, prior to this – even before it is born the child 'is a determined possibility of the father and mother' (*SM*, 56). In everyday life the workers thus find themselves wrapped in a network of mediations that are not simply reducible to the mode and relations of production and which often serve to obfuscate the consciousness between the worker and their work. If Marxism contents itself with the sole perspective of production it will fail, in Sartre's view, 'to find mediations which allow the individual concrete – the particular life – to emerge from the *general* contradictions of productive forces and relations of production' (*SM*, 57).

According to Sartre, orthodox Marxism has tended to study human beings only statistically, considering them 'from the outside with a total scientific objectivity and like an inert object' (1968, 90). In the *CDR* Sartre addresses this complaint to Engels who

> crown[s] his success with the result that he kills the dialectic twice over to make sure it is dead – the first time by claiming to have discovered it in Nature, and the second time by suppressing it within society. (*CDR*, 712)

Although at one point he claims to be agnostic about Engels's attempt to found a dialectic of nature (see *CDR*, 32–3), he makes it clear elsewhere that nature cannot be dialectical since it has no history and no project:

> only the project, as a mediation between two moments of objectivity, can account for history; that is for human creativity . . . In effect we reduce everything to identity . . . or we make of dialectic a celestial law which imposes itself on the universe . . . or we restore to the individual man his power to go beyond his situation. (*SM*, 99)

Engels's dialectic is like 'a celestial law', according to Sartre, because it is not anchored properly in human praxis and so considers 'the Nature of man [as lying] outside him in an a priori law, in an extra human nature, in a history that begins with the nebulae' (*CDR*, 27). As in Althusser's structuralist Marxism, the dialectic is superimposed over the mechanisms of society but suppressed within it, leading to the idea of a self-perpetuating historical law or conatus. Throughout his work, Sartre is critical of all such theories in social science which reduce the historical process to the force of 'hidden realities', as in 'economism' which, according to Sartre, 'reduce[s] the relations of practical multiplicities to simple contradictory determinations . . . and men to pure anti-dialectical moments of the practico-inert' (*CDR*, 788).

In the *CDR* Sartre agrees with Engels that economic conditions are the determining ones 'in the final analysis'. However, Sartre stresses, it is 'the contradictions within them which form the driving force of history' (*SM*, 31). These contradictions translate for Sartre into a series of 'obscure constraints' and 'exigencies' and are not absolute determinations but demands that must be met and supported by praxis. The class struggle, for instance, cannot be explained simply through an impersonal account of external conflicting forces, but draws its reality from praxis: 'this contradictory unity of each in the Other is generated by praxis and praxis alone' (*CDR*, 794). Sartre does not, of course, deny the reality of socio-historical structure, only its independence from the realm of human praxis. In emphasizing the importance of praxis, he demonstrates that economic structures are not static but develop historically through human agency.

Since orthodox Marxism theorizes individuals as mere fragments or 'supports' (Althusser) of the wider social system, it tends, like certain forms of philosophical *Holism* (as in Durkheim's), to grant this system a kind of self-subsistent autonomy. In relation to the holist's claim, for example, that social wholes are irreducible to the sum of their parts, Sartre's own account of social wholes in the *CDR* does allow them the possibility of 'taking on a life of their own'. Under the sway of the practico-inert, for instance, individuals in the series submit their praxis to outward determinations and become, under the institution, a 'forged tool' for the mechanical functioning of the group. In each case, the social whole precedes and conditions individual activity. However, this reveals just one aspect of a wider dialectical process for Sartre since the relations that structures prescribe are always under the threat of possible revolution.

Unlike the holist who grants an ontological, organic status to the group, Sartre argues that 'the group is not a metaphysical reality, but a definite practical relation of men to an objective and to each other' (*CDR*, 404n.). In Sartre's view, there is no 'hyperorganism' in human collectives, no kind of exterior substance independent of specific human agents – no relation without things that are related.[3] Socio-historical structures always depend for their existence on the totalizing projects of the human agents who are subject to them.

In Sartre's analysis of the fused group, the group hangs together since it contains 'a definite practical relation of men to an objective and to each other' (*CDR*, 404n.). This constitutes a 'form of inter-individual reality' (*CDR*, 367) founded upon a 'practical determination of everyone by everyone, by all and by oneself from the point of view of a common praxis' (*CDR*, 506). There is no hidden reality behind the existence of the group, Sartre insists, only a continuous totalizing on the part of each member from the viewpoint of a collective project. Once this 'practical determination of a common praxis' is no longer sustained in the totalizing projects of its members, the free fluidity of fusion gives way to the coagulated alterity of the series and the organized/institutional collective. Having lost its practical basis, the group has to consolidate itself through a system of rights and duties and, ultimately, through force and terror. Since there exists no ontological basis for the direct assimilation of individual praxis into the organicity of the whole, to refuse dissolution within the group is effectively to legitimize violence as a means of group integration and cohesion (see *CDR*, 613, 630). Sartre's analysis of the ontological conditions of group life can be seen in this way to differ significantly from the holist and orthodox Marxist account. For Sartre, collectives are not substances but a set of ongoing practical relations between individuals while, in the holist's account, they are organic autonomous wholes ontologically prior to the individuals who are no more than abstract reflections or fragments of them.

However, it is not just in contrast to holism that Sartre's social philosophy in the *CDR* can be usefully juxtaposed, but also in relation to the kind of *methodological individualism* (MI) Sartre himself utilizes in *BN*. As we saw in the previous chapter, Sartre delineates only the individual constitution of the social world in *BN* and does not consider sufficiently how this world rebounds back upon the subject with its own set of demands. As such, Sartre extrapolates the social entirely from the individual and the interpersonal and configures it as no more than the temporary site on which individuals meet and freely define their identities.

In this respect, his theoretical framework in *BN* can be placed alongside other theories of MI (e.g. Popper, Hayek) in which social facts are seen as simply the logical constructs of facts about individuals. Social phenomena are reduced to their individual constituent parts and collective entities, such as the army or the market, are seen essentially as theoretical constructs which do not define real relations. The market, for example, is seen only as a theoretical entity, directly founded upon and collapsible into the preferences of individuals and their private dispositions.

Sartre's work in the *CDR* does not sever this explanatory link to the individual, but nor does it deprive the individual of social oxygen as MI tends to do. Once original choices are enacted, they are absorbed into the practico-inert field, become reified and rebound back upon individuals in the form of *de facto* compulsions and prescribed relations. In a state of war, for instance, individuals are thrown into specific relations which connect to the practico-inert field. As in a gladiatorial ring, they are dominated by the force of their prescribed relation which compels them to fight. They are thrown into a reality of 'individuals-in-relation' that inscribes them into real and definite relations which are not reducible to their individual preferences. As Sartre makes clear throughout the *CDR*, it is impossible to understand the structure of relations between individuals unless 'the ensemble of material circumstances' on which it is established has been defined (*CDR*, 255).

In Sartre's analysis of collectivities, entities such as the army are more than purely theoretical constructs extrapolated from individuals since they prescribe and necessitate a definite network of 'inter-individual reality'. In the army, individuals find themselves subject to a whole series of compulsions, interdictions, punishments, rewards and violent reprisals which circumscribes their activity – the ultimate sanction of death for desertion, for example, constitutes a definite horizon on which individual (totalizing) projects must fix. Interest is in this way defined through the structure of the practico-inert and cannot be derived entirely from individual subjectivities:

either 'everyone follows his interest', which implies that divisions between men are natural — or it is divisions between men, resulting from the mode of production, which make interest (particular or general, individual or class) appear as a real moment of the relations between men. (*CDR*, 216)

This does not mean, however, that individuals are completely enslaved to their practico-inert field and group structure since these cannot ontologically absorb or annul entirely individual praxis. Interests may be defined in a concrete way by the practico-inert, but they are not always integrated directly or uniformly into the totalizing projects of individuals. In Sartre's social theory structure and collectivities are *nominal* entities which circumscribe human action, but remain forever conditional upon it. Once cemented, they have a nominal reality that is both imperious and yet porous to human praxis. They are not illusory abstractions from facts about individuals (as in MI) and nor do they have 'the type of metaphysical existence' which holists grant them: 'We repeat with Marxism: there are only men and real relations between men' (*SM*, 76).

In the *CDR* Sartre contrasts his own *dialectical reason* with the form of *analytical reason* employed by holism and MI. Analytical reason, in Sartre's view, engenders a fixed immobility in its attempt to understand the social field since it proceeds by dissolving objects into parts and then explains subsequent interaction in terms of causality and force. In MI, for instance, the past is fragmented into a false plurality because it does not connect individual projects to the socio-historical field. The effect of this is to sever the vital link from the past to the present to the future. It is this field, according to Sartre, which constitutes a unified horizon that connects individual projects and which forms a continuum that links the past to the future. As he explains:

I find myself dialectically conditioned by the totalized and totalizing part of the process of human development: as a 'cultured' man . . . I totalize myself on the basis of centuries of history and, in accordance with my culture, I totalize this experience. This means that my life itself is centuries old, since the schemata which permit me to understand, to modify and to totalize my practical undertakings . . . have *entered the present* (present in their effect and past in their completed history). (*CDR*, 54)

MI effectively shifts this reality into the 'inner natures' of private individuals and the plurality of their dispositions. Holism too employs this kind of immobile separation between agency and structure where there is no sense of co-dependence, only relations of exteriority in which praxis is dissolved into the determining force of the objective totality. Sartre argues in the *CDR* that analytical reasoning does have a limited use and can be applied to praxis made passive in the exteriority of the inert (as in the processes of the market, for instance). However, he stresses, it cannot be extended to the multiplicity of praxes which gave rise to structures in the first place. He does acknowledge that there is indeed a skeleton of the inert and quantifiable within social life, but this is not so much individuals themselves, only their relations.

History, totalization and dialectical reason

In the *CDR* Sartre implements his principle of the dialectical circularity between praxis and inertia on the level of the individual, social groups and history. In Sartre's view, orthodox Marxism fails to make history intelligible since it dissolves what is contingent and singular into the universal and necessary – its 'sole purpose is to force the events, the persons, or the acts considered into pre-fabricated moulds' (*SM*, 37). This is most evident, for instance, in what can be seen as the eschatological and teleological basis of Marx's work in which history is granted an internal logic, end-point or necessary course of development.[4]

For Sartre, action always imposes changed conditions and the creation of counterfinalities. There exists to this extent a kind of 'cunning of History' in which history continually escapes its makers and participants experience negatively what may turn out to have positive effects (and vice versa). Unlike the Hegelian 'cunning of History', however, Sartre posits no underlying, single direction to history since it inevitably faces fracture and detotalization stemming from the 'irreducible individuality of the person' (1983, 31). History thus reveals, in Sartre's words:

[an] impossible synthesis of the continuous and discontinuous ... Movement broken by nothingness: birth and death. At the distance of a birth and a death, what was progress becomes proposed solution, that is, closed in on itself and problematic. (*CDR*, 33)

Throughout his work, Sartre eschews a teleological or progressivist model of historical change, focusing instead on the radical contingency of history and on the problematic nature of the notion of progress. In the second volume of the *CDR*, for instance, he questions briefly the idea of progress and puts forward the suggestion that this might be defined as the 'positive transformation of the practical field by me . . . in such a way that, between this new being and this new field, the relations will be better than between me and my field' (*CDR*(2), 410), but does not go on to enlarge upon exactly what 'better' might mean. Considering the question of whether trading-posts constituted an improvement for the Eskimos, Sartre poses the deeper question 'are such comparisons really possible? Do they have any meaning?' (*CDR*(2), 409). Progress is thus always in question for Sartre since fundamentally no single mind or perspective can unite our actions into a single meaning and direction. As he states in the *Cahiers*: 'Deep within himself every man is repelled by the end of History. He wants to make himself and to make the world in a creative ignorance . . . Existentialism does not present itself as the end of History or even as a progress' (1983, 99).

Sartre's usual emphasis on detotalization and on the existential perspective of the individual are, however, offset by other elements in the *Critiques* where he seeks historical unity and sets himself the 'historical task . . . to bring closer the moment when History will have *only one meaning*' (*SM*, 90). To this end, Sartre investigates the possibility of whether opposed collectivities struggling against each other can provide a single history, arguing at one point that history is intelligible only if divergent praxes 'finally appear as partially totalizing and as connected and merged in their very oppositions and diversities by an intelligible totalization from which there is no appeal' (*CDR*, 817). Since this totalization 'can only be the totalization of concrete totalizations effected by a multiplicity of totalizing individualities' (*CDR*, 37), the problem of history is, Sartre states, 'the problem of a totalization without a totalizer' (*CDR*, 817). In the second volume of the *CDR* he continues this quest for historical intelligibility, observing that, if there is no 'unity of the different classes which supports and produces their irreducible conflicts', human history effectively 'decomposes into a plurality of particular histories' (*CDR*(2), 20). His eventual abandonment of the second volume of the *CDR* is commonly seen, however, as a concession of failure on his part to produce a single totalization of this kind that is 'beyond all appeal'.

Where the first volume of the *CDR* essentially outlines a *synchronic* analysis of the dialectical method, the second represents a concrete implementation of this method on a *diachronic* level as Sartre seeks to make intelligible the degeneration of socialism and the rise of Stalin in Bolshevik Russia following the Revolution. The deviation of the Russian Revolution, according to Sartre, is an illustration of the 'petrifying backlash of praxis upon itself' (*CDR(2)*, 129). In the face of capitalist threat and encirclement, the only way to safeguard the revolution 'was to increase pitilessly, day by day, the rate of production' (*CDR(2)*, 129). This gave rise ultimately to social differentiation, function, and hierarchy in the form of 'Stakhanovites, activists and Stalin prizewinners' (*CDR(2)*, 133). Furthermore, as Sartre's analysis of the fused group in the *CDR* suggests, the revolutionary group in Russia was always liable to degenerate into an institution in an attempt to impose authority and unity, the initial construction of socialism thus being marked by 'the indissoluble aggregation of bureaucracy, of Terror, and of the cult of the personality' (*CDR*, 662). In this respect, Sartre suggests that the rise and personal cult of Stalin were an inevitable response to the exigencies of the situation:

> can we say, then, that Stalin was required, even in what was most singular about him, even in the determinations that came to him from his milieu, from his childhood, from the *private* features of his adventure . . . ? Was *that former Georgian seminarist* really necessary? There will be a temptation to answer yes . . . (*CDR(2)*, 215–16)

In view of this, critical attention has been brought to the necessitarian tone of Sartre's analysis of history in the second volume of the *CDR* which, in Aronson's view, 'leaves him morally too neutral in the face of Stalin's brutality' (1980, 285) and in which, according to Dobson, 'historical actors are *displaced* to the point where control over objectives and their realisation is, at best, tenuous' (1997, 14). As Dobson himself notes earlier (1997, 8), however, the second volume of Sartre's *CDR* is not completely lacking in moral judgement for he does stress at times the personal responsibility of Stalin, who was not 'the instrument of the situation – of History – as Marxists too often think; but, on the contrary, inasmuch as Stalin made himself the man of the situation by the reply he gave to the exigencies of the moment' (*CDR*(2), 196). Sartre's moral judgement can thus be found in the space between the objective demands of the situation and Stalin's actual practice. Although the revolutionary regime had to increase production to meet the threat of an encircling capitalist enemy:

> ten million tons of pig-iron obtained by threats and bloody measures of coercion (executions, concentration camps, etc.) were *on no account* comparable to ten million tons of pig-iron obtained in the same perspective, and by an authoritarian government, but without coercive measures. (*CDR*(2), 207)

Thus, in spite of the sometimes necessitarian tone of Sartre's analysis of Bolshevik Russia, he does not abandon completely his existential perspective of personal responsibility and historical contingency. In the second volume of the *CDR* Sartre theorizes two sources of historical deviation – praxis being deviated by its own results and the influence of personal factors. Although he provides little sense of control over the first of these, it is this second element which introduces historical responsibility into Sartre's scheme. Even though, for Sartre, 'circumstances determine the individual's powers' (*CDR*(2), 219), he continues to work against a purely functionalist account of history in the second volume of the *Critique*, maintaining that, even under conditions of scarcity, people will always 'overflow' the objective historical task (*CDR*(2), 219).

The social world of postmodernism

One of the main features of postmodernist theory is its suspicion of (and in some cases direct hostility towards) Marxism as a radical theory of social explanation. As a 'mirror image' of capitalism, Marxism is attacked for its modernist assumptions of rationality, social coherence and 'productivism' (that is, its over-reliance on the model of production and the labour-process as an explanatory basis of social life), as well as for its 'macro-theoretical', universalizing and totalizing methods.

In this section I examine criticisms of Marxism and modernism found in Foucault's genealogical analysis of modern society and in Baudrillard's semiological revolt against Marxism. In many ways, Foucault's genealogy and Baudrillard's semiology can be viewed as important and useful indicators of a growing dissatisfaction with Marxism and Marxist explanations of modern society. In Foucault's genealogy, Marxist understandings of power are called into question since they are seen to rely too exclusively on macro-theoretical concerns about political economy and the repressive nature of state power. The effect of this, in Foucault's view, is that Marxism neglects the *productive* aspect of power (the fact that it produces domains of objects, discourses, etc.) and thus fails to uncover modes of domination in modern society that extend beyond the state and the realm of political economy. Baudrillard takes up and extends this criticism of Marxism while in turn criticizing Foucault's own theory of power in *Forget Foucault* for omitting key mechanisms of power and social reproduction, such as the media, fashion, semiotics, leisure and consumption, that loom large in contemporary postmodern society.

Where the attitude of Affirmative postmodernists like Foucault, Derrida, Deleuze and Guattari towards Marxism can largely be seen as ambivalent,[5] Sceptics like Baudrillard are generally much less forgiving and much more directly hostile. Although Baudrillard was initially favourably disposed towards Marxism in his work of the 1960s (offering his own semiological analysis as a supplementary theoretical addition to Marxist analysis) in his later work this attitude becomes one of fundamental opposition. To this extent, Baudrillard's depiction of a postmodern society characterized by simulation, implosion and hyperreality presents a social landscape which, he argues, is no longer amenable to modernist theories (like Marx's) that base their understanding on a productivist model.

Foucault's genealogy
According to Foucault, the origin of what we call truth or knowledge is bound up inextricably with domination, subjugation and the relationship of forces — that is, *power*: 'Between techniques of knowledge and strategies of power, there is no exteriority' (1978, 98). Basing his genealogy on the Nietzschean conception that there is no essence to things or no immobile form of things developing throughout history,

Foucault argues that any particular claim to know something involves the attempt to put a specific grid upon it and thus exclude or subjugate other possible grids. In this sense, knowledge always involves a relation of force in that it is always bound up with an attempt to determine the world and others in it in a particular way.

For Foucault, knowledge (particularly that of the human and social sciences) and power-relations constitute one another by rendering the social world into a form that is both knowable and governable, each being dependent on the other. If something is established as an area of investigation, this is only because relations of power have constituted it as a 'possible object'. Conversely, power can be exercised only over something that 'techniques of knowledge and procedures of discourse [are] capable of investing in' (1978, 98). In the case of incarceration which Foucault studies in *Discipline and Punish*, discourse and power interpenetrate by the process in which incarceration develops to manage inmates, leading to new discourses (criminology), which then study prisoners 'scientifically' and finally influence the administration of prisons. Discourses of incarceration become institutionalized in the form of the human sciences and serve as guides for the implementation of policy. According to Foucault, the 'scientific' discourses of criminology, psychology, clinical medicine, population theory, political economy, modern biology, psychoanalysis and psychiatry are all implicated to this end in 'the power of constituting domains of objects' (1972, 234).

Prima facie, Foucault's genealogical analysis of power-relations seems consonant with the Marxist demand to uncover modes and relations of power within class society. Foucault's general argument in *Discipline and Punish* that the penal system and its associated disciplines in capitalist society were implemented not because of a 'humanitarian awakening' but as a 'regulated practice' to reaffirm the power of the ruling class seems consistent with Marx's analysis of class exploitation and division. However, Foucault's analysis of power is most commonly seen as a rival account to the Marxist one where power is viewed as an instrument wielded over the oppressed and exploited that would disappear through a transformation in the mode of production. For Foucault, such a transformation would result in a continuation of power-relations – they would simply assume new forms and guises. There can be no liberating escape from power-relations as Marxism tends to suppose since all forms of truth and practice are linked in a circular way with systems of power which produce and sustain them, and to effects of power which they induce and which in turn extend them. As Foucault emphasizes, power is not just an instrument of prohibition and repression which functions negatively, but one which *produces*:

> I would distinguish myself from para-Marxists like Marcuse who give the notion of repression an exaggerated role – because power would be a fragile thing if its only function were to repress . . . Far from preventing knowledge, power produces it. (1980, 59)

According to the standard Marxist account developed by Marcuse and the Frankfurt School, a thoroughgoing critique of ideology (that uncovers the distortion of capitalist ideology and the ways in which this leads to repression and false consciousness) implies the possibility of a non-ideological true consciousness or discourse. For Foucault, this type of thinking is mistaken since it implies that knowledge can be disinterested and configures truth accordingly as an *absence* of power-relations. In Foucault's form of *Ideologiekritik*, all discourses are secreted and shaped by socio-political interests and so are always enmeshed in networks of power: 'There is no power-relation without the correlative constitution of a field of knowledge, nor any knowledge that does not presuppose and constitute at the same time power-relations' (1977a, 27). The Foucauldian account of power/knowledge is then different from both standard Marxist and liberal analysis, both of which see knowledge as subversive of power and as a standpoint from which we are able to egress networks of power. Foucault offers no such panacea of truth which is 'objective', 'disinterested' and not implicated in the constitution of definite power-relations:

> Truth is a thing of this world . . . it induces regular effects of power. Each society has its own regime of truth, its 'general politics' of truth: that is the type of discourse which it accepts and makes function as true. (1980, 131)

Within Foucault's Nietzschean perspective, knowledge is not seen as an exercise in attaining true consciousness, but as a means of undermining and capturing authority – an attempt to control, define and constitute persons. It is, as such, more like a weapon than a pair of glasses: 'theory does not express, translate, or serve to apply to practice: it is practice' (1977b, 208).

In Foucault's view, the purpose of an analysis of power is 'not to formulate the global systematic theory which holds everything in place, but to analyse the specificity of mechanisms of power . . . to build little by little a strategic knowledge' (1980, 145). He maintains that there is no definite, focal point of power, only endless networks and circulations – 'power comes from below . . . power is not something that is acquired, seized or shared . . . power is exercised from innumerable points . . . ' (1978, 94). Power should be seen not as the homogenous domination of one class over another but as a net-like, circulating organization that does not reduce directly to a consequence of legislation and social structure. In order to understand the larger structures of power (which Marxists address) it is necessary first to analyse in their specificity the *micro-structures* of power that precede and form the foundation for larger structures – to conduct what Foucault refers to as an *ascending* analysis of power: 'starting, that is, from its infinitesimal mechanisms . . . and then see how these mechanisms of power have been – and continue to be – invested, colonised, utilised, involuted, transformed, displaced, extended, etc., by ever more general mechanisms' (1980, 99). Within Foucault's labyrinth of power, power no longer comes from above, simply excluding, but is an immanent process tied to knowledge and discourse which operates as a technique on all levels of society. Individuals are themselves the products of power-relations since the practices and institutional discourses that define them are also definite means of government over them. Since individuals have no fixed essence or nature, their self-constitution is the result of subliminal socialization. Power-relations individuate persons and prescribe them definite characters through a process of what Foucault calls *normalization*. In his study of madness, for instance, he explains how the mad are confined as a consequence of moral perception (their 'body of unreason' was seen as incapable of labour) and how their subjectivity comes to be defined in turn as an object of psychological observation and knowledge through the subjection of the body in confinement. Foucault points out how the body is in this way the *axis* of a political field of subjectification – 'power-relations have an immediate hold upon it, they invest it, mask it, train it, torture it, force it to carry out tasks, to perform ceremonies, to emit signs' (1977a, 25).

Before he begins to analyse those 'discontinuous processes' of normalizing power in modern society, Foucault describes how power in the sovereign state of the monarch had been very different from this. According to Foucault, the juridico-discursive power of the monarch was 'the right to put to death and let live' (1978, 136). Since in the sovereign state the king represented a physical embodiment of power, power was embodied in the public space and the act of punishment enacted within it – public executions, violent reprisals, ritualized humiliations, torture, etc. Crimes were seen in this state as a personal injury to the king for they were thought to violate the political order (and a wider cosmic order) of which the king was a physical embodiment. Punishment thus became construed not as reparation or deterrence but as a rightful balancing, a setting right of the cosmic order. Foucault presents the full brutality of this punitive power in the opening pages of *Discipline and Punish* where he describes the drastic and horrific punishments handed down to the attempted regicide, Damiens.

Although coercion was bloody and dramatic in the sovereign state, it was, according to Foucault, only an intermittent power, 'a discontinuous, rambling, global system with little hold on detail' (1980, 151). In contrast to this old punitive power, Foucault explores how the modern age requires a different means of controlling individuals. The power of the monarch to determine life or death was transformed in the modern age into 'a power that exerts a positive influence on life, that endeavors to administer, optimize, and multiply it, subjecting it to precise controls and comprehensive regulations' (1978, 137). Where the old power of the monarch depended on the public space, the new power which exemplifies the modern age operates by universal surveillance. Power has retreated from the visible order and is now concealed, dispersed to innumerable points.

Foucault sees this transition to the modern age as involving the substitution of the drama of bloody punishment for deeper, more constant levels of control. As he points out, the penal reforms of Enlightenment humanism did not just seek to punish, but 'to punish better; to punish with an attenuated severity perhaps, but in order to punish with more universality and necessity; to insert the power to punish more deeply in the social body' (1977a, 82). Punitive functions can be seen in this way to have shifted from the body to the mind in order to grip tighter. The 'fundamental reference [of] the philosophers and jurists of the eighteenth century' was, Foucault argues, 'not to the state of nature, but to the meticulously subordinated cogs of a machine, not to the primal social contract, but to permanent coercions, not to fundamental rights, but to automatic docility' (1977a, 169).

The transition from the old power to the new is not seen as emancipation by Foucault since he perceives the penal reforms of the Enlightenment to be themselves totalitarian blueprints. Under the ideal of humanitarian reform came a whole network of 'moral technologies' which were the means of a new mode of control. The modern individual is born into a vast array of regulations in which he is measured, disciplined, examined and classified in order to normalize him or her and make him or her a better subject of control:

> Historically, the process by which the bourgeosie became (in the eighteenth century) the politically dominant class was marked by the establishment of an explicit, coded and formally egalitarian juridical framework, made possible by the organization of a parliamentary, representative regime. But the development and generalization of disciplinary mechanisms constituted the other, dark side of these processes. The general juridical form that guaranteed a system of rights that were egalitarian in principle was supported by these tiny, everyday, physical mechanisms, by all those systems of micro-power that are essentially non-egalitarian and asymmetrical that we call disciplines. (1977a, 216–7)

Modern society is seen by Foucault as an essentially 'disciplinary society', based upon a 'micro-physics of power' (1977a, 26) that disseminates a range of detailed, meticulous techniques for the subjection of individuals, independent of regimes and institutions but transferable across them. In *Discipline and Punish* Foucault connects the formation of modern disciplinary society with the Marxist understanding of the structural effects of the mode of production (1977a, 25). As mentioned earlier, it is possible to understand Foucault's work as a continuation of the Marxist project to uncover forms of domination and networks of power in class society. According to Foucault, however, although Marxism shows how capitalism oppresses the poor (by transforming their traditional rights into crimes against property, for instance – as Marx argued in *The Case of the Wood Theft Laws*), it does not go beyond the mode of production to make intelligible forms of domination which occur at other points of the social space. By contenting itself with the macro-structures of class society, Marxism fails to explain adequately the micro-structures of disciplinary practice upon which the larger structures are parasitic:

> If one describes all these phenomena of power as dependent on the state apparatus, this means grasping them as essentially repressive . . . I don't want to say that the state is unimportant; what I want to say is that relations of power, and hence the analysis that must be made of them, necessarily extend beyond the limits of the state. In two senses: first of all because the state, for all the omnipotence of its apparatuses, is far from being able to occupy the whole field of actual relations, and further because the state can only operate on the basis of other, already existing power-relations. (1984, 63–4)

Foucault's concern with the 'superstructural' functions of capitalist society and with forms of normalizing power focused on the body and identity (which he terms 'bio-power) points to a form of analysis that uncovers deeper forms of domination which permeate the social field to affect marginalized and oppressed groups beyond the proletariat and the labour-process. His analysis of the 'micro-structures of power' is intended to undermine power 'where it is most invisible and insidious' in modern disciplinary society by bringing to attention subtle and invidious mechanisms of power which are not directly apprehensible to a descending structural analysis (1977b, 53).

In many respects, the disciplinary society Foucault describes can be located on the cusp of our present postmodern reality. This is certainly the verdict of Deleuze who, in a short article published in 1990, situates it at the point between the past and the present – it is, he argues, part of what we are but also of what we are ceasing to be (1995, 178–9). As Deleuze observes, we are moving from a disciplinary society to a control society – from one based on discipline, institutions, closed spaces and the 'concentrative production' of machines to one based on control, technology, computers and the 'metaproduction' of information and signs (1995, 180), evident, for instance, in the way that the bounded spaces of the mental hospital and the prison are giving way to the unbounded control of community care and electronic modes of sur-veillance: 'Control is short-term and rapidly shifting, but at the same time continuous and unbounded, whereas discipline was long-term, infinite and discontinuous' (1995, 181).

Deleuze's 'Postscript on Control Societies' bears similarity to some of the ruminations of Baudrillard who, like Deleuze, theorizes control rather than discipline as the definitive feature of contemporary capitalist societies. Where Foucault focuses on the disciplinary institutions (e.g. the prison, the asylum, the school) that emerged out of the eighteenth and nineteenth centuries in Europe, Baudrillard turns instead to developments in twentieth-century capitalism that have ushered in new mechanisms of power and social reproduction centred on the media, semiotics and consumption.

Baudrillard's semiology

Until 1972, Baudrillard's project can be seen as an attempt to reconstruct Marxism by synthesizing the Marxian critique of political economy with forms of semiological analysis to make it a more effective basis for the critique of modern capitalism. Like Barthes, Baudrillard investigates the commodification of everyday life under capitalism and analyses the signs that are organized into systems of signification in modern consumer society. To Marx's distinction between 'use-value' (the utility of objects) and 'exchange-value' (the monetary worth of objects), he adds the category of 'sign-value' whereby commodities signify social status and power. The neglect of this axis of symbolic exchange leaves Marxism incomplete, in Baudrillard's view, and unable to break out beyond a restrictive logic of political economy. By confining value to the dichotomy of use-value and exchange-value and championing the former as a utopian other to the latter, Marx failed to realize, he argues, that use-value itself is a construct of the system of exchange-value which produces a rationalized system of needs and objects that integrate individuals into the capitalist social order:

> by maintaining use value as the category of incomparability, Marxist analysis has contributed to the mythology (a veritable rationalist

mystique) that allows the relation of the individual to objects conceived as use values to pass for a concrete and objective – in sum 'natural' – relation between man's needs and the function proper to the object. (1981, 134)

Baudrillard attempts to undo the opposition between use-value and exchange-value insofar as the former is conceived by Marx as the ahistorical outside of historical systems of exchange, rooted in natural, unalienated needs. For Baudrillard, all needs (including personal ones) are socially mediated and deeply influenced by the 'consummative mobilisation' of capitalist society (1981, 135). Against the importance given to the concept of need in modernist social theory, he proposes that 'an accurate theory of objects will not be established upon a theory of needs and their satisfaction, but upon a theory of prestations and signification' (1981, 30). The fundamental basis to consumption, he emphasizes, 'is not use value, the relation to needs', but 'symbolic exchange value' (1981, 30).

After 1972, Baudrillard's attitude towards Marxism darkens as he becomes increasingly critical of its one-sided 'productivist' logic. In *The Mirror of Production* he argues that 'a revolution has occurred in the Capitalist world without our Marxists having wanted to comprehend it'. Modern capitalism, he states, has moved 'from the form-commodity to the form-sign, from the abstraction of the exchange of material products under the law of general equivalence to the operationalization of all exchanges under the law of the code'. In a regime of controlled signs and codifications under which all aspects of life have been systematically incorporated, we are now faced with 'a structure of control and of power much more subtle and more totalitarian than that of exploitation'. We live in conditions where 'the symbolic destruction of all social relations' is threatened 'not so much by the ownership of the means of production but by the control of the code' (1975, 121, 122).

In Baudrillard's view, Marxism dilutes its conceptual grasp of the social field by refusing to displace all importance from the mode of production and the category of labour. To get beyond this, Marxism must slay the sacred cow of labour and open its boundaries to the significance of language, symbolization and visual signification within social exchange. By defining the proletarian in terms of his labour power alone, Marx effectively falls back on 'an essence which in fact [the working-class] was assigned by the bourgeois class' (1975, 156). Marx(ism) is in this sense transfixed by a bourgeois work ethic and so obstructs the comprehension, analysis and development of wider forms of human exchange. This shows, Baudrillard comments, 'how the Marxist dialectic can lead to the purest Christian ethic' — the 'aberrant sanctification of work' has been 'the secret vice of Marxist political and economic strategy from the beginning' (1975, 36). The pivotal conception of the labouring subject (*homo faber*) in Marx is itself an effect of the guiding rationality of capitalism:

> man is not only quantitatively exploited as a productive force by the system of capitalist political economy, but is also metaphysically overdetermined as a producer by the code of political economy. In the last instance, the system rationalises its power here. (1975, 31)

Marxism and capitalism are seen, then, as 'mirror images' of a single modernist logic centred on production, the former representing merely a more efficient and equitable organization of production than the latter, rather than a different sort of society with different aims, values and life activities. The genuine revolutionary alternative to capitalism is, Baudrillard argues, a society based not on a system of production but on a system of symbolic exchange that breaks with all utilitarian imperatives and grounds itself in the Nietzschean realm of Dionysis, play, experiment, festivity.[6]

In Baudrillard's texts of the early and mid-1970s, a fundamental dividing line in history is presupposed between premodern symbolic societies (organized around practices of symbolic exchange, such as gift-giving, festivals, etc.) and modern productivist societies (organized around production and a system of political economy). This dividing line effectively calls into question the Marxian philosophy of history (which posits the primacy of production in all societies) and the Marxian concept of socialism (which defines socialism in terms of the labour-process). In a manner similar to Foucault (in *The History of Sexuality*) and Deleuze and Guattari (in *A Thousand Plateaus*), Baudrillard breaks the continuous logic of Marxist (modernist) history by bringing attention to 'pre-historical' forms of existence and society that do not conform to the paradigm of production, reducing in the process Marx's universalizing, trans-historical assumption that 'what men are . . . coincides with their production' (Marx and Engels, 1965, 42) to a specific cultural and historical viewpoint. Indeed, he maintains, Marx's idea that labour is the basis of all societies is 'arbitrary and strange' since 'the analysis of all primitive or archaic organisations contradicts it, as does the feudal symbolic order and even that of our societies' (Baudrillard, 1975, 29). Confronted by 'the absolute idealism of labour', Marx's dialectical materialism ends up as no more than 'a dialectical idealism of productive forces' (1975, 29).

From the 1980s onwards, Baudrillard's work takes a decidedly postmodern turn. Although his texts of the 1960s and 1970s can be seen to contain many postmodern themes in a state of gestation (focusing on the consumer society, the media, cybernetics etc.), it is not until the 1980s that Baudrillard begins to adopt the discourse of postmodernity and to sketch out the contours of a new postmodern age of simulation. The passage from modern society to postmodern society is, he argues, a 'passage from a *metallurgic* into a *semiurgic* society' (1987, 185) — that is, from a society based on production and controlled by the industrial bourgeoisie to one dominated by computers, information, and cybernetic and technological systems which are structured by models, codes and signs that are seemingly beyond the control of any group. A semiurgic postmodern society describes a contemporary landscape where the circulation of signs disseminated through models and codes has come to dominate social life.

In articulating his idea of postmodern society, Baudrillard makes use of three important defining concepts, *simulation*, *implosion* and *hyperreality*, which, he argues form an important part of our present postmodern experience. According to Baudrillard, simulation 'is no longer that of a territory, a referential being or a substance. It is the generation by models of a real without origins or reality; a hyperreal' (1983a, 2). Postmodern society is simulational to the extent that codes or models actually structure experience and erode distinctions between the model and the real. The boundary between image (simulation) and reality implodes as models (such as Disneyland, simulated environments, etc.) become more 'real' than their instantiations in the social world (1983a, 25–7). Hyperreality thus describes a condition where models become a deter-minant of the real through the generation of 'ideal types' (such as 'ideal sex' as portrayed in sex manuals or the 'ideal home' as portrayed in magazines) and simulations (e.g. opinion polls, soap operas).

As Baudrillard perceives it, the boundaries between reality and unreality, politics and images, event and simulation, have imploded. Where modern society (the western industrial world) was previously marked by 'explosion' through the expansion of national boundaries, production, science and technology and the differentiation of social spheres, discourse and value, postmodern society is 'imploded' to the extent that previous boundaries and distinctions have collapsed in an age where meaning and messages neutralize one another in an uninterrupted flow of information, entertainment, advertising and politics. In this postmodern society saturated by the dissemination of media messages and semiurgy, the apathetic masses have become 'a sullen silent majority' in which all meaning, messages and solicitations implode as they become bored and indifferent to the constant messages and attempts to solicit them to work, vote, buy, consume or register an opinion.[7]

In his *In the Shadows of the Silent Majorities* Baudrillard proclaims that the social has disappeared as it has become absorbed into the void of the apathetic masses, signalling the implosion of distinctions between polit- ical ideologies, classes and cultural forms and between media semiurgy and the real itself. Indeed, the masses, he argues, signify no more than a simulational object constituted 'in the form of anticipated responses [and] circular signals' which circumscribe its existence (1983a, 33):

> All contemporary systems function on this nebulous entity, on this floating substance whose existence is no longer social, but statistical, and whose only mode of appearance is that of the survey. A simulation on the horizon of the social, or rather on whose horizon the social has already disappeared. (1983a, 19–20)

Against Marx's notion of the proletariat as a primary historical and social agent, Baudrillard argues that

> [t]o want to specify the term 'mass' is a mistake — it is to provide meaning for that which has none. One says: 'the mass of workers'. But the mass is never that of workers, or of any other social subject or object . . . The mass is without attribute, predicate, quality, reference.

It has nothing to do with any *real* population, body, or specific social aggregate. (1983a, 5–6)

Baudrillard's revolt against modernity thus develops and steadily deepens as we trace his writings through the 1960s and 1970s to the 1980s and beyond. In his earlier work modern society is contrasted to a very different historical landscape, that of the symbolic society, in which he finds a remedial counter-logic – the logic of symbolic exchange as opposed to the logic of production. After his 'postmodern turn' in the 1980s, Baudrillard moves on to describe the features of a new post-modern age radically different in form from the productivist age of modern society.

In an article 'On Nihilism', first delivered as a lecture in 1980, Baudrillard presents modernity as 'the radical destruction of appearances, the disenchantment of the world and its abandonment to the violence of interpretation and history' (1984, 38). He goes on to characterize the modern period as the era of Marx and Freud who both employed depth models to demystify reality and reveal the prime underlying forces behind appearances. For Freud this prime force was the libidinal unconscious whereas for Marx the economic substructure forms the underlying base for superstructural (epi)phenomena such as politics and culture. In this way, modernity was founded on a paradigm of meaning grounded in the certainty of a depth force (the dialectics of history, the economy, the unconscious, desire). In opposition to this modernist quest for depth meaning, Baudrillard heralds a 'second revolution, that of the twentieth century, of postmodernity, which is the immense process of the destruction of meaning, equal to the earlier destruction of appearances. Whoever lives by meaning dies by meaning' (1984, 38–9).

In Baudrillard's view, postmodernity is devoid of meaning since everything is visible, explicit, transparent, obscene and in a state of constant flux. Meaning, by contrast, requires depth, a prime force, an unseen dimension, a stable foundation or a base model. Along with the disappearance of meaning in postmodernity, Baudrillard pronounces the end of history and the advent of a new postmodern post-historical existence (1987, 67ff.).[8] Since there are no longer any stable structures, base meanings or nexuses of causality through which it is possible to delineate historical trajectories or lines of development, everything is subject to indeterminism and to a vertiginous proliferation of interpretations: 'Suddenly there is a curve in the road, a turning point. Somewhere, the real scene has been lost, the scene where you had rules for the game and some solid stakes that everybody could rely on' (1987, 69). Baudrillard's postmodern theory can be seen in this respect as a theory of *disappearance* in which the key features of modernity — production, the real, meaning, the social, history — are viewed as having come to an end and as no longer relevant to the new, depthless, transparent, entropic, simulational, hyperreal and imploded social landscape that he characterizes as postmodernity:

> The end of labor. The end of production. The end of political economy. The end of the signifier/signified dialectic which facilitates the accumulation of knowledge and meaning . . . And at the same time, the end of the exchange value/use value dialectic which is the only thing that makes accumulation and social production possible. The end of the linear dimension of discourse. The end of the linear dimension of the commodity. The end of the classic era of the sign. The end of the era of production. (in Best and Kellner, 1997, 103)

The postmodern Critique: *rationality, totalization and universality*
In general terms, postmodernists raise two main objections against the idea of modern reason:

1. Reason is a product of the Enlightenment and modern science and engenders an oppressive, totalitarian and utilitarian logic which excludes emotion, feeling, affectivity, imagination and play.
2. Modern reason assumes universalism and excludes cultural diversity whereas postmodernists assume that foundations change from one cultural episteme to another.

Like Weber, the Frankfurt School and Heidegger before them, postmodernists point critically to the logic of control and domination inherent within modern (capitalist) rationality. This rationality, they argue, is 'one-dimensional', instrumental and utilitarian, bound up inextricably within the assumptions of modern (Newtonian) science.

As Adorno and Horkheimer point out in *The Dialectic of Enlightenment,* the Enlightenment conception of reason rests on a 'logic of identity', the hidden structure of which is the will to mastery and control since it seeks to deny, repress and violate that which is singular, different and other. This 'hidden logic' of Enlightenment reason is intrinsically repressive and totalitarian, turning inexorably from the domination of nature into the domination of people and societies. Heidegger echoes this view, arguing that modern agriculture has become a 'setting-upon' nature, a 'motorized food industry – in essence the same as the manufacturing of corpses in gas chambers and extermination camps, the same as blockading and starving of nations, the same as the manufacture of hydrogen bombs' (in Bernstein, 1991, 130).

Advocates of postmodern science reject the assumptions intrinsic to modern scientific rationality of Newtonian determinism (the world conceived as a mechanical causal grid), Cartesian dualism (the radical separation of subject and object, spirit and matter) and representational epistemology (the idea that science accurately represents or 'pictures' the true state of things), in favour of principles of chaos, indeterminacy and hermeneutics, calling for a 're-enchantment' of nature which has been denuded of depth by modern utilitarian calculation.[9] Recent French post-structuralists, such as Luce Irigaray and Hélène Cixous, have continued this critique of modern scientific rationality, lamenting the incessant way in which modern science, confident of its rationality, has suppressed the seminal voices of intuition, emotion, enchantment and magic. In contrast to the modern rationality of work, science, utility and material need, postmodernists follow an *aesthetic rationality* akin to that proposed by Nietzsche, which resides in the Dionysian realm of affective energies, emotional discharge, symbolic exchange, intoxication, play and mimesis. This can be evidenced clearly in Lyotard's early work where the idea of a 'libidinal economy' which valorizes fragmentation, desire, intensity and plurality is put forward as an antidote to the modern obsession with reason and unity:

> We don't want to destroy capital because it isn't rational, but because it is. Reason and power are one and the same thing. You may disguise the one with dialectics . . . but you will still have the other in all its crudeness: jails, taboos, public weal, selection, genocide. (1984b, 11)

This postmodern assault upon reason has led some, most notably Jürgen Habermas, to characterize postmodernism as fundamentally irrationalist and thus consistent with the anti-Enlightenment ideologies of Fascist Germany. In Habermas's view, Enlightenment rationality exhibits both progressive features (democracy, critical reason, cultural differentiation) and regressive ones (the invasive colonization of the lifeworld and the extension of instrumental rationality). To this end, he criticizes postmodernism for abandoning reason altogether rather than undertaking a reconstruction of reason that preserves its progressive features (which Habermas tries to achieve with his own theory of 'communicative rationality'). The postmodern critique of reason is thus, in Habermas's view, far too undifferentiated in its rejection of reason, giving rise ultimately to a dangerous form of irrationalism that offers no safeguard against fascism and authoritarianism.

In Lyotard's view, however, control and domination are intrinsic to the very form of reason, aspects of which Habermas seeks to defend. Modern reason, he argues in *The Postmodern Condition*, is bound up with the notions of *totalization* and *universalism*, providing justification for modernist discourses (capitalism and Marxism) that legitimate their positions by appeal to 'meta-discourses':

> I will use the term *modern* to designate any science that legitimates itself with reference to a meta-discourse . . . making an explicit appeal to some grand-narrative, such as the dialectics of Spirit, the hermeneutics of meaning, the emancipation of the rational or working subject, or the creation of wealth. (1984a, xxii)

Meta-discourses are 'totalizing' in the sense that they attempt to explain the entire socio-historical field through reference to one particular viewpoint or theory, thus disqualifying antagonistic or plural perspectives. In Marxism, for example, history and society are reduced to the viewpoint of production and the proletariat. The effect of this is to reduce history to an eschatological scheme of meanings (the growth of productive forces, the destiny of the proletariat, the inevitability of communism) conceived in progressivist, linear and universal terms. For Lyotard and other postmodernists, these discourses are totalitarian in the sense that they attempt to silence and subjugate other voices or perspectives by advocating universal rules and criteria that exclude the marginal, the minority and the oppositional. Marxism functions in this way by equating historical destiny and social meaning with the viewpoint of one group (the proletariat), thus effectively denying or silencing alternative perspectives (e.g. feminism) and closing off future possibilities for practices of freedom.

Like Foucault, Lyotard puts forward a *micro-logical* strategy for social and political theory which eschews universalism, totalization and the formulation of grand narratives, seeking instead to construct a patchwork of local, minor and diverse narratives in which all voices and perspectives can be heard. Universalism, according to Lyotard, involves the imposition of a coercive, homogenizing consensus and 'does violence to the heterogeneity of language-games' (1984a, 75). In *The Differend* he argues (following Kant and Wittgenstein) that different domains of judgement, such as theoretical, practical, and aesthetic, have their own autonomy, rules, criteria and procedures of justification – therefore no single method, set of concepts or theory has privileged status in disparate domains. There is, in Lyotard's view, always a point of difference (the differend) between two heterogeneous languages, narratives or 'phrase regimes', a gap of incommensurability where no criteria exist for a 'meta-judgement'. Thus the task of theory and of politics is, he argues, to testify to the differend in order to resist the injustice which silences those who do not speak the terms of the dominant language. In opposition to the totalizing grand narratives of modern theory (and Habermas's idea of a 'communicative consensus'), Lyotard urges us to 'wage a war on totality': 'let us bear witness to the unpresentable; let us activate the differences and save the honour of the name' (1984a, 82). Postmodern theory, he states, 'refines our sensitivity to differences and reinforces our ability to tolerate the incommensurable. Its principle is not the expert's homology, but the inventor's paralogy' (1984a, xxv).

Sartre and postmodern social theory

Criticisms of Marxism found in the post-structuralist texts of Derrida, Foucault, Deleuze, Guattari, Baudrillard and Lyotard highlight three main flaws in its explanatory framework:

1. Marxism is insufficient for explaining the nature of our contemporary world which has moved, in Baudrillard's words, 'from a capitalist-productivist society' based on the domination of the bourgeoisie to 'a neo-capitalist cybernetic order that aims now at total control' (1983b, 111).

2. By placing too much emphasis on the sphere of political economy, the state and the realm of production, Marxism is not only unable to account for sources of domination and power that exist beyond the labour-process, but is itself the 'mirror image' (Baudrillard) or 'reverse discourse' (Foucault) of capitalism insofar as it reproduces the labour-centric and instrumental logic that lies at the heart of modern capitalist rationality.

3. Marxist history is teleological in the sense that it grants history an internal logic (the growth of productive forces, the Destiny of the Proletariat) and end-point (the future communist society). As a consequence, it tends to conceive historical development in the Enlightenment terms of (linear) progress and is reductive in the sense that it confines historical understanding to the single aspect of production, thus closing off other aspects of historical intelligibility (e.g. symbolic exchange) that do not conform to the model of political economy.

As we saw in the last section, Sartre is also critical of the teleological assumptions of Marxist history which, in his view, effectively deny history its radical contingency. His criticisms of Marxist teleology connect in this way to the postmodernist project of erasing historical grand narratives which posit an animus or inevitable direction to historical change. Like Foucault and other postmodernists, Sartre exhibits extreme scepticism towards the Enlightenment idea of modern scientific progress, showing instead (through his concept of 'counterfinality' in the CDR, for example) how what might appear to one generation as progress becomes 'closed in on itself and problematic' (1983, 33) to the next.[10]

This difference between Sartrean and Marxist history relates back to a difference on the philosophical level regarding their understanding of alienation. For Marx, as Sartre points out, alienation 'begins with exploitation' under capitalist production (CDR, 227). It is seen in this way as a contingent historical occurrence which relates to the condition of the subject under capitalism rather than being an intrinsic quality of the human condition. Alienation represents, for Marx, an inversion of subject/object relations where, under capitalist commodification and production, labour becomes dominated by dead matter, violating the workers' human nature by altering their status from 'person' to 'thing' and leaving their creative praxis unobjectified. Free unalienated labour, by contrast, involves the objectification of one's essential powers and the imposition of an enduring human shape on the non-human (matter).

In Sartre's philosophy, however, there is a Hegelian undercurrent to the idea of objectification since what is objectified eventually becomes alien and hostile to the free praxis which shaped it. The reification of human praxis into the form of totalized matter and the practico-inert thus points, according to Sartre, to a form of alienation which is 'a constant characteristic of all kinds of objectification' (CDR, 227). By working upon the environment to satisfy need, 'man returns to himself as Other' (CDR, 227):

There is no doubt that man ... discovers himself as Other in the world of objectivity; totalized matter as an inert objectification that perpetuates itself by inertia, is in effect a non-man, and even, if you like, a counter-man. (CDR, 285)

Where Marx tends to see only the positive, transformative aspects of objectification, Sartre focuses also on its possible negative and alienating features. For Sartre, action always creates counterfinalities which, as the 'inner cancers' of praxis (CDR(2), 58), reify that action into an objective and alienating practico-inert reality. Objectification thus represents both the 'necessity of freedom' (CDR, 480) and its 'progressive alienation ... to necessity' (CDR, 672):

Man creates himself through the intermediary of his action on the world. That is what one can concede to the Marxists. But, at the same time, humanity being a detotalized totality, there is an internal theft of (one's) work, thus the image that man has of himself is perpetually alienated. (1983, 129)

To this end, Sartre's concept of alienation introduces a deeper comprehension of social misery into Marxist theory and can be seen in general terms as an attempt to make intelligible all the forms through which praxis becomes lost and opposed to its creators.[11] In contrast to Marx, Sartre does not see alienation simply as a specific historical consequence of the capitalist mode of production, but as a phenomenon that permeates the entirety of one's being-with-others insofar as we share a common practico-inert reality. Thus, in opposition to Marx's somewhat eschatological pronouncements concerning the end of forms of alienation under communism, Sartre questions whether 'the disappearance of capitalist forms of alienation' must 'be identified with the suppression of all forms of alienation?' (CDR, 307n.).

Sartre's analysis of alienation bears a similarity in this respect to the work of Foucault and Baudrillard which both focus on modes of alienation and oppression tied to forms of knowledge, discourse and exchange that operate on all levels of society (families, groups, etc.) and extend beyond the narrow aspect of production. For Foucault, for instance, power would not disappear in Marx's future communist society since it is always a kind of potential or actual 'unspoken warfare' which invests itself productively and multifariously in the social field, always liable to congeal and reinscribe conflict in 'social institutions, in economic inequalities, in language, in the bodies of each and every one of us' (1980, 87–8).

In his later work Sartre displays a critical attitude towards the form of *economism* which infects Marxist thinking. Although he agrees with the basic Marxist formula that '[t]he mode of production of material life dominates the production of social, political and intellectual life' (SM, 33–4), he is keen to emphasize that the converse is equally true: 'the economic is afloat in religion and ethics' (1983, 50). His theory of *mediations* in the CDR is designed in this way to avoid Marxist reduction-isms of the social field by giving each sector of capitalist society its due weight and relative autonomy in the overall dialectical scheme – the family, for instance, must be shown as both a sector of the totality and as generating its own specific forms of domination. On an epistemological level, Sartre's categorial apparatus for understanding this process is the concept of *totalization* in which perception involves the drawing together of disparate acts into a meaningful whole. Thus, a true dialectical understanding of society, in Sartre's view, would make intelligible the 'micro-contexts' of social life and draw these together to see how they continue to affect and in turn be affected by the wider 'macro-structures' of society which Marxists tend to focus on exclusively.

In the years that followed the publication of the *CDR* until his death in 1980, Sartre's growing scepticism towards Marxism in many ways mirrors the abandonment of Marxism in postmodernist thinking. In an interview given in 1975 this scepticism hardens into overt criticism as Sartre argues that he was previously wrong in thinking existentialism to be 'only an enclave of Marxism', stating emphatically that 'I have never thought like a Marxist, not even in the *Critique de la Raison dialectique*' (1981b, 20, 24). Sartre also suggests in this interview that society has changed dramatically since the epoch in which Marx wrote and that 'the analysis of national and international capitalism in 1848 has little to do with the capitalism of today' (1981b, 21). He thus concludes, in a manner similar to that of Foucault, Baudrillard and others, that Marxism has outlived its time and that 'there are too many difficulties in preserving the Marxism of today' (1981b, 20–1).

Through their common critique of Marxism it is possible to discern a number of similarities between Sartrean and postmodernist social theory. On the level of history, both avoid a teleological or grand narrative approach to historical change, preferring instead a pluralized historical account which stresses detotalization, perspectivism, indeterminacy, contingency and circularity.[12] Indeed, it is these latter two features of *contingency* and *circularity* that unite Sartre's analysis of history most clearly with that of Foucault and other postmodernists. For these thinkers, the contingency of things reveals a world with no natural order or true original state – thus 'the order of things' is imposed not by those things themselves, but by the socially and historically conditioned frameworks human societies impose on them.[13] The consequence of this is that all things are subject to change and reconstitution since there is no essential form or eidetic pattern to things. As all structures and ideas are, according to Foucault, the products of a temporal imagination negotiating its contingent, temporal existence, they can always be dismantled, transformed and demystified to expose their psychological, social and historical origins – 'Because they are made, they can be unmade, assuming we know how they were made' (1979, 252).

For Sartre, as we have seen, history reveals the dialectical *circularity* of praxis and inertia, a 'perpetual double movement of regrouping and petrification' (*CDR*, 643) in which projects of collective freedom become crystallized into hegemonic, institutional structures of seriality. These themes of circularity and crystallization are also present in the work of Foucault and Deleuze and Guattari who, like Sartre, set out to comprehend and identify the mechanisms of inertia in social life that become institutionalized, ossified and restrictive to future practices of liberty: 'we strike and knock against the most solid obstacles, the system cracks at another point, we persist. It seems that we're winning, but then the institution is rebuilt; we must start again' (Foucault, 1977b, 230). For Foucault, this circularity is conceived as a 'permanent provocation' between power and resistance, for Deleuze and Guattari, as a dual process of territorialization/deterritorialization, and, for Sartre, as a dialectical movement 'of interiority and exteriority' (*CDR*, 57).

It is not, however, just in relation to the question of history that Sartre's work bears close similarity to postmodernist theory, for they both unite also around the common aim of avoiding economic reductionism. For Sceptical postmodernists like Baudrillard, this revolt against economism generally takes the form of an outright rejection of political economy, while in less extreme variants (Foucault, Deleuze and Guattari), it articulates the need to supplement the macro-structures of economic categories with those found in the micro-contexts of everyday life. In his later work, Sartre is much closer to the strategy of supplementation suggested by Affirmative postmodernists like Foucault and Deleuze than he is to the extreme form of abandonment advocated by Baudrillard and other Sceptics. The trouble with Marxism, in Sartre's view, is not that it attaches importance to the realm of political economy as a determining factor in social life, but that it attaches *too much* importance to it, thus effectively reducing those other determining factors (family, groups, culture) to mere reflections of the economic base. In doing so, Marxism ultimately 'lacks any hierarchy of mediation which would permit it to grasp the process which produces the person and his product inside a class within a given society at a given historical moment' (*SM*, 56). Sartre observes in this context how the basic projects of the individual are formed well before they enter the workplace: 'Today's Marxists are concerned only with adults; reading them, one would believe that we are born at the age when we earn our first wages. They have forgotten their own childhoods' (*SM*, 62). A renewed Marxism, according to Sartre, would account properly for the numerous mediations (family, ethnic, community, cultural) that can serve to obfuscate the class-consciousness and rational self-interest of the worker or individual. In the case of the family, for instance, we must

> discove[r] the point of insertion for man and his class – that is, the particular family – as a mediation between the universal class and the individual. The family in fact is constituted by and in the general movement of History, but is experienced, on the other hand, as an absolute in the depth and opaqueness of childhood. (*SM*, 62)

Although Sartre did not explicitly adopt the discourse of postmodernity, he does concur with the postmodern idea that Marx's (production-centric) analysis is no longer adequate to explain the nature of contemporary (multinational) capitalism (Sartre, 1981b, 21). Like Foucault and Baudrillard, he provides a deeper understanding of sources of control and alienation in contemporary capitalist society that lie outside the production process and relate to the micrological contexts of everyday life in which people find themselves subject to a myriad of ideological interpellations.

Critical considerations

In this chapter I have looked at Sartre's social theory as it evolves from his early existentialist perspective in *BN* to a more collective-based conception in the *CDR*. As Deleuze observes, Sartre succeeds in this way in progressing beyond the abstract individualism of his early work and so 'provid[es] Being and Nothingness with its necessary complement in the sense that collective exigencies come to complete the subjectivity of the individual' (in Majumdar, 1997, 42n.41). Indeed, the form of abstract individualism we find in *BN* later becomes a critical target for Sartre in the *CDR*. As I suggested earlier, Sartre's social theory of Dialectical Nominalism provides a key heuristic apparatus that overcomes the opposition of methodological individualism and holism in social theory, enabling us to grasp the full complexity of a social field which comprises both freedom and necessity, agency and structure, individuals and groups.

The key concepts that form the basis of Sartre's Dialectical Nominalism (the practico-inert, the progressive–regressive method, totalization and mediation) allow us in this respect to comprehend the social field from a wider standpoint than that afforded by Marxist theory (and its reductionist tendencies). In later years, Sartre added to this conceptual apparatus through his notion of 'objective spirit' which, he argues, comprises 'those structured ensembles [that] jeopardize the exploited classes to the extent that they intrude into each individual from without and impose themselves in the memory as ramparts against any coming to awareness' (1974c, 47). In this respect, both Sartrean and postmodernist theory offer valuable insights into forms of alienation and control in capitalist society that are overlooked by the purely economic perspective of Marxist theory. Baudrillard, in particular, illuminates contemporary forms of control associated with the circulation of signs, information and cultural codes of meaning which require a different form of understanding than that afforded by the productivist logic employed by Marxists.

In the case of some forms of postmodernism, however, the link between cultural and economic hegemony is severed altogether – the social field is detotalized or fragmented to such an extent that any kind of systematic viewpoint based on connecting the different spheres of social influence is denied. Alongside this guiding principle of detotalization, some postmodernists also emphasize the idea of radical *discontinuity* wherein the nature of postmodern society is seen as fundamentally different from, and thus discontinuous with, that of modern (industrial) society.[14] To this end, postmodernism tends, in its more extreme forms, to call for a complete dissolution of modernist categories (totalization, systematicity, continuity, narrative, foundationalism, determinacy) which, it is claimed, are no longer relevant in explaining and understanding the nature of contemporary postmodern society.

In reaction to this postmodern thesis of radical discontinuity and detotalization, Fredric Jameson, most notably, has called for a more dialectical approach to the question of postmodernism which contextualizes it within the development of capitalism while engaging postmodern positions to rethink Marxist theory and politics in the contemporary era.

In Jameson's view, postmodernism is not merely a new aesthetic style, but rather a new stage of 'cultural development of the logic of late capitalism' (1984, 85), based on cultural fragmentation, the predominance of images and simulacra, the schizophrenic breakdown of the subject and the colonization of the unconscious. Unlike Baudrillard, however, (who sees postmodernism as a rupture in history), Jameson analyses discontinuity as a reconfiguration of a prior logic and describes historical ruptures in terms of continuity and discontinuity. His 'postmodern Marxism' defends the idea of *narrative* in this way since it enables us to make connections between historical events and conceptualize them within a larger milieu outside of which they are incomprehensible. The use of narrative, he argues, allows us to comprehend 'the lost unity of social life' and to 'demonstrate that widely distant elements of the social totality are ultimately part of the same global historical process' (Jameson, 1981, 226).

In an attempt to overcome the difficulties associated with the postmodern principle of detotalization, Jameson defends a *totalizing methodology* as essential to map the homogenizing and systemic effects of late capitalism itself. The postmodern emphasis on difference, particularity and heterogeneity (which, Jameson argues, cannot be genuinely understood outside a relational and systemic context) can serve in this respect to reify singularity and divert attention from the tendencies of capitalism towards sameness, uniformity and generality (e.g. mass production and consumption, social conformity, propaganda, global market relations, the mass media). Jameson concludes that a totalizing viewpoint is essential for political groups in order to understand, to address, and to unite against the systematic nature of contemporary global capitalism and that 'without a conception of the social totality (and the possibility of transforming a whole system), no Socialist politics is possible' (1988, 355).

Jameson's ideas of totalization, narrative and cognitive mapping can be seen in many ways to bear close similarity to Sartre's own principles of totalization, mediation and dialectical reason adumbrated in the *CDR*. As Jameson notes in *Postmodernism, or the Cultural Logic of Late Capitalism*, Sartre's concept of totalization designates a trans-historical experience of the 'unification inherent in human action' and is as such integral to the experience of subjects in the postmodern era:

> Totalizing, in Sartre, is, strictly speaking, that process whereby, actively impelled by the project, an agent negates the specific object or item and reincorporates it into the larger project-in-course. Philosophically, and barring some genuine mutation of the species, it is hard to see how human activity under the third, or postmodern, stage of capitalism could elude or evade this very general formula, although some of postmodernism's ideal images – schizophrenia above all – are clearly calculated to rebuke it and to stand as unassimilable and unsubsumable under it. (1984, 333)

As we have seen, totalization is a synthesizing activity for Sartre which draws disparate elements together into a meaningful, complex whole. This means understanding specific social phenomena as constitutive parts or mediations within a wider social totality and mapping the relative influence each has in the overall dialectical scheme of things. Sartre's theory of mediations points to a form of dialectical understanding in which we can comprehend how structures and relations of capitalist society constitute specific phenomena and how their analytical dissection can shed light on broader forces. In contrast to this dialectical form of analysis, postmodernism tends only to map marginal and micro-phenomena, thus ignoring the more systemic features of contemporary capitalist society.

By over-extending the principle of detotalization, postmodernists find themselves in the throes of what Habermas has called a 'performative contradiction' – utilizing global and totalizing concepts as they simultaneously prohibit them. This can be seen in Lyotard's idea of 'postmodernity' and in Foucault's idea of the 'disciplinary society' which, to a certain extent, both rely on some form of grand narrative or periodizing and totalizing horizon. In spite of his stated theoretical preference for detotalization and heterogeneity in *Discipline and Punish*, for instance, Foucault remains captive to a totalizing impulse reflected most of all in the way that he extends 'dispositifs' of power ubiquitously across the social field. In *Power/Knowledge* he reiterates this totalizing discourse of a 'disciplinary society', speaking of 'the global functioning of . . . a society of normalization' and characterizing modern society as one in which 'domination is organized into a more-or-less coherent and unitary strategic form' (1980, 107, 142).

Responding to criticisms of this kind levelled at his idea of 'the post-modern condition', Lyotard has argued at length that the '[p]ostmodern is not taken in a periodizing sense' (Lyotard and Thébaud, 1985, 16) but more as a *rewriting* of the modern:

> As you know, I made use of the word 'postmodern': it was but a provocative way to put the struggle in the foreground of the field of knowledge. Postmodernity is not a new age, it is the rewriting of some features modernity had tried or pretended to gain, particularly in founding its legitimation upon the purpose of the general emancipation of mankind. But such a rewriting, as has already been said, was for a long time active in modernity itself. (1987, 8–9)

> A work can become modern, only if it is first postmodern. Post-modernism thus understood is not modernism at its end but in a nascent state, and this state is constant. (1984a, 79)

Like Lyotard, Foucault refrains from presenting the postmodern as a historical era separate from modernity, viewing it rather as a (counter-) attitude within modernity, 'a mode of relating to contemporary reality; a voluntary choice made by certain people; . . . a way of thinking and feeling; a way, too, of acting and belonging that at one and the same time marks a relation of belonging and presents itself as a task'. Thus, according to Foucault:

> rather than seeking to distinguish the 'modern era' from the 'pre-modern' or 'postmodern' . . . it would be more useful to try to find out how the attitude of modernity, ever since its formation, has found itself struggling with attitudes of 'countermodernity'. (1984, 39)

As Jameson (1984) points out, however, the idea of a 'postmodern condition' signifies more than just an attitude, condition of knowledge or 'one more stage of modernism proper' since it is bound up in historical terms with a process of social transformation (which Lyotard himself recognizes) that has given rise to a new social landscape and 'dominant cultural logic, or hegemonic norm':

> even if all constitutive features of postmodernism were identical and continuous with those of an older modernism . . . the two phenomena

would still remain utterly distinct in their meaning and social function, owing to the very different positioning of postmodernism in the economic system of late capital, and beyond that, to the transformation of the very sphere of culture in contemporary society. (1984, 57)

Thus, it might be said, despite their celebration of heterogeneity and plurality, both Foucault and Lyotard find themselves in the throes of an ambiguous and contradictory totalizing impulse, denying and withdrawing from the totalizing viewpoint that their defining concepts imply.

Like Jameson, Sartre shows a way beyond this impasse of postmodernist social theory by implementing postmodern insights into the influence of cultural and micro-contexts while situating them within a wider dialectical horizon which grasps the systemic nature of the social totality in which they combine and unfold. Unlike most postmodernists, Sartre retains a balanced, dialectical view of the continuing importance of narrative and totalization as key explanatory tools in social theory. By abandoning these notions completely, postmodernism fails to make an adequate distinction between different kinds of narrative or between 'general' and 'totalistic' theories,[15] thus effectively closing off further understanding and blurring vital distinctions. As Jameson shows, without some notion of a comprehensive narrative that draws together disparate elements into a general viewpoint, postmodernism condemns itself to a form of hermetic particularism that fragments and splinters a social field which under late capitalism has become ever more systematic, homogenous and globalized.

This can be seen too in the postmodernist revolt against reason where, by rejecting reason at the outset, postmodernists generally fail to provide a critical account or examination of different forms of rationality and the different social effects they engender. In response to this, which, as Habermas argues, propels postmodernism towards the dangers of irrationalism, Foucault came to question this complete rejection of reason in postmodernist thinking, warning against both the total abandonment and the uncritical acceptance of modern rationality: 'If it is extremely dangerous to say that Reason is the enemy that should be eliminated, it is just as dangerous to say that any critical questioning risks sending us into irrationality' (1984, 249). Thus, the function of critical thought, according to Foucault, is to theorize 'this sort of revolving door of rationality that refers us to its necessity, its indispensability, and at the same time to its intrinsic dangers':

> What is this Reason that we use? What are its historical effects? What are its limits, and what are its dangers? How can we exist as rational beings, fortunately committed to practicing a rationality that is unfortunately crisscrossed by intrinsic dangers? (1984, 249)

Like Foucault, Derrida also came to reject a simplistic abandonment of reason and denied being an enemy of reason. Although his work sets about challenging the rationality of established conceptual distinctions or institutional practices, the task of criticism, he argues, involves a 'double gesture' of rationally formulating questions about the limits and effects of rational endeavours (1983, 16). He explicitly acknowledges in this respect that his own theoretical efforts conform to the principle of reason and warns others who would share in these efforts against dissolving reason – 'Those who venture along this path, it seems to me, need not set themselves up in opposition to the principle of reason, nor need they give way to "irrationalism" ' (1983, 17).

In the *CDR* Sartre contributes significantly to this project of critical thought outlined by Foucault and Derrida, articulating a form of reason (dialectical reason) which, in contrast to a modern analytical reason that 'freely shapes the world while remaining free from the consequences of its action' (*CDR*, 71) emphasizes the essential co-dependence of humans and their world. In this respect, Sartre configures modern rationality and provides a form of rationality which combats scientific, instrumental rationality without lapsing into irrationalism.

In certain respects, it is possible to discern a distinctly Nietzschean and postmodernist colouration in Sartre's form of dialectical reason. In the same way that postmodernists criticize the idea of objectivity in social theory, insisting that each observer brings a social and biological biography to the act of viewing, Sartrean dialectical reason also emphasizes the perspective of the theorist[16] – it 'can and must be anyone's reflexive experience' (*CDR*, 48). For Sartre, the act of totalization is both subjective (in the sense that it is limited by the particular insertions of the individual in history and society) and objective (in that this can become a project for everyone if they choose to adopt it). We should understand 'dialectical investigation', he argues, 'as a praxis elucidating itself in order to control its own development' (*CDR*, 220). It is not an objective or disinterested comprehension of an external state of affairs, but always leads back to the subject in his need to choose a course of action:

> So in a sense, man submits to the dialectic as to an enemy power; in another sense he *creates* it; and if dialectical Reason is the Reason of History, this contradiction must itself be lived dialectically, which means that man must be controlled by the dialectic insofar as he *creates* it, and *create* it insofar as he is controlled by it. (*CDR*, 35)

In criticizing Sartre, commentators usually focus on two main elements of his work in the *CDR* which, they argue, detract significantly from the heuristic value of his overall project — these are, his negative theorization of need (Aronson, 1980; McBride, 1991) and his individualism (Aronson, 1980; Simont, 1985). In McBride's view, Sartre's equation of needs with nature as something essentially negative is 'one of the less attractive or defensible aspects of his thought from beginning to end'. This is related closely to his concept of scarcity which, McBride argues, has two main difficulties: 'the vagueness of the notion' and 'the consequent difficulty of envisioning its overcoming' (1991, 109–10). In the *CDR*, for instance, Sartre takes issue with Marx's and Engels's treatment of scarcity, arguing that it is more than the mode of production which determines it:

> this scarcity (of the product in relation to man) exists as a fundamental determination of man: we know that the socialization of production does not eliminate it, unless in the course of a long dialectical process of which we do not yet know the outcome. (*CDR*, 138–9)

Elsewhere, Sartre presents scarcity as a kind of inert material fact, a historical fate which social transformation would not obviate:

> the whole of human development, at least up to now, has been a bitter struggle against scarcity. (*CDR*, 123)

> any history free of scarcity . . . is as unknown to us as that of another species living on another planet. (*CDR* (2), 22)

Given that, for Sartre, a condition of scarcity 'realizes the passive totality of the individuals within a collectivity as an impossibility of co-existence' (CDR, 129), this, it might be argued, effectively contextualizes in a historical sense his earlier ontological denial of *Mitsein* in *BN* by reinscribing conflict as an essential condition of social existence. In other places, however, Sartre is less deterministic in entertaining the possible overcoming of scarcity, acknowledging that our history is just one history among all possible histories and that it is thus impossible to demonstrate *a priori* 'that all histories must be conditioned by scarcity' (CDR (2), 22): 'relations of immediate abundance between other practical organisms and other milieux are not inconceivable a priori' (CDR, 735).

Sartre's analysis of scarcity (like his social theory in general) can be seen in this light to oscillate between modernist and postmodernist poles. On the one hand, Sartre stresses the modernist element of *necessity* (taking scarcity as a given material fact) and yet, on the other, he configures it in postmodern fashion as a *contingent* construct.[17] However, Sartre's emphasis usually lies with the element of necessity in the *CDR* and it can be argued that he generally gives *too much* weight to the determining influence of scarcity in human relations and thus insufficient consideration to its contingent and historically specific nature. Although, as he rightly shows, scarcity can plunge human relations into hostility, stamping them with the hallmark of matter, he is too hasty in outlining the necessity with which it imposes 'an impossibility of co-existence' within a collectivity. Indeed, in the *CDR*, Sartre generally gives a hyperbolic and necessitarian emphasis to the determining influence of scarcity:

> In fact nothing – neither great wild beasts nor microbes – can be more terrible for man than an intelligent, carnivorous, cruel species which could understand and outwit human intelligence and whose goal would be precisely the destruction of man. That species is obviously our own as grasped by every man in Others within the milieu of scarcity. (CDR, 132)

However, although conditions of scarcity often demand that a material situation be overturned, they do not determine the specific means whereby individuals and groups will effect this overturning. This is indeed suggested, I think, by Sartre's own example of the Chinese peasants in the *CDR* where, acting purely as separate individuals, each becomes a threat to the others and surrenders their fate to the counterfinality of matter. Acting collectively by joining their labour in a common plan would not, by contrast, give rise to the same situation of mutual hostility. As a collective group they are able to discuss and revise their individual needs in the light of a collective rationality not to despoil and exploit the landscape and so become the victims of a likely and disastrous counterfinality. Even in very extreme, atypical examples of scarcity, individuals and groups need not descend into violence, threat or 'an impossibility of co-existence' in a straightforward or predictable way. It is not inconceivable, for instance, that a group of people shipwrecked on a barren desert island might decide among themselves (albeit reluctantly) upon a collective plan of cannibalism or suicide. Although this is clearly an intractable and horrific situation, it need not automatically plunge relations into a state of abject or outright hostility. Sartre would of course be wrong to disregard scarcity entirely, but his continual emphasis on eradicating it and on its importance in determining human relations can neglect the ways in which humans can overcome its negative prescriptions by subscribing to a collective rationale.

Thus, as McBride suggests, Sartre's theorization of scarcity suffers both from ambivalence (in regard to the possibility of overcoming it) and from the underdeveloped 'vagueness of the notion'. His ambivalence stems from the contradiction between the necessary and conflictual nature of scarcity and the possibility of a harmonious 'fully human community' that he consistently argued for and struggled for in his work and in his life. The vagueness of his conception relates to the way in which he fails to define or to distinguish between different degrees or kinds of scarcity (e.g. geographical (positional), material, emotional, etc.) or to elaborate concrete means or specific collective strategies to combat these.

From a postmodernist perspective, Sartre's consistent attachment to the importance of scarcity in the *CDR* reveals a certain Marxist and modernist bias within his work. As Baudrillard argues in *The Mirror of Production*, for instance, scarcity is not a material fact, but rather a theoretical construct of modern invention, an 'idealist over-determination by political economy' that does predominate in non-productivist societies based on symbolic exchange (1975, 59). Cixous'

(1986) idea of a 'gift-giving economy' is put forward in a similar vein to articulate a set of economic principles that refuses to accept the modern assumption of the givenness of conditions of scarcity.[18] From this perspective, Sartre's theorization of need and scarcity in the *CDR* entrenches itself within a modernist perspective that takes need as a direct and material given and which thus fails to consider both the positive aspects of need and the ways in which all needs (including personal ones) are deeply influenced by the 'consummative mobilisation' of capitalist society (Baudrillard, 1983a, 135).[19]

As Lévi-Strauss argues in *The Savage Mind* (1966, 324–57), Sartre's work in the *CDR*, though having relevance to our modern western societies, by no means pertains to all human cultures. This lack of historical and cultural scope can be seen most clearly in the way that Sartre devotes so much space in his analysis of history to Stalin and Bolshevik Russia unlike Foucault, Deleuze and Guattari and Baudrillard, for instance, who range far beyond this limited fragment of modern history in their overall historical trajectories. Indeed, the way in which the ghost of Stalin haunts and dominates Sartre's historical analysis has led certain commentators to focus critically on what they discern to be its narrowly individualist perspective.[20]

In the main, it is the lack of underlying sociality in Sartre's work that causes him to focus so much attention on the individual praxis of Stalin. Since his dialectic of the group in the *CDR* ignores any prior form of social co-operation, it is almost inevitable that Sartre perceives a sovereign individual (Stalin) as necessary to preserve the group's purposes. What this reveals is the limited and restrictive way in which Sartre conceives sociality (intersubjectivity). Although his account of the fused group (in which the identity and praxis of the individual are confirmed, enabled, strengthened and 'synthetically enriched' by the common totalizing project) advances well beyond the abstract form of individualism in *BN* and points to a more communal-based logic in the *CDR*, Sartre gives this group only a *reactive* ephemeral status. There is fusion, he insists, only when there is an imminent or actual danger – the group emerges when serial multiplicity yields an 'impossibility of living':

> insofar as the individuals within a given milieu are directly threatened
> . . . by the impossibility of life, their radical unity . . . is the inflexible

negation of this impossibility . . . thus the group constitutes itself as the radical impossibility of living, which threatens serial multiplicity. (*CDR*, 341)

This 'group identification', Sartre insists, should not be conceived in terms of 'altruism and egoism', but is 'engraved in the practico-inert field' (*CDR*, 368), produced by the dialectical relation between the praxis of an oppressive group and the progressive integration of individuals as 'mediating others' into a totality which comes to be the (oppressed) fused group. By restricting group identification to a purely reactive status, however, Sartre omits both those concepts (such as love, friendship, kinship) through which we can reach an organicity of communal relations as well as vital, enriching experiences of intersubjectivity that arise from spontaneous collective gatherings or festivals. These come about not when 'individuals in a milieu are directly threatened' (*CDR*, 341), as Sartre asserts, but are based on expressions of (Nietzschean) play and symbolic exchange. They are not in this sense motivated (or constituted) by fear and are not directly 'engraved in the practico-inert field', but instead involve a fluid and reciprocal context for artistic exchange, projects of solidarity or activities of mutual identification. Unfortunately, Sartre leads us to think that humans are united by the fact of their materiality alone – 'we are united by the fact that we all live in a world which is determined by scarcity' (*CDR*, 136) – and not in any deeper, more substantive way. Lacking an adequate theory of sociality in his work, it is not surprising that his attempt to bring the full reality and unity of class-conflict into historical view in the second volume of the *Critique* was doomed to failure. From his denial of a primordial *Mitsein* or sociality in *BN* to a restrictive conception of it in the *CDR*, Sartre does not break free from a pathological individualism that suffuses his main philosophical texts.

In the next chapter I examine some of the merits and the difficulties that arise from Sartre's individualist perspective as they relate to his political theory, as well as his subsequent attempts to overcome this individualism in the *Cahiers* and elsewhere.

Political Theory and Practice

a philosophy remains efficacious so long as the praxis which has engendered it, which supports it, and which is clarified by it, is still alive. (*SM*, 5–6)

Socialism: masculine noun, a cultural genre, born in Paris in 1848, died in Paris in 1968. (Lévy, 1977, 8)

Sartre, Marxism, the PCF and 1968

In the Preface to the *CDR* Sartre describes Marxism as 'the unsurpassable philosophy of our time' and places his own existentialism as a subordinate enclave within Marxism, 'a parasitical system living on the margin of Knowledge, which at first it opposed but into which today it seeks to be integrated' (*SM*, 8). Previous to this, however, Sartre's early work generally expresses indifference towards Marxism and, after the 1960s, this allegiance towards Marxism steadily and progressively wanes.

When criticizing Marxism, it is not always clear to whom Sartre addresses his complaints, whether to Marx himself or simply to the Stalinist orthodox form it had come to assume under the aegis of the PCF in France. In *Search for a Method* Sartre declares a kinship with Marx and generally complains about the distortion of his thought in the hands of its 'official interpreters' (*SM*, 17), but in the main text of the *CDR*, as we saw in the last chapter, he takes issue in a number of respects with Marx and Engels directly. In the overall trajectory of Sartre's work, the *CDR* represents an important transition point in this respect as it contains both the fullest expression of Sartre's (rejuvenated) philosophical Marxism and yet at the same time highlights a number of theoretical problems within Marxism which, at a later date, would be perceived by Sartre as profound inadequacies (1981b). Although Sartre clearly is closer to the humanist

Marxism of Marx than to the orthodox Marxism of Stalin or Plekhanov, it is difficult to ascertain the precise extent to which his growing disillusionment with Marxism post-1960s was generated by a philosophical hostility towards Marxism in general or simply through a reaction to the actual practices of (Stalinist) Marxism in the form of the PCF and other Communist Parties.

This is further complicated by the fact that, like many other French intellectuals at the time, Sartre's relationship to the PCF was not itself consistent, veering between the extremes of enthusiastic support and hostile denunciation. For some French intellectuals like Foucault, Lyotard, Guattari and Baudrillard, the actual political practices of the PCF were eventually perceived as the logical outcome of a theoretical system, Marxism, which was only partially revolutionary and which was intimately bound up with the capitalist rationality it sought to contest. For others like Henri Lefebvre, Louis Althusser and Roger Garaudy, Marxism itself was not perceived to be the problem, merely its distorted embodiment in the form of the PCF (they were all prominent members of the PCF for a number of years before being expelled for 'heretical practices'). In Sartre's case, both these elements are present, but after 1968, he is generally more content to criticize and withdraw from Marxist categories rather than 'renew' them as was his stated aim in the CDR.

In general terms, Sartre's attitudes towards the PCF can be divided into three main periods which progress from ambivalence and antagonism in the 1940s, to uncritical and enthusiastic support in the early 1950s, and finally to growing hostility and repudiation after 1956. In this first period which constitutes his main 'existentialist phase', his political outlook was a broadly anarchist one in which his strong sense of independence prevented him from forming relations with political organizations. As Sartre later recalled, he and Simone de Beauvoir attended few marches in this period and observed the Communist Party from afar: 'We were communist sympathizers without a shadow of a doubt, but we weren't members. The idea never entered our heads' (1980, 31). Unlike his close friend, Paul Nizan, for instance, Sartre could not silence his dissenting voice and submit to a party line.

Although Sartre's work of this period exposes the negative and sordid features of bourgeois life, his narrow individualist perspective effectively debars any form of collective solidarity or positive social existence by placing conflict at the heart of our being-with-others. Reacting to this, Communist critics took Sartre to be a representative of the bourgeoisie, publicly denouncing him in the Communist press as a 'writing hyena', 'lubricious viper', 'viscous rat' and 'gravedigger of the young'.[1] Sartre responded critically in turn to the PCF, stating in *What is Literature?* that '[t]he politics of Stalinist communism are incompatible with the honest practice of the literary craft' (1978, 256).

This relation of political indifference and critical hostility between Sartre and the PCF soon changed in the 1950s, however, precipitated both by the shift in Sartre's philosophical perspective from individualist to more social categories and by the Cold War political climate in France. The most significant event in this latter respect was the frame-up and arrest in 1952 of the Communist leader, Jacques Duclos, by the French state which impelled Sartre towards a 'radical conversion' to Communism and towards a hatred and disgust for his own class, the bourgeoisie, which, he stated, 'would only die with me' (1965, 288). From then on, the intensity and divisive nature of the Cold War climate in France compelled Sartre to take sides and to view anti-Communism as a form of treason to the masses: 'An anti-Communist is a rat' (1977, 287). Stuck between the Cold War polarities of Stalinist Communism and capitalism, Sartre describes the difficulty of the situation in the following way: 'Either the USSR was not the country of socialism, in which case socialism didn't exist anywhere and doubtless, wasn't possible: or else, socialism was *that*, this abominable monster, this police state, the power of beasts of prey' (1977, 275).

Sartre's growing radicalism and politicization in this period can be glimpsed first of all in *What is Literature?* which, as Contat notes, signifies 'a politicised act of faith in literature as pointing the way to man's future' (1996, 15). In this text, Sartre outlines the necessity for 'committed writing', viewing literature as a 'conducting wire' to socialist democracy (1978, 268). Art, he maintains, leads to reflection (which is 'an essential condition of action' (1978, 153)) and discloses the images which society tries to hide from itself:

> If society sees itself and, in particular, sees itself as seen, there is, by
> virtue of this very fact, a contesting of the established values of the

regime. The writer presents it with its image; he calls upon it to assume it or to change itself. (1978, 75)

Since art and society are inseparably bound together, each work of art implicitly contains a valuative stance on the existing order of things. Thus, Sartre argues, writers do not need to eulogize the existing order to help maintain it, merely not speak out against it (1978, 19). This theory of commitment was extended further and applied to concrete political action in *The Communists and Peace* where Sartre wholeheartedly endorses the PCF as the guardian and agent of proletarian liberation. Here, Sartre argues that the Communist Party is exactly how it should be: authoritarian and structured, centralized and consisting of paid militants who act upon and represent the true interests of the working class. Only an organization 'as the pure and simple incarnation of praxis', Sartre argues, can prevent the masses from sinking into apathy and resignation (1968, 115).

Sartre's uncritical support for the PCF in this text and in the early 1950s is construed by most commentators as a significant aberration in his political thinking. Merleau-Ponty, most notably, severely criticizes Sartre's 'Ultra-Bolshevism' in *The Adventures of the Dialectic* where he charges Sartre with providing a justification for Stalinism in philosophical terms by reinforcing what Merleau-Ponty describes as his earlier *pour-soi/en-soi* distinction between the party (as pure action) and workers (as inert and isolated). In Sartre's later political phase post-1960s, this image of a passive proletariat in need of control and orchestration by an active centralized party was 'turned on its head', Sartre inverting the image to show the party as inert and conservative and the ordinary masses as socialism's true practical and revolutionary agent.

Despite Sartre's 'Ultra-Bolshevism' in *The Communists and Peace*, it is still possible in overall terms to take a positive view of Sartre's political project in the 1950s, the defining features of which were his growing radicalism and his deepening sense of socialist principle. Although Sartre's period as an uncritical apologist for the PCF in the early 1950s can be seen as a regrettable phase in his political trajectory that he would later distance himself from, this period was only a short one and also one in which Cold War polarities impelled intellectuals to take sides with either capitalism or Communism. The intensity of this Cold War atmosphere charged the air with a political electricity, illustrated by the clamour to assign a political valence to Sartre's *Les mains sales* in 1948. Despite the fact that it was not Sartre's intended meaning, certain French critics were keen to give it an objective meaning of anti-Communism. With this in mind, Sartre's support for the PCF in the 1950s can be seen as an attempt on his part to confirm his consistent opposition to capitalism and to disprove the constant attacks on him in the Communist press (especially *L'Humanité*) that branded him as a representative of the bourgeoisie and an agent of the government and Wall Street.

In much the same manner as the arrest of Duclos in 1952 was a catalytic event in Sartre's support for the PCF, the Soviet invasion of Hungary in 1956 effectively ended this support and signalled the beginning of a third phase in Sartre's political thinking characterized by a growing critical awareness of inherent inadequacies in Marxist political practice and by a return to an anarchistic outlook similar in some respects to the one he had adopted in the 1930s. The inadequacies of Marxist political practice came most visibly into focus in the events beginning in May 1968 in France where Sartre and many other French intellectuals turned against the PCF for acting to obstruct and to divert the revolution. The student revolts of May 1968 which spread to other sections of French society at large were, in Sartre's view, 'a radical contestation of every established value of the university and society' which linked positive social change to the radical upsurge of the imagination (1969, 62):

> What is interesting about your action is that it is putting imagination in power . . . Something has come out of you which is confounding, shaking up, rejecting everything which has made our society what it is today. It's what I would call an extension of the field of possibilities. (in Aronson, 1980, 312–13)

Unlike traditional struggles conducted by and directed through the central organ of the party which aimed to seize the apparatus of power, the revolts of 1968 were spontaneous, decentralized and non-hierarchical, seeking not to seize power directly but to contest and dismantle it across the entire social field. To this extent, 1968 signified a new form of political practice which differed significantly from the centralizing, authoritarian framework of the PCF and traditional Leninist practice.

As several French commentators noted at the time,[2] Sartre's *CDR* can be viewed as a theoretical inspiration for the practices of 1968.

In particular, his analysis of group structure in the *CDR* can be seen as a direct criticism of the centralizing, authoritarian and institutional nature of the party structure. The positive forms of reciprocity and collectivity engendered in the fused group point to a very different form of social life than the degenerated forms of seriality and 'vertical otherness' Sartre identifies with the organized/institutional group. Indeed, in later years this opposition to authority and institutionality became the basis of Sartre's political outlook:

> If a revolutionary party must exist today, it should have the least possible resemblance to an institution, and it should contest all institutionality − outside itself, but first of all within itself. What must be developed in people is not the respect for a supposed revolutionary *order*, but rather the spirit of revolt against all order. (1974b, 47−8)

In the 1970s, Sartre moved towards an ultra-left *gauchiste* position and worked closely with Maoist groups in France, famously distributing *La Cause du Peuple* in the streets of Paris under the threat of arrest by the government. During this time he continued to vilify the PCF, accusing it of being 'in league with the government against the Maoists' and declaring it to be 'the largest conservative party in France' (1974a, 60). Despite the fact Sartre begins his essay in *Situations* ('Les Maos en France') with the disclaimer that he is not a Maoist, in this text he stresses three main points of agreement with the Maoists − their espousal of violence as a justified form of political self-defence ('a Socialist cannot but be violent, for his goal is one that the ruling-class utterly repudiates' (1977 (10), 97)), their spontaneity and their anti-authoritarian morality.

The socialism of Sartre's later political period can be viewed in this light as a Marxism of an unusual and dubious kind in so much as it disturbs, modifies and calls into question Marxist forms of understanding in the process of renewing them. Indeed, Sartre's libertarian form of Socialism has more in common with certain forms of anarchism than it does with traditional forms of Marxism, viewing hierarchy, organization and authority as the main obstacles to reciprocity, fusion and freedom.

In Sartre's overall political trajectory, it is possible to find contrasting elements of change, evolution and consistency. As his work evolves, he steadily abandons the limited framework of individualism which characterizes his early political outlook and moves towards socialism as a collective means of overcoming individual alienation. In the late 1940s, his early mood of detachment changes into one of activism and commitment, culminating in his practical involvement with Maoist and student groups in 1968 and the 1970s. For a brief period in the 1950s, Sartre directed this growing sense of commitment towards the PCF, adopting a pro-party position which he would abandon entirely in his later political phase.

The consistency that runs throughout Sartre's political project from the 1930s onwards can be found most of all in his growing independence and radicalism – even in his period of support for the PCF, he did not hold a party card. In his later political phase this sense of independence is woven into a framework of political anarchism which, unlike the anarchism of his early years, is now linked to a project of collective freedom, solidarity and commitment. Reviewing his political trajectory in the 1970s, Sartre himself identifies anarchism as the basis of his overall political outlook:

I have never accepted any authority over me and I've always thought that anarchy, that is, a society without structures of authority, must be brought about. (1977 (10), 156)

If one rereads all my books, one will realize that I have not changed profoundly, and that I have always remained an anarchist. (1977 (10), 24)

The politics of postmodernism

The postmodernist revolt against Marxism as a totalistic theory of society is carried over into the political sphere where it is viewed as a totalitarian and centralizing discourse. According to Foucault, for instance, Marxism involves 'the coercion of a theoretical, unitary, formal and scientific discourse' which has 'the inhibiting effect of global, *totalitarian* theories' (1980, 80–1). Since Marxism locates power centrally in the productive and economic base of society, it effectively confines possibilities for revolt within this narrow sphere. This can be seen in Marx's tendency to reduce political agency to the singular aspect of the proletariat and to equate alienation suffered by society at large with the specific alienations suffered by the proletariat in the realm of production:

> A class must be formed which has radical chains, a class *in* civil society which is not a class *of* civil society, a class which is a dissolution of all classes, a sphere of society which has a universal character because its sufferings are universal, and which does not claim a particular redress because the wrong which is done to it is not a particular wrong but wrong in general . . . This dissolution of society, as a particular class, is the proletariat. (1975, 256–7)

For Foucault, by contrast, since power is dispersed everywhere in the social field, decentred and plural, so in turn must be forms of political organization and struggle. Foucault, Deleuze, Guattari and Lyotard all put forward in this vein a micro-logical strategy of political struggle designed to recover autonomous, local and marginal discourses, knowledges and voices suppressed through totalizing narratives. Their 'theoretical rupture' with the macro-strategies of Marxism exhibits a deep concern with centralization – in praising Foucault's theory of power, for instance, which breaks with the idea of a single central point of power, Deleuze describes the way in which Foucault provides 'a theoretical revolution directed not only at bourgeois theories of the state, but at the Marxist conception of power and the relation to the state'. For Deleuze,

> [t]he theoretical privilege that Marxism accords the state as an apparatus of power brings with it its own practical conception of the directing, centralizing Party, proceeding to the conquest of state power, but, conversely, this organizational conception of the Party is justified by this theory of power. (1975, 1212)

The political events of 1968 in France (and elsewhere) serve as a useful focal point through which we can view these changes in political understanding put forward by post-structuralists and postmodernists. As Foucault states, the events of 1968 signalled a different kind of strategy of political resistance which was 'profoundly anti-Marxist' (1980, 57) in the sense that it was a spontaneous, largely unorganized and non-hierarchical revolution which did not seek to replace one dominant political 'truth' (capitalism) with another (the Marxism of the *Parti Communiste Français*), but which sought instead to contest power multifariously across the entire fabric of social life. It involved a *decentralized* contestation of power rather than an attempt to 'overthrow the enemy' through an orchestrated conquest of state power directed by and mediated through the central organ of the party. It was, in other words, local, decentralized, diffuse, immediate, spontaneous and organic, arising from the creation of new forms of reciprocity which subverted power rather than from an organized struggle to appropriate the central, existing power of the state – a form of politics as a 'transgressive festival' or a 'display of excessive expenditure' far removed from the calculating and instrumental Jacobin/Leninist framework of modern politics.[3] As Lyotard stated in the 1970s, the movement of 1968 was, above all, a struggle against 'big politics' and traditional forms of social and political representation:

> If the May 1968 movement can continue to mean anything, it is because it extended criticism to a number of forms of representation, to the union, the party, the institution of culture in general, which 'big politics', including Trotskyism and Maoism, either ignored or considered merely secondary. On the contrary, the movement of May 1968 found these forms of representation to be immediate and persistent obstacles to the liberation of potential critical energy. (1973, 307)

The growing disillusionment with Marxism among French intellectuals following 1968 can be seen in the rise to prominence of *Les Nouveaux Philosophes* such as André Glucksmann, Philippe Sollers and Benny Lévy who all rejected it as inescapably a philosophy and a practice of domination. In *Les maîtres penseurs,* for instance, Glucksmann (like Albert Camus many years before in *L'homme révolté*) blames Hegel for the totalizing propensities of Marxist philosophy, seeing in the 'text' of German philosophy the seeds of all totalitarian evil, whether 'left' or 'right':

> The 'Germany' in which fascism was born is not a territory or a population, but a text and a textual relation . . . found in the modern

brains of this planet, in the Pentagon in Washington, as much as in some God-forsaken concentration camp in the Cambodian country-side. (1977, 48)

Above all, the *Nouveaux Philosophes* lambasted Marxism for its neglect of the individual as a creative being and as a repository for authentic values. For Sollers, who had previously been associated with the revolutionary Tel Quel group, Marxism's 'rage to enslave that which speaks and lives' turned his political view towards America as a progressive horizon for individual freedom. Lévy and Glucksmann similarly dismissed all forms of socialism and Marxism as totalitarian despite the availability of socialist discourses (such as Sartre's) which were non-elitist and which condemned totalitarian Communism. Although the *Nouveaux Philosophes'* reading of Nietzsche provides little in the way of theoretical insight or political guidance, the brief popularity of Lévy and Glucksmann's work following 1968 reflected a very real and widespread disenchantment with the political practice and logic of Marxism. Thus, it was not only those like Sollers who moved to the Right but also those remaining on the Left (such as Barthes, Lacan, Foucault, Deleuze, Guattari and Derrida) who often defined themselves in opposition to the monolithic centralism characteristic of French Marxism and the PCF.

The politics of postmodernism can be read as a kind of postscript to May 1968 in that they reflect this movement away from Marxism and shift focus away from the sphere of political economy to that of culture and everyday life. Like the protagonists of 1968, postmodernists have no faith in conventional political parties and forms of organization (whether of the Left or Right) because, as Tucker states, they 'are bound to become bureaucratic, corrupt, and undemocratic' (1990, 76). Equally, they share a preference for decentralization and plurality, stressing, in their more Sceptical forms, non-participation or play and euphoria as the best alternatives to traditional modern political action.

In some cases, the politics of postmodernism have been inscribed within the dialogue of the Right focusing upon the obsolescence of Marxist theory and Communism, or (as in 'Third World' postmodern movements) upon the notion of an idealized traditional society which encourages a reminiscence of the past as a means to overcome the present (see Vattimo, 1988, Chapter 10)). For critical Marxists such as Eagleton,

Callinicos and Harvey, postmodernism fits neatly in this sense with the culture and ideology of a new conservatism where ironic detachment, non-participation, indifference and apathy are seen as the only effective means for strategic resistance. In the case of Affirmative postmodernists (e.g. Foucault, Deleuze, Laclau and Mouffe), forms of progressive (socialist) political organization are not abandoned altogether – they do, however, decentre the position of labour maintaining, along with Guattari and Negri, that 'the discourse of worker's centrality and hege-mony are thoroughly defunct' and that the traditional working classes 'no longer represent a social majority' (1990, 122, 127). In Guattari's view, a postmodern 'micro-politics' shifts focus away from the (Marxist) discourse of the proletariat towards the discourses of the marginalized and excluded, setting loose 'a whole host of expressions and experi-mentations – those of children, of schizophrenics, of homosexuals, or prisoners, or misfits of every kind – that all work to penetrate and enter into the semiology of the dominant order' (1984, 184).

The variety of perspectives found within postmodern political think-ing means that it is not always easy to decide upon the political valence of postmodernism. Although both Sceptical and Affirmative forms involve a critique of Marxism, in Sceptical forms this tends to be accompanied by a shift towards the Right or some form of political quietism whereas Affirmative versions incline, like Sartre's anarchistic form of socialism, towards a more *gauchiste* position. Thus, rather than being necessarily conservative as Harvey, Habermas and others suggest, postmodern political positions range from those like Foucault who seek to radicalize Marx to Sceptics like Lyotard who want to lay him to rest. In spite of this variety, however, there are some common features that unite postmodern political thinking, namely the preference postmodernists hold for the notions of *micro-politics*, *plurality*, *difference* and *locality*. Added to this is a general postmodern concern for *identity politics* that draws its animus from the sphere of culture and everyday life and inveighs against the modern political logic of class politics and political economy.

Sartre and postmodern political theory

As we have seen, the events of 1968 in France can be viewed in many ways as an expression of both Sartrean and postmodernist political themes. In Sartre's case, it is clearly evident and beyond doubt that, in Ronald Aronson's words, 'every political bone in his body had been aiming at this movement for over twenty years' (1995, 28). Prior to this in the early 1960s, Sartre's political experience had undoubtedly been darkened by the Cold War witch-hunts of the 1950s and by the subsequent realization that the Soviet Union and the PCF were more enemies than agents of a free socialist society. The *CDR* is often seen in this light to be imbued with this sense of darkness, particularly with regard to Sartre's account of the ephemeral and fragile nature of group fusion which leads him to conclude that the initial construction of socialism 'could only be the indissoluble aggregation of bureaucracy, of Terror, and of the cult of the personality' (*CDR*, 662). As we saw in the last chapter, however, determination and necessity comprise just one aspect of Sartre's dialectical method in the *CDR* and constantly remain open to the radical upsurge of praxis which disturbs and overturns the social inertia of the practico-inert. In this respect, the revolutionary praxis of 1968 focused attention on the perennial possibility of affirmative praxis and political agency at a time when the intellectual paradigm was dominated by structuralism which was proclaiming the death of the subject. A year later in 1969 structuralism began to lose its intellectual dominance, Lévi-Strauss bemoaning the fact that 'the position of the youth now corresponds to that of Sartre'.[4]

The active spirit of revolt engendered in the struggles of 1968 effectively put into question the structuralist dissolution of agency and no longer made it possible to think abstractly of social structures as frozen synchronies and as unilateral determinants of social action that simply construct subjects who are without desire, interest or a determinate impulse for freedom. This plunged (post-)structuralism into a kind of farcical return to Zeno's paradox — agency was clearly there and palpable, but how could it be accounted for? As a result of this inherent difficulty, the more Affirmative post-structuralists such as Foucault steered their work away from structuralist methods and embarked upon reconstructing an affirmative account of agency which could explain this experience of subjective revolt:

> there is a plurality of resistances, each of them a special case: resistances that are possible, necessary, improbable; others that are spontaneous,

savage, solitary, concerted, rampant, or violent; still others that are quick to compromise, interested, or sacrificial. (Foucault, 1978, 96)

Without the political opening of those years, I would perhaps not have had the courage to take up the thread of these problems and to pursue my inquiry in the direction of punishment, prisons and discipline. (Foucault, in Ferry and Renaut, 1990, xix)

In *Negotiations* Deleuze echoes this view of Foucault, acknowledging the importance of 1968 as an inspiration for the writing of *Anti-Oedipus:*

Anti-Oedipus was about the univocity of the real, a sort of Spinozism of the unconscious. And I think '68 was this discovery itself. The people who hate '68, or say it was a mistake, see it as something symbolic or imaginary. But that's precisely what it wasn't, it was pure reality breaking through. (1995, 144–5)

In this way, the Sartrean themes of freedom and subjectivity were brought into focus and reinvigorated in the struggles of 1968 at a time when, intellectually, they were being dissolved by the dominant structuralist paradigm. After 1968 these themes were taken up by the more Affirmative postmodernists such as Foucault, Deleuze and Derrida, whose earlier relation of antipathy towards Sartre turned into one of respect in the 1970s. More Sceptical postmodernists like Baudrillard, however, continued the assault on the subject inaugurated by structuralism, characterizing the postmodern age as one marked by the loss of agency and by the death of meaning.

The political uprisings of 1968 had a profound influence on the eventual shape of West European politics that followed it, bringing into critical focus the issues of sexual politics, the environment and ecology, workers' control and co-operative movements, the politics of culture and the question of alienation. Following 1968 in France, for instance, gay and feminist movements sprang up in the early 1970s (e.g. '*Front Homosexuel Révolutionnaire*' in 1971 and '*Choisir*' in 1972), signifying a shift in political consciousness away from the central domain of political economy towards more plural and diverse forms of politicization centred on the issue of identity. In Foucault's view, this marked a movement beyond the narrow focus of production that brought into view 'the full range of hidden mechanisms through which a society conveys its knowledges and ensures its survival under the mask of knowledge: newspapers, television, technical schools, and the lycée' (1977b, 225).

In the 1970s, post-structuralists like Foucault, Deleuze, Guattari and Lyotard built these insights into a micrological political strategy aimed at recovering discourses, knowledges and voices suppressed through totalizing narratives and at breaking the control of disciplinary powers over the body through the creation of new modes of desire, pleasure and expression. For Foucault, this meant combining a *discourse politics* that contests hegemonic discourses which serve to normalize identities with a *politics of the body* that explores the transgressive potential of somatic pleasure. For Deleuze and Guattari in *Anti-Oedipus* and *A Thousand Plateaus*, this points to a *politics of desire* which is seen as essential to combat the way in which capitalism and fascism instantiate themselves at all levels in society to impede the flow of revolutionary forces and produce reactionary subjectivities. A rationalist macro-politics, they argue, leaves the terrain of desire, culture and everyday life uncontested and thus neglects the crucial space in which subjects are produced and controlled and in which fascist subjectivities originate and take hold:

> Hitler got the fascists sexually aroused. Flags, nations, armies, banks get a lot of people aroused. A revolutionary machine is nothing if it does not acquire as least as much force as these coercive machines have for producing breaks and mobilizing flows. (Deleuze and Guattari, 1983, 293)

This postmodern turn towards micro-politics involves a rejection, as we have seen, of traditional Marxist approaches to political strategy. Reflecting on the events of 1968 in France, Deleuze and Guattari echoed the view of those, like Sartre, who attacked the PCF for its conservative and authoritarian nature. This, they argue, stems largely from the limited macro-perspective of the PCF — since the 'objective conditions' for the struggles of 1968 were not ripe (capital and class contradictions had not yet reached a 'crisis stage'), they were rejected by the PCF as diversionary or immature instead of being seen as necessary preconditions for a macro-political revolution.

This is reflected too in Marxist interpretations of fascism which, according to Deleuze and Guattari, by relying exclusively on macropolitical explanations in terms of the state, overt political repression and the crisis of capitalist accumulation, neglect the psychological element of fascism as a deformation of desire and as a subjective condition produced in capitalist society, a form of modern power which is 'without doubt capitalism's most fantastic attempt at economic and political reterritorialization' (1983, 258). Fascism cannot be explained simply as a form of ideology or false consciousness but should be seen as a real assemblage of forces and desire which invests itself on both molar and molecular levels:

> fascism is inseparable from a proliferation of molecular focuses in interaction, which skip from point to point, *before* beginning to resonate together in the National Socialist State. Rural fascism and city or neighbourhood fascism, youth fascism and war veteran's fascism, fascism of the Left and fascism of the Right, fascism of the couple, family, school, and office. (Deleuze and Guattari, 1987, 214)

In a manner similar to Reich, Deleuze and Guattari argue that the masses were not duped or deluded by a false consciousness (as Marxists suppose) but wanted fascism at a certain time and under certain conditions in the sense that it connected with certain modes of desire which mapped onto general assemblages of collective desire in German society at that time. In *Economie Libidinale* Lyotard also follows this line of argument, theorizing the experience of workers under capitalism not as a case of false consciousness but as a configuration of libidinal forces which work through social groups:

> look at the English proletariat ... [they] enjoyed the hysterical, masochistic, whatever exhaustion it was of *hanging on* in the mines, in the foundries, in the factories in hell, they enjoyed it, enjoyed the destruction of their organic body which was indeed imposed upon them, they enjoyed the decomposition of their personal identity, the identity that the peasant tradition had constructed for them, enjoyed the dissolution of their families and villages, and enjoyed the new monstrous *anonymity* of the suburbs and the pubs in the morning and evening. (1974, 111)

As Guattari states in *Molecular Revolution*, it is not necessary to believe in the capitalist system to realize that co-operating with it is the easiest way to satisfy one's immediate needs. Truths for people are expressed essentially in terms of desires and pragmatic concerns that tend to reproduce the dominant machinic mode of production (1984, 163). Since Marxist revolutionary strategy neglects the plane of desire, it fails to grasp the unconscious as a locus of repression not only in social life, but also within subjects and groups. Thus it is possible to have subjects who are revolutionary in their class-interests and objectives, but reactionary or authoritarian in their modes of desire. To this end, in a manner similar to Sartre's reflections on the seriality that haunts the fused group, Deleuze and Guattari speak of revolutionary struggles where 'groups and individuals contain micro fascisms just waiting to crystallize' (1987, 9). Those who fail to liberate desire and so reproduce hierarchy and authority in the course of struggle are seen by Deleuze and Guattari as *subjugated groups* while those with 'molecular libidinal investments' are seen as *subject groups*. In the same way that, for Sartre, the fused group must permanently struggle against seriality, Deleuze and Guattari argue that, to stay as subject groups, revolutionary groups must avoid the 'molar pole' of investment with structured lines of movement and stratified flows and stay within the 'molecular pole' of decoded flows, schizophrenic intensities and revolutionary social investments (1987, 11).

The fear of social congealment is something that unites Sartre's political outlook closely with that of postmodernists like Foucault, Deleuze and Guattari. In Foucault's terms, this process of congealment is seen as a movement in social life which inclines 'always towards order', in Deleuze and Guattari's as the 'reterritorialization of desire', while in Sartre's it represents the dialectical movement towards inertia, organization, seriality and the institution. Efforts of resistance are seen in this way to have only a temporary resonance as they become 'absorbed by the dominant structure' (Foucault, 1977, 232). The drive to stabilize the achievements of revolutionary resistance most often forecloses options for the ongoing practice of liberty that extends and alters those achievements. As Foucault explains:

> I've always been a little distrustful of the general theme of liberation
> ... I do not mean to say that liberation or such and such a form of

liberation does not exist. When a colonial people tries to free itself of its colonizer that is truly an act of liberation, in the strict sense of the word. But we also know that, in this extremely precise example, this act of liberation is not sufficient to establish the practices of liberty that will later on be necessary for this people, this society and these individuals to decide upon receivable and acceptable forms of their existence or political society. (1988, 2–3)

This fear of congealment and inertia gives rise in Sartre and in postmodernists to a deep scepticism concerning Marxist accounts of proletarian revolution – in particular, the idea of a centralized proletarian conquest of state power. As a centralized, institutional organ of state power, a 'Dictatorship of the Proletariat' would, according to Sartre, be impelled towards Stalinization, terror and seriality (CDR, 662). To illustrate this, he points to the experience of the sailors of Kronstadt in 1921 in Bolshevik Russia who, by attempting to return to the revolutionary ideals of 1917, were labelled as insurrectionists and counter-revolutionaries and subsequently massacred: 'if the group is really to constitute itself by an effective praxis, it will liquidate alterities within it, and it will eliminate procrastinators and oppositionists' (CDR, 403). Rather than, in Engels's famous statement, 'wither away', the proletarian state is much more inclined to augment and crystallize itself in the urge towards consolidation and a functional stability.

The solution Sartre, Foucault, Deleuze and Guattari all propose to this problem of congealment is a form of *permanent revolution* in which an ethic of permanent resistance is required to prevent the limits that give form to the self, groups and the community from hardening. The price of liberty is seen to entail a constant activism and perpetual vigilance with regard to ourselves and to our relations with others since all knowledge and social forms are potentially dangerous as instruments of authority and grounds of exclusion. As Foucault states:

The ethico-political choice we have to make every day is to determine which is the main danger ... My point is not everything is bad, but that everything is dangerous ... If everything is dangerous, then we always have something to do. So my position leads not to apathy, but to a hyper- and pessimistic activism. (1984, 343)

Many commentators have drawn attention to the pessimistic vision that pervades both Sartrean and postmodernist political theory. In postmodern theory the form of this pessimism changes from those, like Baudrillard, who speak from the dark side of postmodernity and advocate nihilism to those, like Foucault, who tether their underlying pessimism to an affirmative political vision. In Baudrillard's Sceptical postmodernism, for instance, the response to the 'melancholic tonality' of the 'present systems of simulation, programming and information' (1984, 39) is to give up the attempt to change and control the world and to adopt instead the 'fatal strategies' of objects:

> a system is abolished by pursuing it into hyperlogic, by forcing it into an excessive practice which is equivalent to a brutal amortization. 'You want us to consume – OK, let's consume always more, and anything whatsoever; for any useless and absurd purpose'. (Baudrillard, 1983a, 46)

In the view of his liberal critics (e.g. Merquior, 1985; Walzer, 1979), Foucault can be placed alongside the Sceptical postmodernists like Baudrillard who offer a grim vision of the iron cage of contemporary society but 'no plans or projects for turning the cage into something more like a human home' (Walzer, 1979, 207). However, in his later years, Foucault insisted at length that his political vision is not a dystopian one of inevitable oppression:

> The problem is not trying to dissolve them [relations of power] in the utopia of a perfectly transparent communication, but to give one's self the rules of law, the techniques of management, and also the ethics, the *ethos*, the practice of self, which would allow these games of power to be played with a minimum of domination. (Foucalt, in Schrift, 1995, 53)

Optimism is founded in this way for Foucault in the recognition that since things have no essential pattern or pre-inscribed nature, they can always be changed – we can always modify entrenched power structures 'in determinate conditions and according to a precise strategy' (Foucalt, 1988, 123):

There is an optimism that consists in saying things couldn't be better. My optimism would consist rather in saying that so many things can be changed, fragile as they are, bound up more with circumstances than necessities, more arbitrary than self-evident, more a matter of complex, but temporary, historical circumstances than with inevitable anthropological constraints. (Foucault, 1988, 156)

Thus, although the postmodern pessimism of Foucault stems from the recognition that projects of freedom are always liable to become congealed and absorbed by the dominant power structure, his optimism is based conversely upon the recognition of the fragile, contingent and temporary nature of all structures – 'as soon as there is a power relation, there is a possibility of resistance' (1988, 123). Similarly, for Deleuze and Guattari, since desire is 'revolutionary in its essence' and operates 'in the domain of free synthesis where everything is possible' (1983, 116, 54), it cannot be contained entirely within the segregative and restrictive connections and relations that capitalist society imposes: 'there is no social system that does not leak in all directions' (Deleuze and Guattari, 1987, 204). Multiple lines of escape and transformation are in this way always possible – 'power centres are defined much more by what escapes them or by their impotence than by their zone of power' (1987, 217).

Sartre's outlook also swings between the moods of pessimism and optimism, the latter founded primarily on what Sartre takes to be the irrepressibility of freedom and the former on what he sees as its inevitable passage towards alienation. In a political sense, his activist stance to change the world inclines him towards optimism while philosophically, his pessimism comes to the fore as he focuses upon the various ways by which freedom congeals into necessity. Like Foucault, however, Sartre's political optimism is tempered by a pessimism that places him at a distance from the Enlightenment champions of progress and utopia. As Aronson comments:

It is obvious that Sartre's Marxism shared none of the deep optimism of a Marx, Engels, or Lenin. He was at his best when explaining negativity – say, the oppressive weight of the practico-inert. After a brief period of entertaining the most positive hopes – such as his

visions of the City of Ends and of a society in permanent revolution –
Sartre returned to the negative as the natural focus of attention and
the natural tenor of his analysis. (1980, 287)

In a late interview in the 1970s, Sartre himself concurs generally with
this interpretation:

> Freedom is all the time! It is there, and when it fails, this means that it
> has alienated itself all over again! . . . I know what I must tear myself
> away from, but I do not quite know what for. Or to put it another
> way, the thing that is least well founded in me is optimism, the reality
> of the future. I have this optimism but I cannot find a basis for it. And
> that's the heart of the matter. (1991, 95)

In the political visions of Sartre, Foucault, Derrida, Deleuze and
Guattari, projects of freedom cannot be fully articulated or determined
in advance in the form of a utopian blueprint since, once established,
they can soon become imperious and restrictive to future practices of
liberty. Attempts to prescribe and to predetermine the concrete form
of a future political existence have the ultimate effect of restricting the
possibilities of a future that is in principle unknowable since no code or
blueprint can anticipate or justify the specific choices, dangers and situations we will be faced with. To this end, Derrida advocates that we
should pursue a logic of 'undecidability' which, he argues, serves not as a
mask for nihilism or indifference but as a constant ethical-political
reminder that 'a decision can only come to being in a space that exceeds
the calculable program that would destroy all responsibility by transforming it into a programmable effect of determinate causes' (Derrida,
1988, 116). In Foucault's view, what is needed in political theory is a kind
of politics which refrains from offering political blueprints and which
concentrates instead on the creation of 'new schemas of politicisation':

> Political analysis and criticism have in large measure still to be
> invented – so too have the strategies which will make it possible to
> modify the relations of force, to co-ordinate them in such a way that
> such a modification is possible and can be inscribed in reality. That is
> to say, the problem is not so much that of defining a political

'position' (which is to choose from a pre-existing set of possibilities) but to imagine and to bring into being new schemas of politicisation. If 'politicisation' means falling back on ready-made choices and institutions, then the effort of analysis in uncovering the relations of force and mechanisms of power is not worthwhile. To the vast new techniques of power correlated with multinational economies and bureaucratic states, one must oppose a politicisation which will take new forms. (1980, 190)

The political logic that they distil in order to create new forms of politicization that do not fall back on the ready-made choices of capitalism and Stalinist Communism is, in each case, a form of anarchism which stresses spontaneity and a concern for individual autonomy. For Foucault, this yields a radically egalitarian political project that aspires to an anarchic freedom from governance, for Deleuze and Guattari, it involves 'nomadic' forms of existence that resist attempts by state powers to pin them down and keep them in place, while, for Sartre, it points to a form of social life which is anti-hierarchical and libertarian and not dependent for its functioning on the economic, political or social dominance of some over others.

The main feature of the postmodern schema of politicization outlined by Foucault, Deleuze, Guattari and others is the way in which political struggle is extended to all areas of social life beyond the productive order. This new logic of political practice avoids what Laclau and Mouffe (1987) call 'the centring tendency' in liberal and Marxist discourse which works against the democratic tendency in politics, serving to subjugate the knowledges and discourses of the marginalized by reducing their plural experiences to the viewpoint and destiny of the proletariat. As Laclau and Mouffe observe:

There is no *unique* privileged position from which a uniform continuity of effects will follow, concluding with the transformation of society as a whole. All struggles, whether those of workers or other political subjects, left to themselves, have a partial character, and can be articulated to very different discourses. It is this articulation which gives them their character, not the place from which they come. There is therefore no subject – nor further, any 'necessity' – which is absolutely radical and irrecuperable by the dominant order, and which constitutes an absolutely guaranteed point of departure for a total transformation. (1985, 169)

In view of this, postmodernists call for new political alliances that decentre the position of labour, arguing that the proletariat 'no longer represent a social majority' and that 'the discourse of workers' centrality and hegemony are thoroughly defunct' (Guattari and Negri, 1990, 127, 122). As Baudrillard points out, the tactic and meaning of work in the new phase of capitalism have changed dramatically. Instead of workers being at the centre of the revolt, it is now those who are excluded from work, the marginalized, who represent a threat to the dominant order. It is thus the 'reverse of Capitalism's initial situation' (1975, 132) in that the forces of opposition are not themselves located in the structure. Since disaffection and subversion arise primarily from sites outside the productive order, there is no longer a paradigmatic revolutionary class-subject to which all struggles can be related or reduced. Subversion is in this sense 'transversal', spanning across plural groupings and not connected necessarily to the economic base or productive order (1975, 132).

The question of Sartre's relation to postmodernist politics has divided commentators between those like Aronson who posit Sartre as 'one of the Godparents' of a plural and radical postmodern movement, and those such as Birchall who emphasize his Marxism and reject his assimilation to 'the currently fashionable ideals' of postmodernist 'identity politics'.[5] As we will see in the next section, Sartre's politics do not always fit easily into a postmodern framework. This is particularly so in relation to his strong attachment to the category of *need* as a cornerstone of political morality which postmodernists are inherently suspicious of, judging it to contain a distinctly modernist and instrumentalist bias. During Sartre's middle political phase it is certainly true, as Birchall points out, that Sartre adopts a strongly Marxist viewpoint, particularly in *The Communists and Peace* where he endorses the practice of the PCF and where he places himself at a distance from anti-Marxist critiques of the ideology of productivity.

Either side of this middle phase, however, Sartre's attitude towards Marxism is much more lukewarm, beginning in the 1930s with indifference and ending in the 1970s with disenchantment and apostasy.

In Sartre's early existentialist phase, the ideas of identity and subjective freedom are at the forefront of his investigation which, through the concept of Bad Faith outlined in *BN*, probes the dynamic of psychological inertia. Although *BN* lacks the cultural or social perspective of post-modernism which looks at the processes through which identities are culturally formed, it does explore the psychological aspect of how identities are subjectively constituted. In this respect, by focusing on the conditions of subjective (and objective) identity, Sartre's existentialism helps to fill the void in Marxist theory which relates, as Wilhelm Reich put it, to 'what happens "in people's heads", or in the psychical structures of human beings who are subjected to [social] processes' (1972, 284).

Sartre's valuative ideal of authenticity points to a form of identity politics which, like Foucault's attempt 'to give your existence the most beautiful form possible' (1984, 353), involves recognizing those conditions and limits (facticity) that have made us what we are and working upon, stretching and transgressing those limits through 'projects of freedom' (Sartre), 'limit-experiences' (Foucault) or 'lines of flight' (Deleuze and Guattari) that deliver us to those limits without attempting to exist securely beyond them. For Foucault, Deleuze and Guattari, the body is the prime locus in which power relations invest themselves, forcing it 'to carry out tasks, to perform ceremonies, to emit signs' (Foucault, 1977a, 25). For Sartre too, the body represents the 'outer objective shell' of the individual which others (and society) manipulate, condition, objectify and mould through the imposition of the (normalizing) gaze.

In Sartre's later political phase, the praxis which engenders, supports and is clarified by Marxism is barely kept alive, eroded by the practices of the PCF and by a growing awareness of theoretical inadequacies and closures within Marxist theory itself. Sartre does hold on to a form of socialism, but one entirely different from the party-based, labour-centric bias of traditional Marxist/Leninist political practice. As we saw in the last section, his personal and theoretical involvement with the 'anti-Marxist' struggles of 1968 was significant. What impressed Sartre most of all about this movement was the way it rallied against pre-existing political choices to explore the imaginative possibilities of new modes of politicization. The socialism of Sartre's later years reveals a political project that is consistent with this aim, moving beyond the traditional focus of Marxism to uncover and to struggle against wider forms of oppression in society. Sartre's libertarian political discourse shares in this respect a clear affinity with the dialogue of Affirmative postmodernism which, in Aronson's words, is 'feminist, pro-gay liberation, anti-racist and ecological'[6] (1995, 34).

Critical considerations

The postmodern revolt against modern political theory can be seen in terms of a fundamental opposition between *micro-politics* and *macro-politics*. Where modern political theory is based on a macro-analysis of the state and political economy, micro-analysis focuses on the 'infinitesimal mechanisms of power' (Foucault, 1980, 99) that produce, construct and maintain identities. From the postmodern perspective, Marxist macro-analysis omits key mechanisms of power in capitalist society and is complicit in the very condition of modernity that made the bourgeois *Homo Economicus* a subject. Thus, in Lyotard's view, the Marxist concept of revolution is crippled by an inadequate approach 'which has become, and perhaps always was, empty: the idea that one could actually overturn relations merely within the sphere of political economy and therefore the (tacit) idea that this sphere must be maintained' (1974, 145). From the Marxist viewpoint, the micro-struggles advocated by postmodernists are ineffective and diversionary since they do not attack power at its source and fail to take account of the wider political and economic contexts in which they are waged.

These points of tension between Marxist macro-politics and postmodern micro-politics can be seen in part through criticisms made by Alex Callinicos of Foucault's political search for artistic self-invention. In Callinicos's view, this postmodern search is abstract and insufficiently political in that it ignores the political constraints and 'the matter of the brute inequalities in resources' that set limits to the process of self-creation within class divisions (1989, 90). Thus, Callinicos argues:

> to invite a hospital porter in Birmingham, a car-worker in São Paolo, a social security clerk in Chicago, or a street child in Bombay to make a work of art of their lives would be an insult — unless linked to

precisely the kind of strategy for global change, which ... post-structuralism rejects. (1989, 90–1)

While Callinicos is right to bring attention to the wider political and economic constraints that often serve to limit or obstruct projects of self-development (which postmodernists often give insufficient consideration to or ignore altogether), it is also the case that the relation between economic resources and the scope for self-development is not as straightforward or as predictable as some Marxists may suppose. Following Callinicos, it is true to a certain extent that people who lack productive resources and must sell their labour power in capitalist society do have their scope for self-invention drastically reduced. The street child in Bombay, for instance, is limited in her ability to pursue projects of self-creation due to the fact that she must beg, steal, or prostitute her body each day in order to get the few basic material goods on which her day-to-day survival depends. She is clearly disadvantaged in this respect unlike the aristocrat, for instance, who has all the time, opportunity, resource and expectation to develop her powers and to exercise her autonomy. The street child cannot make her existence into 'a work of art' since this existence depends upon selling herself in order to get the basic things she needs – as Marx said, her freedom can begin only when the mundane material necessities of her life have been taken care of.

However, while it may be true that those who do not have access to productive resources and have to sell their labour power are fundamentally constrained in pursuing autonomous projects, these are not a matter of economic resource or of productive freedom alone. As is clear from Foucault's analysis of power, those who are not constrained in this way, and who enjoy a privileged position in the structure of capitalist relations, are still bound by normative constraints and tied to normalized subjectivities that offer no more than the illusion of self-cultivation. This can also be glimpsed in part in Hegel's narrative of master and slave. Although the slave has no resource of his own and must spend his time and energies labouring for the master's material requirements, he experiences the confirmation of his subjectivity within the scope of his praxis which enables him to develop his powers and capabilities. The master, by contrast, cannot find such a means of self-confirmation – as he becomes more abstracted from his creative, productive powers and is given over to the pleasures of consumption, he becomes less autonomous and ultimately, in Hegel's account, more dependent on the subjectivity of the slave.[7]

Another, more concrete example of this can be seen in the case of travel which, by taking us beyond the bounds of our own culture and landscape, is a possible means to a deeper and multifaceted self-understanding, enabling us to develop ourselves in ways that parochialism leaves unexplored by throwing us into strange and new situations to which we have to respond. A woman, for example, who has vast economic resources would typically use them to travel in luxury – a chauffeured car, a corporate hotel, etc. During her travels, money takes care of all her needs to the extent that she need not engage with the local culture or even utter a single word of a foreign language in the process. If, by contrast, she travels with little money in the cheapest way possible, she constantly needs to draw upon and develop her powers of communication. Her lack of resources compels her to become more resourceful. She has no private limousine waiting to take her on arrival to a hotel suite but must instead define new limits for her powers by finding her way around unknown territory – she must communicate with others of a different culture, interpret new signs and learn the skills of practical survival in an alien environment. In the absence of familiar commodities, she has to fashion objects through her own praxis, improvising and building upon latent skills.

Projects of self-cultivation can be seen in this way to have an ambivalent relation to the provision of economic resources. A superfluity of material resource can disincline individuals from developing their skills 'in all directions', leading instead to the easy option of consumption. On the other hand, insufficient access to material resource can significantly obstruct projects of self-development in the sense that most projects require, or are at least enhanced by, some access to materials and also in the sense that those who have no material resource have to sell their labour power (and their time) in order to provide for the basic necessities of life.

It is interesting to note in this context that one of Foucault's 'heroes of self-invention', Diogenes the Cynic, had only a bath-tub to call his own. Although liberation in the realm of economic and material production may be an important condition for pursuing active modes of self-invention, it is not always a sufficient one since there are other sources of oppression in the social field that obstruct self-invention which extend beyond 'social institutions [and] economic inequalities' (Foucault, 1980, 87). Foucault's 'microphysics of power' aims to reveal to this extent how mechanisms of social power constrain individuals as they normalize them through discourses, knowledges and techniques centred upon the body. Women, for instance, do not just experience constraints upon their autonomy as proletarians, but also experience constraints of gender (as do men). These constraints exercise a 'bio-power' over women's bodies in which women are constrained to internalize a male gaze which enforces norms of feminine bodily gestures, sizes, appetites and appearances that involve what Judith Butler calls 'the repeated stylization of the body' into forms that have congealed to such an extent they are seen as natural. More pay, better welfare, equal rights in the workplace would not liberate women entirely from forms of oppression since there is also the crucial issue of (gender) identity at stake.

By bringing the question of identity into critical focus, postmodern micro-politics has proved valuable in understanding and articulating the concerns and potential strategies of resistance for oppressed groups which macro-political analysis tends to ignore or to reduce to an entirely economic context. Foucault's idea of the 'reverse discourse', for instance, constitutes an important form of analysis that enables us to think about the nature and efficacy of 'discourses of resistance' in ways which can illuminate political strategies of emancipation. Through his analysis of the reverse discourse, Foucault draws attention to the ways in which oppressed groups often contest their domination by using the premises of the dominant discourse, and thus, even as they challenge, invoke the legitimizing discourse of the oppressor. This can be seen, for example, in attempts to project homosexuality into public visibility which have served to reinforce the perception of homosexuals as overtly sexual beings by identifying themselves with the dominant discourse that reduces them to sexual essentialism. In the first volume of *The History of Sexuality* Foucault shows how the idea or 'truth' of homosexuality appeared as a discourse which claimed homosexuality as *natural* in terms of the dominant discourse, thus serving to reinforce the 'prevailing medical discourse' (1978, 101).

Postmodernists could in this sense respond to the criticisms Callinicos levels at Foucault by claiming that a preoccupation with material and economic constraints itself reveals a 'reverse discourse' which legitimates the capitalist conception of human beings as *economic beings*. Insofar as Marxists adhere to the notion of labour as a transcendent category, they place themselves under the spell of the bourgeois work-ethic and become, in Adorno's phrase, 'the carriers of capitalist propaganda'. As we saw in the last chapter, this is manifested in the way Marxists reproduce the logic of capitalism by championing industrialization and the growth of productive forces even though the facts of industrial production give the agrarian conception of the 'fully-developed individual' outlined by Marx and Engels in *The German Ideology* a wholly unrealistic connotation. What Marxism omits, from a postmodern perspective, is the recognition that projects of self-development depend as much on experiential and discursive modes of self-understanding as on the development of productive capabilities. As Foucault states:

> it is false to say, 'with that famous post-Hegelian' [Marx], that the concrete existence of man is labour. For the life and time of man are not by nature labour but pleasure, restlessness, merry-making, rest, needs, accidents, desires, violent acts, robberies, etc. (1979, 62)

From a Marxist perspective, however, the micro-political strategies of postmodernists are ineffectual since they leave the wider macro-structures that condition micro-contexts in place. It can be questioned, for instance, whether the postmodern strategy of resurrecting local, subjugated knowledges is enough in itself to bring about concrete and effective political change for marginalized and oppressed groups. The fate of these groups cannot be decided simply on the level of competing discourses for vital to their advancement is the specific economic, cultural and political climate in which they voice their resistance. Workers who are dependent financially on their employers cannot wage equal contests of discourse for they are constrained in what they do and say by the fact that others have control over their economic situation. Economic ownership and political inequality serve in this way to obstruct equal contest between different forms of discourse. Since the dominant group has a monopoly over the means of cultural production and circulation (what Baudrillard calls 'the control of the Code'), marginal or subjugated discourses are always open to distortion, misrepresentation or absorption, whatever the force of their contestation.

These difficulties within postmodern political theory are reflected in the eventual powerlessness of the movements of 1968 to effect widespread change in the larger structures of power in France. Indeed, from a Marxist viewpoint, some, such as Regis Debray, reject the 'humanist view' of 1968 put forward by Sartre and others (that views 1968 as an expression of subjective freedom in revolt against the system) adopting instead a functionalist approach to 1968 which theorizes it as an effect of the capitalist system, a kind of pseudo-revolution and point of transition in the development of bourgeois individualism – the 'Cradle of the New Bourgeois Society'. Ferry and Renaut suggest to this end that, 'in its defence of the subject against the system', 1968 'is linked in a certain way to contemporary individualism' (1990, xxiii).

Building on these weaknesses, critics of postmodernism point to the individualist nature of postmodern micro-politics. Echoing Callinicos's complaint (1989, 90–1) of the lack of collective goals, strategies and aspirations in postmodern micro-politics, Bernstein states, for instance, that 'although there is a strong undercurrent . . . that gravitates towards ethical-political issues' there is in the end 'an absence of an intellectual resource for a collective "macro-political" strategy' (1991, 6). Commenting on Foucault in particular, Grimshaw points to the necessity in postmodern thinking to give an account of political existence which rejects 'unproblematic universalism' (recognizing the dangers and absences in so-called 'universal ideals') but which includes the notions of mutuality and collectivity as regulative and organizing principles. Foucault's only alternative to universalism, she adds, is 'the rather uninspiring idea of a solipsistic fashioning of a regimen for individual life' (1993, 68). By emphasizing the idea of difference over that of solidarity or community and by viewing the social field as something imposed rather than as a positive field for self-constitution, postmodernists tend to lack an adequate account of intersubjectivity. This can be seen clearly in Baudrillard's characterization of individuals as disconnected and 'undifferentiated particles within the mass' (1983a, 39) as well as in Foucault's incipient resistance to the normalizing 'discourse of the other'.

These difficulties arise in Foucault's postmodern political project due to the fact that he conflates socialization with normalization by failing to make a distinction between necessary forms of constraint essential in any process of individual socialization and forms of power which mark the coercive restraint of needs, desires and abilities. In this way, as Eagleton comments, Foucault is 'deeply sceptical of the utopian dream that heterogeneity could ever be released from the categories of normalisation and institutions, the forms of discursive and non-discursive domestication – which alone lend it social embodiment' (1990, 386). Since his 'vigorously self-mastering individual remains wholly monadic', his vision of society is, according to Eagleton, 'just an assemblage of autonomous self-disciplining agents, with no sense that their self-realization might flourish within bonds of mutuality' (1990, 390). Although Deleuze and Guattari do not conform exactly to this individualist paradigm within postmodernist thinking in that they generally seek to intensify and to mobilize social flows rather than impede them, their account of intersubjectivity is nonetheless generally left undeveloped. Similarly, Lyotard's theoretical framework of heterogeneity, difference and dissensus which he puts forward in his later work as a normative form of political logic offers little in the way of collective strategy or intersubjective understanding.

In view of this lack of a collective logic in postmodernist theory, one can raise the question of the extent to which the postmodern emphasis on difference and heterogeneity gives rise to particularism and hermetic irrelevancy.[8] Without an underlying basis of intersubjectivity, differences can become reified, producing rigid barriers and divisions within groups and individuals that obscure common interests and obstruct projects of solidarity. This can be seen in the emergence of so-called 'Third World' postmodern political movements which emphasize national, cultural, racial and religious differences. Although the form of this particularism need not necessarily culminate in the extreme forms of nationalism and religious fundamentalism associated with these postmodern movements, the care for difference advocated by postmodernists tends to obscure what all human beings have in common regardless of race, gender or cultural influences.[9] Ferry and Renaut comment in this respect that '[w]hen only exaggerated differences survive, then everyone's other becomes "wholly other", the "barbarian" ' (1990, 120). It is only within a relational context of common experience that we are able to empathize and undertake projects of solidarity with others – when the other becomes 'wholly other' our ability to empathize in this way is severely restricted.[10]

For the more Affirmative postmodernists such as Foucault and Deleuze, these difficulties, though evident, are less systemic than they are for Sceptical postmodernists, like Baudrillard, who deny the possibility of collective agency altogether. Deleuze and Guattari, for instance, emphasize the need to overcome familial and other privatized boundaries in order to open up desiring processes that intensify social relations. Desire, they argue, is collective and is present in bonds that exist between people even if these bonds degenerate into sclerosis and betrayal (1994, 177). Collective activity is particularly emphasized by Guattari as a means to overcome the fragmentation and privatization of life under capitalism through the creation of new forms of subjectivity that intensify affective and aesthetic relations with others (Guattari and Negri, 1990, 122). Similarly, Foucault argues in places for new forms of collective experimentation and living, maintaining that the question of promoting new subjectivities is not merely a private ethical question but also 'political . . . social, philosophical' (1984, 216).

In William Connolly's view, Foucault's postmodern care for difference should not be premised on the 'demonisation of the other' as Ferry and Renaut and others suggest. According to Connolly, a Foucauldian politics based on 'an ethic of cultivation . . . of care for the contingency of things' entails a respect for 'agonistic openness' which affirms contest between different modes of life (1991, 383). In relations of 'agonistic openness', the other does not constitute a disabling threat to my identity but provides an alternative and enriching perspective through which I am able to grasp my own limits. Respect for others is based accordingly on a notion of indebtedness to those who prevent limits from congealing by sustaining contest between different ideas and identities (1993, 382–3). Through 'a cultivation of care for difference', Connolly argues, we are able to respect others by seeing them as embodying and living out some of the possibilities and richness of life that we had to forego in order to be who we are (1991, 64).

In spite of these qualifications, however, which insulate a postmodern politics of difference from certain charges of monadic individualism, there is still a sense in which it yields only a very thin conception of intersubjectivity. By viewing intersubjectivity from the perspective of difference and strategic agonism alone, this effectively overlooks the many techniques of subjectification that do not rely primarily on contradistinction from the other. What postmodernism lacks in this sense is an account of what people have *in common*, without which it is ultimately impelled towards an individualist logic that yields scarce resource for projects of collective freedom.

According to Sartre in *Anti-Semite and Jew*:

> What men have in common is not a 'nature' but a condition, that is, an ensemble of limits and restrictions: the inevitability of death, the necessity of working for a living, of living in a world already inhabited by other men. (1965, 72)

In common with postmodernism, Sartre is well known for his rejection of universalism – even in his later socialist phase 'Universality . . . is only an economy of means. But it does not refer to any species or genus' (*CDR* (2), 194). In his early existentialist phase, this rejection takes the restrictive form of an atomistic individualism in which 'we are always . . . in a state of instability in relation to the Other' (*BN*, 408). As his work evolves, however, Sartre adopts a much more discernibly Marxist viewpoint which focuses on our shared common inherence in the world of (totalized) matter. Since we all live in a common world, we are all subject to 'the limitations which apriori define man's fundamental situation in the universe'. It is this shared human condition, according to Sartre, that makes the most diverse projects of individuals 'comprehensible to everyone' (1966b, 303, 304).

In the post-war years, Sartre came a long way in exorcising the spectre of individualism that haunts his early work. In *Existentialism and Humanism*, for instance, he maintains that 'freedom unrecognized remains abstract' and argues for a 'universal freedom conditional' in which our freedom 'depends entirely on the freedom of others and their freedom depends on ours' (1966b, 307). In the *CDR* Sartre's account of group fusion denotes a positive form of reciprocity in which the other represents the extension and reflection of my own possibilities. In the *Cahiers* he no longer conceives of individuals as 'out of reach and radically separated' (*BN*, 482) but argues that community and co-operation between people are possible on the basis of a 'mutual recognition of each other's freedom'. This recognition, he argues, represents the 'refusal to consider the original conflict between freedoms by way of the Look as something impossible to surpass' (1983, 274, 280). When I work with another in the realization of a common aim 'I am put in such a position that I *recognize* the other's freedom without being pierced [by] a look' (1983, 271). In this way, conflict is seen by Sartre no longer as an ontological necessity but as a historical adjunct of alienation. Through a recognition of the other's freedom it is possible, he argues, to achieve an 'authentic love' which 'signifies something wholly other than a desire to appropriate' (1983, 362).

Despite this shift towards intersubjectivity and socialism in Sartre's later political outlook, however, which places him at a distance from certain forms of postmodern individualism, he never manages fully to break out of the individualist framework of his early philosophy. This is evident, as Aronson notes, on 'a methodological . . . a theoretical as well as political' level (1995, 27). In the *CDR* Sartre grants group fusion only a reactive transitory status, contending that group identification should not be conceived in terms of 'altruism and egoism' but is 'engraved in the practico-inert field' (*CDR*, 368). Similarly, in Sartre's idea of a universal human condition which he puts forward in *Anti-Semite and Jew*, this condition is conceived only negatively as 'an ensemble of limits and restrictions' (1965, 72). This negative perception arises mainly from the limited way Sartre theorizes need as something which is necessarily burdensome and materially based (potentially causing conflict between individuals in conditions of scarcity) rather than as something which can unite humans through common experiences of joy, friendship, sacrifice, love, partnership, generosity or pleasure. Thus, although Sartre's idea of a universal human condition (premised on the universality of needs) contrasts favourably with some postmodernist accounts that reject the category of need altogether (and with this, the possibility of a common project), Sartre tends to theorize collectivity in a limited way, influenced strongly by a Marxist perspective which equates need with material need.

While it is clear that Sartre's later work attempts to break open the privatized boundaries of individuals in society (his critique of the serial and institutional group in the *CDR* shows how people are fundamentally separated in capitalist society while being together in groups), sociality remains a problematic concept for Sartre. Despite the fact that he no longer demonizes the other as he had done in *BN*, he continues to regard sociality more as a threat than as an occasion for cohesiveness and social harmony. This is due to the fact that, although Sartre shows a growing awareness of the affirmative dimensions of collective life, he never fully gets beyond a limited appreciation of them, ever aware of the constant threat of seriality. This gives Sartre's social world a strange and ambiguous character – the cohesion that he sees as essential for effective political action is hard to attain and, once realized, it is permanently haunted by the threat of dissolution. Indeed, in a late interview Sartre himself reflects on the general tendency in his work to separate individuals rather than unite them:

> I do not see any reason to speak of intersubjectivity once subjectivities are separated. Intersubjectivity assumes a communion that almost reaches a kind of identification, in any case a unity ... I see the separation but I do not see the union. (1981b, 43–4)

In this chapter I have traced the trajectory of Sartre's political thought as it evolves from the detached individualist anarchism of his early period through the committed Marxism of his middle period to the libertarian socialism of his later years. Within this trajectory, Sartre's attitude towards Marxism changes from initial indifference to uncritical allegiance and finally to suspicion and disillusionment. In this respect, Sartre's later political perspective reflects the general disenchantment with Marxism evident in postmodernist thinking. In common with the postmodern micrological strategies of Foucault, Deleuze, Guattari and Lyotard, Sartre's post-1968 political philosophy elaborates a new form of politicization which opposes the labour-centric bias and centralizing strategies of traditional Marxist and liberal political practice. Both Sartrean and postmodernist political theory distil a new form of political logic that illuminates and contests contemporary mechanisms of power in capitalist society that Marxist theory overlooks. This new form of 'discourse' or 'identity' politics has proved valuable to oppressed and marginal groups in capitalist society (e.g. prisoners, women, homo-sexuals, the mad, etc.) whose oppression is not reducible entirely to a substructural, economic explanation.

This concern with identity in Sartrean and postmodernist politics shifts the focus of attention towards the individual. In doing so, they both articulate vital forms of individuality that often differ significantly from the restrictive forms of bourgeois individualism which they oppose. Furthermore, Sartre's analysis of group life in the *CDR* illustrates well the complex and shifting dialectical relation between individual and group which, within modernist political theory, is polarized into the simple dichotomy of 'self-interest' (liberalism) and 'species-being' (Marxism).[11] Sartre, Foucault, Deleuze and Guattari all bring into focus the dangers of collectivity (the 'hegemony of the group') in preserving a space for a form of individuality that avoids the restrictive egoism and self-interest of the bourgeois subject.

The problem with this, however, is that this turn towards the individual in Sartrean and postmodernist political theory tends to be accompanied by a shift away from the collective. Although no longer blind to positive forms of community, Sartre shows only a limited appreciation of them in the *CDR* and elsewhere. Like Foucault, he tends to equate socialization with normalization at the outset and thus lacks a positive underlying conception of sociality. This can be seen clearly in the way that both Sartre and Foucault view the 'gaze of the Other' from a negative perspective. Sartre is particularly guilty of this since he draws ontological conclusions from his analysis of the gaze in *BN* whereas Foucault refrains from ontological generalizations, contenting himself in *Discipline and Punish* with a specific analysis of the institutional gaze within the Panopticon. However, both these thinkers fail to offset the negative, normalizing functions of the gaze with an equal appreciation of the more positive, enriching aspects of being-seen by others. In certain contexts, the presence of the other constitutes a vital and edifying element in the confirmation of individual subjectivity and does not represent an imminent normalizing threat. If, for example, I am lost and completely alone with little food, water or resource to survive, the gaze of another human might signify a much-needed external recognition of my subjective needs and desires. The other would in this circumstance represent neither the anonymous and alienating other described by Sartre nor the authoritarian, institutional other found in the Panopticon, but one who makes possible my subjective confirmation by perceiving me as a (human) subject in need of help.

Indeed, in other circumstances, it is the *removal* rather than the imposition of the gaze that gives rise to alienation, as when we are being ignored or ostracised. In *BN* Sartre disregards these positive aspects of the gaze completely, viewing the gaze of the other instead as one which necessarily alienates me and causes my universe to 'disintegrate' (*BN*, 255). The care for difference advocated by postmodernists can, as Connolly suggests, precipitate a vital form of respect for others but this alone is not sufficient to guarantee concrete projects of solidarity or collective exchanges of reciprocity since it neglects the crucial ways in which our being-with-others is premised on what we share and have in common with others rather than on how we differ from them. One can cite here Foucault's comments in *The Order of Things* that 'if everything were absolute diversity, thought would be doomed to singularity . . . and absolute monotony' (1970, 119). Indeed, it is only the presence of the other that gives face, meaning, form and contrast to an individual's own sense of personal identity and individuality. Sartre himself recognizes this in the *CDR* when he argues forcefully against the isolated 'Robinsonade' individual of bourgeois mystification (see *CDR*, 677–8).

In lacking a sense of collective identity, the postmodern strategy of difference, heterogeneity, plurality and diversity can incline towards reproducing standard liberal conceptions of the political process that configure it as a form of 'alliance politics' between separate and disparate groups. Moreover, since postmodern political struggles lack the concept of a collective totality, they are liable either to induce reformism (transforming only isolated parts of the system) or to reproduce existing repressive dynamics (e.g. the continued existence of bureaucracy, racism, sexism or homophobia in 'existing Socialist societies').[12] This has led the more Affirmative postmodernists like Foucault (1980) and Guattari (1986) to attack the 'social abandonism' of postmodernism which renders collective political action impossible by multiplying differences. In a contemporary world dominated by multinational capitalism that tends towards sameness, homogeneity, uniformity and generality, the postmodern emphasis on difference and particularity can serve as an obfuscating fiction which reifies specificity and diverts attention away from the processes of globalization, social conformity and mass consumption. Lacking an adequate theory of collectivity and totality, postmodernist politics thus finds itself in the danger, as Foucault acknowledges, 'of remaining at the level of conjectural struggles [and] of being unable to develop these struggles for the lack of a global strategy or outside support' (1980, 130).

4

Sartre, un Homme Postmoderne?

> freedom represents something that doesn't exist but that
> gradually creates itself, something that has always been
> present in me and that will leave me only when I die. And I
> think that all other men are like me, but that the degree of
> awareness and clarity with which this freedom appears to
> them varies according to the circumstances, according to
> their origins, their development, and their knowledge.
> (Sartre, in Beauvoir, 1984, 361)

In this book, I have sketched a picture in which two Sartres emerge alongside one another: the Old Sartre – aggressive and totalistic, Cartesian and
classical, modernist and Marxist, an optimist and grand-thinker – and
a New postmodern Sartre who is changing and plural, aestheticized
and splintered, aporetic and anarchistic, a pessimist and arch-decon-
structionist. Like two pugilists in a boxing ring, they shadow one another,
join together, clash, contend and struggle for primacy within individual
texts and in his work taken as a whole.[1] However, as I have presented it,
there is no clear resolution or victorious end to this fight but an ongoing
agonism of differences and emphases that rise and fall as Sartre's critical
perspective shifts.

In standard interpretations of Sartre, only the face of the Old classical
Sartre is recognized – that is, the humanist Sartre resolutely opposed to
the postmodern trickeries of the French post-structuralists. This view
still bears a strong influence and is evident, for instance, in Andrew
Dobson's (1993) book *Jean-Paul Sartre and the Politics of Reason* where
Sartre is presented as a Master constructionist impelled by an Enlightenment animus that is distinctly anti-postmodern. Against this view, I have
argued that there are strong postmodern elements in Sartre's work that
span the broad theoretical range from his analysis of the subject through

his theory of history to his understanding of political life, making him, to use Fredric Jameson's phrase, a 'hidden origin' of important theoretical manœuvres in postmodernist theory.

In *The Dismemberment of Orpheus* (1982), Ihab Hassan constructs an interesting and authoritative shorthand list that enables us to contrast the differences between modernism and postmodernism. Here is an abridged version of this:

Modernism	*Postmodernism*
Purpose	Play
Presence	Absence
Transcendence	Immanence
Centring	Dispersal
Synthesis	Antithesis
Art object/Finished work	Process/Performance/Happening
Design	Chance
Hierarchy	Anarchy
Distance	Participation

If we apply this list to Sartre's work, his postmodernist markings come readily into view. In Sartre's early philosophy, *Transcendence* is a dominant motif that, as we saw in Chapter 1, finds expression in an idealist theory of freedom. Although Sartre never abandons his notion of the possibility of 'going beyond existing circumstances', the concept of *Immanence* assumes a far greater prominence in his post-war philosophy culminating in an encumbered subject which, like the decentred subject theorized by the French post-structuralists, is shot through with social, historical, linguistic and semiotic codes. Even in his early philosophy, the Sartrean subject is marked by the features of *dispersal* and *absence* — consciousness is, Sartre insists, 'diasporique' (*BN*, 182), non-identical (*BN*, 713) and has 'its being outside it, before it and behind' (*BN*, 179). *Purpose* and *play* both appear as important themes at different times in Sartre's philosophy, the former being most evident in the *CDR* where he adopts a praxis-based model of agency and the latter in his earlier existentialist texts where he assumes a more aestheticist leaning.

Despite the strong Marxist coloration of Sartre's social philosophy in the *CDR*, the concepts of *process* and *antithesis* capture well the essence and features of the Sartrean dialectic. The concept of totalization that looms large in Sartre's dialectic involves *synthesis* insofar as it consists in drawing disparate elements into a meaningful totality but is always, as McBride notes, a 'process word' (1997, 332) denoting activity, *performance* and *happening* and thus does not refer to a rigorously completed or definable entity. Similarly, in contrast to the Hegelian dialectic, the Sartrean dialectic invokes no ultimate synthesis of its constituent parts (*pour-soi* and *en-soi*) that proceeds towards a state of perfected human consciousness or the 'end of history'. As we saw in Chapter 2, Sartre's theory of history conceives the historical process in terms of contingency, *chance*, negation and circularity, criticizing linear accounts that give history a progressivist telos or intrinsic pattern of *design*.

The political logic of Sartre's work also displays a discernibly postmodern ethos insofar as it is premised on the eradication of *hierarchy* and *distance*. This blossoms into a form of political activism which drew him towards political Marxism in the 1940s and 1950s but eventually drove him away following May 1968. As we saw in Chapter 3, Sartre's archetype of the *fused group* and Deleuze and Guattari's idea of the *subject group* can be seen as guiding theoretical models for a new form of political practice that emerged out of the student revolts of 1968 which, unlike the hierarchical, authoritarian structures of modern political practice, involves fluid, egalitarian, *anarchic*, reciprocal and *participatory* forms of political organization. Although Sartre did not explicitly adopt the dialogue of micro-politics advocated by Foucault, Lyotard and others, his political project, both before and after the war, is generally consistent with it, moving beyond the traditional focus of Marxist theory to uncover and contest wider sources of power and domination in the social field that extend beyond the productive order and serve to 'jeopardise the exploited classes to the extent that they intrude into each individual from without and impose themselves in the memory as ramparts against any coming to awareness' (1974c, 47).

These similarities that span across the broad theoretical range of the subject, social theory, history and politics clearly mark a determinate and significant postmodern element in Sartre's thinking which is present from the outset in the 1930s but intensifies as his work evolves. They point unreservedly to a New postmodern Sartre and to an urgent need to reposition his traditional place among the heroic standard-bearers of modern philosophy.

In a manner faithful to Sartre's method in the *CDR*, my intention in this thesis has been to provide a *dialectical* interpretation of his work which traces the intensities, tensions and changing emphasis within the relational interplay of the postmodern and the modern. In the trajectory of Sartre's work from the 1930s to the 1970s these modern and post-modern elements intensify or recede according to a particular text or to a specific emphasis within a single text. As we have seen, the *CDR* contains both modern and postmodern themes, utilizing, developing, clarifying and reinvigorating Marxist theory as it simultaneously probes its weak-nesses and calls into question its basic methods.

Similarly, although *BN* reproduces features of a Cartesian framework, there are other significant elements in this work that move beyond this framework and connect with later postmodernist themes – in particular, Sartre's critique of 'the idea of the self as something which is given to us' (Foucault, 1983, 64).

This dialectical view of changing intensities and emphases can also be applied to postmodernists like Foucault and Deleuze and Guattari whose work incorporates a mixture of postmodern, premodern and modern elements. In Foucault's work, for instance, it is possible to discern elem-ents of change as it evolves from his early archaeology to his genealogy and finally to his later ethical work. In his passage from archaeology to genealogy, his focus changes significantly from showing how the subject is fundamentally constructed to a form of analysis that seeks to draw out the political consequences of subjectification in order to help form resistances to subjectifying practices. In the transition from genealogy to ethics, Foucault replaces subjectivity in the confined body with the constitution of subjectivity in the self-consciousness of desire and switches in this sense from impersonal explanations for why people act as they do to the reflective practices whereby individuals train them-selves. In this later ethical period, Foucault even returns to Kant (a previous target of his critique of modernity in *Les mots et les choses*) as a critical means of identifying 'that thread that may connect us with the

Enlightenment' (1984, 42). This can also be seen in the case of Lyotard who begins in the 1960s with a radical anti-modernist Nietzscheanism but ends up in the 1980s voicing the mantra of Kant's critical Enlightenment project.

To clarify the complexity of this modern/postmodern constellation in the work of the French post-structuralists, I have used the distinction between Affirmative and Sceptical forms of postmodernism to contrast those who reconfigure, rework and transform modernist categories such as the subject, freedom and reason with those who tend to dissolve them as Sceptics do. It is the way in which the more extreme, Sceptical forms of postmodernism dissolve completely these modernist categories that has prompted some Affirmatives like Guattari to distance themselves from the discourse of the postmodern. Despite agreeing with postmodernism in general that a 'certain idea of progress and of modernity has gone bankrupt' (1986, 40), in his essay 'The Postmodern Dead End' (1986), for instance, Guattari identifies the popular discourse of postmodernism as a cynical and reactionary fad which engenders an ethics of non-commitment that paralyses affirmative political action when social repression and ecological crises are escalating. In the 1980s, both Lyotard and Foucault similarly distanced themselves from some of the fashionable *bon mots* of the postmodern discourse.[2]

In spite of these 'constellated similarities' between Sartrean and some forms of Affirmative postmodern theory, there is nonetheless a greater intensity and gravity towards the modern in Sartre's work than in the work of Foucault, Deleuze and Guattari, for instance. In the area of the subject, Sartre maintains a consistent attachment to some form of humanism and freedom which contrasts with the anti-humanist dialogue sometimes taken up by the French post-structuralists even though he prefigures many of the themes of the 'decentred subject' which they later adopt. In this respect, as I argued in Chapter 1, Sartre's assiduous efforts to probe the complex dimensions of (subjective) freedom and his endeavour to resurrect a theory of autonomy in the face of its progressive alienation through Bad Faith (*BN*) or through the determining force of the practico-inert (*CDR*) contrast favourably with the extreme anti-humanism of the 1960s in which Foucault and others, like Nietzsche's madman in the market-place, proclaimed the Death of the Subject and the end of meaningful agency.

Without doubt, the humanist insignia of Sartre's work is something that sits uncomfortably with the general postmodern outlook. According to Derrida, for instance, by making 'man' into a supreme value or measure, 'humanism' is essentially a form of exclusion and racism since it excludes women, children and animals and defines 'humanity' according to specific cultural norms (1989, 62, 70). Derrida's critique of humanism links up in this respect with Lévi-Strauss's criticisms of Sartre in *The Savage Mind* where Sartre's *CDR* is seen as ethnocentric since, as Lévi-Strauss observes, it excludes from the 'properly human' all previous, supposedly 'ahistorical' societies of 'repetition' (see 1966, 324–57).

Although Sartre is consistently vitriolic towards forms of humanism associated with bourgeois individualism, there is nonetheless a discernible *anthropocentric* bias in his work which places him much closer to the modernist paradigm. This is evident most of all in the way he consistently distinguishes the human realm from the rest of nature in his work, valorizing the former as *pour-soi*, active and transformational, and associating the latter with the brute, inert qualities of matter. As Boundas points out, this demonstrates a noticeable difference between 'the Sartrean prose of the *is* and *is not*' and 'the poststructuralist, minoritarian discourse of the *and*' (1997, 339–40). Indeed, Sartre's Cartesian theorization of nature clearly estranges him from the postmodern quest to re-enchant nature and to resurrect it from the denuding, utilitarian and analytical logic of modern science.

This is, however, (at least partially) offset by other elements in his work – in particular his notion of *dialectical reason* – which inveigh against the analytical reason of modern science and move beyond a simplified Cartesianism. Although Sartre clearly elevates the human above the non-human throughout his work, he does, however, reject forms of humanism that serve to exclude and subordinate, arguing in the *CDR* (in tones redolent of Derrida) that 'humanism is the obverse of racism: it is a practice of exclusion' (*CDR*, 702). Thus, in the third volume of *The Family Idiot*, he is quick to dismiss abstract notions of 'humanity':

Humanity *is not* and corresponds diachronically to no concept; what exists is an infinite series whose principle is recurrence, defined precisely by these terms: man is the son of man. For this reason history is perpetually finished, that is to say composed of broken-off sequences each of which is the *divergent* continuation (not mechanically but dialectically) of the preceding one and also its transcendence toward *the same* and *different* ends (which assumes that it is at once *distorted* and *conserved*). (1974c, 346–7)

The complex constellation of modern and postmodern themes in Sartre's work can also be seen in the area of social theory and historical explanation. Central to Sartre's socio-historical theory is the concept of *totalization* which, as we saw in Chapter 2, does not square readily with the postmodern preference for *detotalization*. As a synthesizing activity which draws together disparate elements into a meaningful whole, Sartre's concept of totalization contrasts with postmodernist attempts to fragment, splinter and pluralize the social field. Sartre does at times, of course, emphasize the polyvalence of meanings and the detotalized nature of all alleged totalities, but his intention elsewhere is to give history a single, unitary meaning (see *SM*, 90, *CDR* (2), 20). Whether one ascribes greater emphasis to the element of detotalization in Sartre's work or fixes instead on his attempts to unify history and provide a single meaning, it is clear that his socio-historical outlook incorporates both these elements which intensify and recede as his emphasis changes. Sartre, however, is not the only one who equivocates between totalization and detotalization in this way for it is also possible to glimpse a similar equivocation in Foucault and other post-structuralists who utilize totalizing methods and concepts as they simultaneously prohibit and condemn them.

This complex blend of the modern and the postmodern can also be found in Sartre's political outlook which, as we saw in Chapter 3, gravitates towards the postmodern search for new forms of politicization and political practice while retaining key modernist notions such as need, political freedom, commitment and agency. Sartre shows none of the suspicion postmodernists like Baudrillard exhibit towards the category of need, making it the starting point of his investigation in the *CDR*: 'Everything is to be explained through need; need is the first totalising relation between the material man, and the material ensemble of which he is a part' (*CDR*, 80). The difficulty with Sartre's account of need in the *CDR*, I have argued, is the way in which he tends to equate need with material need alone, thus reproducing standard Marxist interpretations reflected most of all in his consistent emphasis on the necessity of material abundance as a requisite for the possibility of a communist society and his consequent preoccupation with eradicating scarcity. In spite of this, however, Sartre does begin to probe the dynamic of solidarity through the category of need (which creates a shared human condition) and so at least goes some way towards constructing an account of intersubjectivity which is largely absent from the postmodernist account.

In the years that followed the *CDR* up to his death, Sartre developed this idea of need further, integrating it centrally into the framework of a 'Third Ethics' which he outlined in dialogue with Benny Lévy in the 1970s and which he had initially proposed in a lecture given to the Instituto Gramsci in Rome in May 1964 (known as *The Rome Lecture*). In *The Rome Lecture*, for instance, Sartre states: '[t]he root of morality is in need' (1964b, 100). Radical, unalienated needs, he argues, are those that humans possess as members of the human species and belong to 'nude man' irrespective of class, system or culture. They constitute a form of 'human reality' which is 'common to men' (1974b, 342) and allow us to define humanity as 'belonging to a species' (1964b, 88). In his sketch of a 'Third Ethics', Sartre insists that in contrast to his previous ethics, this one is 'a morality of the WE' (1979a, 15). Although he had previously theorized intersubjectivity and communality in the *CDR* and the *Cahiers*, he had insisted that union between individuals is fragile, ephemeral and purely practical, and not constituted in any other, deeper way. In an interview with Michel Sicard shortly before his death, however, Sartre moves beyond this position and posits the existence of an internal *ontological* bond between human beings:

> Ontologically, consciousnesses are not isolated, there are planes where they enter into one another – planes common to two or to *n* consciousnesses . . . [Humans'] perceptions or their thought are in relation one with others, not only by exposure to the other, but because there are penetrations between consciousnesses. (1979a, 15)

Although Sartre's communally based 'Third Ethics' remains a provisional sketch rather than a fully elaborated model, it is indicative of a progressive trajectory in his work towards a more positive account of sociality and intersubjectivity in which 'one must try to learn that one can only seek his being, his life, in living for others' (1979b, 1221–2). This movement towards intersubjectivity in Sartre's later work reveals him once more as a philosopher of change who is able to leave behind previous categorial assumptions by turning his critical vision towards complexity and constellation rather than stasis and univocity.

Another significant respect in which Sartre's political outlook contrasts with the postmodernist view is his search for a primary political agent which, as Pontalis has noted, changes as Sartre's political trajectory evolves. In his early political period this agent is the individual, in his middle phase the Communist Party (PCF), and in his later period, the youth.[3] From a postmodernist viewpoint, this of course clashes directly with the project to pluralize political agency (or to dissolve it altogether, as in the case of Baudrillard) in order to prevent the imposition of the viewpoint of a single hegemonic group. As we saw in Chapter 3, postmodernists decentre the importance of the proletariat as a primary political agent, favouring instead a kind of patchwork alliance between different and disparate discourses, knowledges and groups. By contrast, in *Anti-Semite and Jew* Sartre argues for the prime historical importance and status of the proletariat, arguing that it is not merely one oppressed group among several, but a 'universal class' which holds the key to the liquidation of oppression:

> The reason why the revolutionary adopts the standpoint of the proletariat is first of all because this is his own class, then because it is oppressed, because it is by far the most numerous, so that its fate tends to merge with that of humanity, and finally because the consequences of its victory necessarily entail the suppression of classes. (1965, 72)

Sartre, of course, steadily distances himself from this Marxist viewpoint as his work evolves, turning instead in his final political period to the youth and to student groups as a prime focus for progressive political change. However, although the object of his focus changes as his work evolves, his political project consistently inclines towards *unity* embodied in this idea of a prime political agent – an idea postmodernist political thinking rejects (following Lyotard) as terroristic and exclusionary.

This tension between Sartre's universalizing and unifying political aims and the postmodern preference for multiplicity, difference, fragmentation and plurality can be seen in part in the changing role of the intellectual following 1968 in France which led Sartre to question and revise his own status as a classical intellectual. This came most notably into focus in 1969 where, addressing a meeting of student groups at the Mutualité, he was given the instruction *'Sartre sois bref'* − 'Sartre, be brief'.[4] This small incident was representative of a wider shift in the role and aims of the intellectual that followed 1968. In Foucault's view, this involved a shift away from the 'general' (modern) intellectual who speaks on behalf of all oppressed groups towards the (postmodern) 'specific' intellectual who acts as an advisory within a particular group or form of struggle. In opposition to the unifying aims of the general or classical intellectual, the specific intellectual, Foucault argues, helps to ensure the autonomy of local struggles by recovering 'subjugated' and 'disqualified' knowledges from the hegemony of positivistic sciences, hierarchical political parties and master narratives. While it is clear that Sartre's abiding search for a totalizing consciousness and primary political agent would seem to contravene the pluralist discourse of the specific intel-lectual which Foucault and other postmodernists advocate, it is also the case that 1968 precipitated a change in Sartre's outlook.[5] The events of 1968 made Sartre realize the limitations of his privileged classical intellectual status and made him change his view of the intellectual's role which, he now argued in line with Foucault, must be to serve the masses: 'today I have finally understood that the intellectual . . . must resolve his own problem − or, if you like, negate his intellectual moment in order to achieve a new popular status' (1974a, 227).

In Deleuzian style, I have presented Sartre as a *schizophrenic* thinker whose critical consciousness is split between the modern and the postmodern. Indeed, I have argued that much of the originality and dynamism of his work lies precisely in this tense relationship between modern and postmodern elements. As we have seen throughout this study, Sartre's relation to modernism is a complex one, vacillating between a project to overturn, break open and move beyond modernist modes of understanding and an underlying impetus to hold on to certain modernist ideas and categories. This tension is reflected in the final years of his life which he divided between a political activism that struggled desperately to overthrow the social conditions of capitalist modernity and a classical, academic study of the bourgeois, Flaubert, that was far removed from this activist impulse. Thus, although Sartre was unable to transcend fully his starting points, he was able, as Ronald Aronson has pointed out (1980, 353), to think — and live — them to their limits while immersing himself in our world and its most powerful cross-currents.

In the course of this study, I have attempted to bring some of the weaknesses and limitations of Sartre's philosophy into critical view, examining the ways in which Sartre was unable to transcend the limitations imposed on him by the philosophical, social, historical and political situation of his time. On a theoretical level, this manifests itself in his inability to get beyond some of the theoretical limitations of the (modernist) outlook he inherited from Descartes, Husserl and Marx. On a political level, this came into view in the early 1950s where Sartre's allegiance to the PCF was strongly influenced by the ideological polarities of the Cold War environment. In this sense, although Sartre stretched the parameters of modernism to their limits, articulating new perspectives which prefigured many important themes taken up later by postmodernists like Foucault, Guattari and Derrida, in other respects he was unable to progress fully beyond these limits, reproducing some of the basic assumptions which form the modernist outlook and the classical French tradition of which he was a part.

Despite these limitations, I have endeavoured in overall terms to emphasize the positive value of Sartre's work in understanding and navigating our contemporary postmodern situation. In this respect, I have sought to generalize and extend the heritage of Sartre's work by applying its critical spirit to a time and situation that stretches beyond his own. Whether Sartre himself would have welcomed an application of his work towards this end is, of course, a purely speculative question, but as we have seen throughout this study, there are significant aspects of his work that tend towards a postmodern logic of understanding. Like postmodernists such as Foucault, Deleuze, Derrida, Guattari, Lyotard and Baudrillard, Sartre offers a trenchant critique of the condition of modernity and a deep, searching scepticism towards the project of the Enlightenment. More importantly, however, his work acts as a kind of critical searchlight that shines through the cracks and exposes the fragile foundations of both modern and postmodern excesses.

Thus, there are clearly aspects of postmodernism that are anathema to Sartre's theoretical sensibilities. Beneath the elements of change and evolution in his philosophical outlook, there is a deep and consistent attachment to the idea of human freedom and of transforming the world to bring this about. In the 1960s, this brought Sartre into conflict with (post-)structuralists like Foucault, Derrida and Althusser who were all intent at the time on consigning the figure of 'Man' to the dustbin of history. In the late 1960s and the 1970s, Foucault and others severed their links with structuralism and moved on to the (Sartrean) project of resurrecting the subject and articulating a vision of freedom, relinquishing their hostility and adopting a more positive attitude towards the value of Sartre's work. In an interview in 1968, for instance, Foucault pays homage to Sartre's contribution to intellectual thought in France and views his own work as 'minor' in relation to the 'immensity' of Sartre's:[6]

> I think the immense work and political action of Sartre defines an era ... I would never accept a comparison – even for the sake of a contrast – of the minor work of historical and methodological spade-work that I do with a body of work like his. (*La Quinzaine littéraire*, 46, 1968, 20, in Poster, 1984)

In an article devoted to Sartre entitled 'Il a été mon maître' published in a special 1964 issue of the periodical *Arts*, Deleuze also expresses his admiration for 'the private thinker [who] introduced new themes, a new style, a new polemic and a new way of raising problems as well as a hatred for all modes of "representation" ' (1964, 8–9). He reiterates this in a series of interviews with Claire Parnet published as *Dialogues* in 1977, where he speaks enthusiastically of his respect for Sartre:

> Fortunately there was Sartre. Sartre was our Outside, he was really the breath of fresh air from the backyard ... And Sartre has never stopped being that, not a model, a method or an example, but a little fresh air – a gust of air even when he had just been to the Café Flore – an intellectual who singularly changed the situation of the intellectual. (1987, 12)

Similarly, despite his previous criticisms of Sartre in the 1960s and 1970s, in the lead article for the commemorative fiftieth anniversary issue of *Les temps modernes*, Derrida expresses the 'boundless gratitude' and acknowledges the 'immense debt' he and others owe to Sartre.

He confesses that in previous years he 'wouldn't have dared' admit his affection for Sartre and *Les temps modernes* but that he is now moved to 'do justice' to them and recognize the value of Sartre's philosophical *œuvre* (1996, 44, 40). Even Baudrillard, the arch-Sceptic of postmodernity, acknowledges the enormity of Sartre's influence on post-war French intellectual life and how the 'theory of commitment through Sartre in the 1960s ... had been more or less the point of departure for intellectuals' (in Gane, 1991, 17).

Since his death in 1980, however, commitment has seemingly died with Sartre. The postmodern condition presented by Baudrillard and others is one in which apathy, nihilism, melancholy and withdrawal are seen as appropriate responses to a prevailing situation characterized by meaninglessness, simulation, hyperconformity and the absence of grand narratives which claim a better future for human society. In contrast to Baudrillard's asemic political vision which celebrates the death of meaning and the futility of political action and engagement, Sartre's political itinerary is an evolving story of progressive radicalization, a ceaseless journey to explore the radical possibilities and complex dimensions of freedom with a view to making the world a less alienating and oppressive home.

Shortly before his death in the course of interviews with Benny Lévy (published in English in 1996 as *Hope Now: The 1980 Interviews*), Sartre identifies *hope* (with a quasi-religosity) as a means of overcoming the malaise of apathy and despair that characterizes the postmodern world of the late twentieth century:

> What with the third world war that can break out at any day, and the wretched mess our planet has become, despair has come back to tempt me with the idea that there is no end to it all, that there is no goal, that there are only small, individual objectives that we fight for. We make small revolutions, but there's no human end, there's nothing of concern to human beings, there's only disorder ... In any event, the world seems ugly, evil, and hopeless. Such is the calm despair of an old man who will die in that despair. But the point is, I'm resisting, and I know I shall die in hope. But this hope must be grounded. We must try to explain why the world of today, which is horrible, is only one moment in a long historical development, that

hope has always been one of the dominant forces of revolutions and insurrections, and how I still feel that hope is my conception of the future. (1996, 109–10)

Whether the future conforms to Sartre's 'hope-full' conception remains to be seen, marked as it is, of course, by the feature of contingency that Sartre theorized so effectively throughout his work. In any case, his critical spirit, philosophical guile and gift of dialectical understanding provide us with the inspiration and the means to recover a sense of the authentically human in an increasingly inhuman and cybernetic post-modern world. In the context of Deleuze's remark in *Negotiations* that '[a] thought's logic is like a wind blowing on us, a series of gusts and jolts' (1995, 94), Sartre's thought can be likened to a gust of freedom that blows away constricting webs which bind and entrap. This shines through in the focus of his work which grapples constantly with the problematic of freedom as well as in his personal life where his activism and struggle against oppression thrust him into the forefront of ideological and political controversy in post-war France. Somewhat diminutive and cor-pulent, physically enfeebled and almost blind in his later years, Sartre stood in gladiatorial pose as a resolute defender of the marginalized and downtrodden against the strong arm of the Goliath capitalist state. This made him into an object of vitriolic hatred for the French state which threatened on numerous occasions to imprison him, for pro-colonial groupings on the Right who threatened and ultimately attempted to kill him, and even for those on the Left, such as the orthodox guardians of the Communist faith, who demonized and excommunicated him as a heretic. Through all this, Sartre continued in his own inimitable way to articulate and to refine his telling discourse of freedom. It remains to be seen how this will be taken up and articulated by others in the postmodern configuration of the twenty-first century.

Notes

Introduction

1. See *La Quinzaine littéraire* (May 1966), no. 5, p. 14 and (October 1966), no. 14, p. 4.
2. Christina Howells' interpretation of 'the new Sartre' began a series of articles and essays concerned with exploring the ways in which Sartrean and post-structuralist theory interweave and share common ground. Both Margaret Majumdar (1997) and Peter Caws (1992), for instance, have devoted essays to a reappraisal of the relation between Sartre and (Althusserian) structuralism which (to varying degrees) questions its standard interpretation as one of outright opposition. More recently Marie-Andrée Charbonneau (1999) has brought attention to the common features between Sartre's early work on consciousness and the imagination and Lacan's theory of the subject while Bruce Baugh (1999) has highlighted the similarities between Sartrean consciousness in *BN* and Derrida's theory of *différance* outlined in *Writing and Difference* and other texts.
3. In the text (post-)structuralism is used to denote both structuralist and post-structuralist theory whereas post-structuralism refers only to post-structuralist theory. In general terms, Lévi-Strauss, Lacan and Althusser are regarded as structuralists whereas Foucault, Deleuze and Guattari, Derrida, Lyotard and Baudrillard are seen as post-structuralists. For a more detailed overview, see Harland (1987).
4. See Chancel (1976). In a recent interview Benny Lévy remarked that this sense of division even shows through in Sartre's eyesight – 'his left eye looks one way while his right the other' – and in his name – 'Jean' ('John') refers to the apocalyptic tradition of the Christian Church and 'Paul' to the constructivist tradition (Meerster and Meerster, 2000).
5. In general terms, there are three main approaches to the question of postmodernism. First, there are those who argue for the idea of radical discontinuity with modernity (e.g. Baudrillard), stressing that we are in a totally new era requiring new theories and concepts. Second, there are some who argue that there is no definitive rupture with modernity (e.g. Callinicos),

that we are in a similar condition of modern capitalism which Marx analysed, and that postmodern discourse is in this sense a conservative or irrational ideology which diverts attention away from the systemic nature of capitalism, fitting in neatly with the forms of individualism associated with contemporary consumerism. Finally, some approaches emphasize a dialectic of continuity and discontinuity with modernity (e.g. Laclau and Mouffe, Jameson) and argue that, although there is no definitive rupture, it is still possible to differentiate postmodern from modern positions even though they may share similar aspects since certain features become prominent, intensified or qualitatively different.

In this book I adopt this third (dialectical) approach to the question of postmodernism, viewing it in general terms as a process with degrees of implementation rather than as a fully formed or discrete totality. Following Bernstein, I view the postmodern/modern debate as a kind of *constellation*, 'a juxtaposed rather than integrated cluster of changing elements that resist reduction to a common denominator, essential core, or generative first principle' (1991, 8).

6. This distinction is suggested by Pauline Rosenau in her book *Postmodernism and the Social Sciences* (1992).

Chapter 1

1. See, for instance, Hayim (1980, 23–5) and Howells (1988, 16–18) who both theorize Sartre's concept of *Bad Faith* along these lines.
2. Since consciousness is always *intentional* (requires an object outside of itself) it is in this way incomplete and said to be a 'lack' (see *BN*, 171).
3. Silverman (1980, 85–104) proposes that there are three different stages or 'epistemes' in Sartre's theorization of self and language which relate to an early period (1936–44), a middle stage (1944–52) and a later period (1957–65).
4. See Jopling (1992, 106, 129).
5. In contrast to Foucault, Heidegger views Nietzsche as the last (modernist) metaphysician since his idea of the 'Übermensch' as 'pure will' assumes the metaphysical repetition of humanism. For an interesting discussion of this, see Schrift (1995, 25–8).
6. See Best and Kellner (1991, 90–3) for a critical overview of Deleuze's and Guattari's affirmative project of 'bodies without organs'. In his book on Deleuze and Guattari, Philip Goodchild describes the concept of 'bodies

without organs' as 'an unproductive duration; a site where intensities are distributed; a desiring machine that does not function' (1996, 217).

7. As Megill (1985, 2, 31) points out, it is the 'aestheticist sensibility' in the work of Nietzsche and his French followers (Foucault, Derrida, Deleuze) which defines and unites them most clearly. In certain places, this sensibility even bestows upon art and aesthetic practice an 'ontogenetic' (world-making) significance.

8. See, for instance, Lash (1988), Best and Kellner (1991), Megill (1985) and Rosenau (1992).

9. Simons (1995) uses this phrase (adapted from Milan Kundera's novel *The Unbearable Lightness of Being*) to describe the trajectory of the subject in Foucault's work. Lightness refers, according to Simons, 'to the attempt to exist permanently without limits' and Heaviness 'to a state of total imprisonment within determining limits' (1995, 3).

10. This leads Dews to conclude that '[d]espite his strictures on the absolute autonomy of the self assumed by existentialism, Lacan recognizes in Sartre a fellow Hegelian' (1987, 58).

11. Not all commentators interpret *BN* in this way. Harland (1987, 67) points out, for instance, that in Sartre's existentialism received social signs are seen to run so deep that we can break free from them only by going through the dramatic experience of the Absurd, while Kirsner (1985, 213) argues that Sartre's early emphasis on *ontological* freedom can be seen as an index of how far he thinks *social* freedom has ceased to exist.

12. See Levi (1967, 245ff.).

13. In Soper's view (1986, 74), Sartre's emphasis on the counter-finality and anti-praxis of matter leads him to assume materiality to be necessarily intractable and to see nature as essentially Other and hostile to human purpose. Desan (1966, 90) argues in a similar vein that Sartre effectively transposes his earlier idea of 'L'enfer c'est les autres' onto matter in the *CDR*.

On a less critical note, Kruks (1990, 161) states that Sartre's conception of matter in the *CDR* is less negative than in *BN* since he now sees it to constitute the positive and necessary condition of praxis. However, although Kruks is right to view the *CDR* in this light, it still generally remains the case that Sartre does not get beyond the basic attitude that infuses his literary works which, as Thody comments, 'come back again and again to the same images of sickness and discomfort, of the plethoric unpleasantness of nature' (1992, 31).

14. If every great philosophy, as Nietzsche said, is nothing more than 'the personal confession of its author and a kind of involuntary and unconscious memoir' (1966, 6), this might go some way in explaining Sartre's theoretical

devaluation of nature. As Simone de Beauvoir writes, for instance: 'he abhors – the word isn't too strong – the seething life of insects and the profusion of plants . . . he feels at home only in towns, at the heart of an artificial universe consisting of man-made objects' (in Hayman, 1986, 104).

15. For Adorno and Horkheimer in *The Dialectic of Enlightenment*, this difference between symbolic rationality and modern, instrumental rationality is seen in terms of the historical development of *mimesis* which, they argue, corresponds to three distinct phases.

The first stage, natural mimesis, refers to our primal, instinctual relation to nature in which we mimic nature and camouflage ourselves within it, like the chameleon, through fear of predation. Following Freud's thesis of civilization, Adorno and Horkheimer argue that human societies have slowly and methodically prohibited instinctual behaviour. This came about initially by the organization of mimesis into a symbolic, magical phase in which ceremonies and rites would represent in dance the behaviours, rituals and movements of animals. As with the previous form of mimesis, this involved an attempt to copy or to blend in with the rest of nature. However, in the modern, rational phase of human history, according to Adorno and Horkheimer, instinctual forms have been banished altogether through the imposition of regulative, scientific and behavioural procedures and norms. Mimesis now takes the form in which society threatens nature – control becomes self-preservation through the dominance of nature: 'Society continues threatening nature as the lasting organized compulsion which is reproduced in individuals as rational self-preservation and rebounds on nature as social dominance over it' (1973, 87).

For Adorno and Horkheimer, modern rational mimesis represents an inversion and distortion of the two previous forms of mimesis since it no longer strives to copy or to blend in with nature but instead tries to transform the world into its own image and reduce 'all the power of nature' to 'mere indiscriminate resistance [and] the abstract power of the subject' (1973, 90).

16. André Gorz's 'ecological socialism' is, he has stated, founded upon 'the spirit of Sartrism'. More recently, McBride has called for a more ecological reading of Sartre – as he states, for instance:

It would be a gross exaggeration to pretend that Sartre was ecology-minded in the contemporary sense. Nevertheless there is an important sense in which, in the *Critique*, Sartre introduces an ecological consciousness that neither classical Marxism or classical liberalism . . . developed. (1991, 131–2)

17. Commenting on the lack of an adequate theory of collectivity within postmodernist thinking for instance, Rorty observes that:

> There is no 'we' to be found in Foucault's writing, nor in those of many of his French contemporaries ... It is as if thinkers like Foucault and Lyotard are so afraid of being caught up in one more metanarrative about the fortunes of the 'subject' that they cannot bring themselves to say 'we' long enough to identify with the culture of the generation to which they belong. (1984, 40)

18. According to Grimshaw (1993, 66, 67), Foucault's ethics can be seen as a transition from his earlier genealogical work. In *Discipline and Punish* internalized self-surveillance is seen by Foucault to undermine the autonomy of the subject whereas in *The History of Sexuality* it is seen to constitute it. The trouble is, as Grimshaw notes, this sudden shift remains largely unexplained and does not address the crucial question of when forms of discipline should be seen as exercises of autonomy or of subjection. Without an explanation of this shift, Foucault's defamiliarization of contemporary modes of self-knowledge can become a repetition of them.

    In his theorization of the body, Foucault fails to provide a satisfactory answer as to when a concern for the body is an exercise of self-mastery rather than the result of the internalization of oppressive social norms of bodily appearance that serve to undermine other forms of autonomy. The practice of male body-building, for example, may reveal a body 'totally imprinted by history' — that is, one which has been disciplined by constraining norms of male Herculeanism — or may reveal the aesthetic concerns of the artist and a feeling of 'oneness' between the individual and his body. Unfortunately, Foucault's idea of 'bodies and pleasures' does not show us how to attain the latter without reinforcing the former.

19. For an interesting and detailed overview of Sartre's notion of authenticity see Thomas Anderson's book *Sartre's Two Ethics: From Authenticity to Integral Humanity* (1993).

Chapter 2

1. Against this standard interpretation, Kirsner (1985, 220) suggests that the deeper implication of *Huis Clos* is that hell is not 'other people' but rather 'being alone', illustrated by the fact that Garcin prefers to stay in a hate relationship with Inès than leave and be alone. Similarly, in *Erostratus*,

Hilbert takes up his revolver in a quest for recognition by others and to escape solitude, preferring to be a 'bad somebody' rather than a 'weak non-entity'.

2. As Flynn notes (1984, 121), Sartre does recognize that his social wholes are abstract and that they do interact in the concrete.

3. See Flynn (1984, 125–30). Flynn's book *Sartre and Marxist Existentialism* gives an excellent account of Sartre's social ontology in general.

4. Elster (1986, 93, 191) points in this respect to the 'Hegelian and teleological roots' of Marx's thought, arguing that, although *The German Ideology* is a notable exception to this

> which espouses a robustly anti-teleological view', in his later economic writings, Marx 'reverted to the Hegelianism of his youth, arguing that the immanent purpose of history was to carry mankind through the purgatory of alienation and class conflict towards communism, because full unity could not be achieved in any other way than by a temporary loss of unity.

According to Elster, the communist revolution is seen in this way by Marx as the outcome of a necessary plan of historical development: 'it follows from the central propositions of historical materialism that the communist revolution will occur when and because communist relations of production become optimal for the development of the productive forces' (1986, 159).

Against this interpretation, Callinicos (1989, 36) argues that Marx abandoned 'the teleological metaphysic' after 1844:

> historical materialism is a non-teleological theory of social evolution; not only does it deny that capitalism is the final stage of historical development, but communism, the classless society which Marx believed would be the outcome of socialist revolution, is not the inevitable consequence of the contradictions of capitalism, since an alternative exists, what Marx called 'the mutual ruination of the contending classes', Rosa Luxemburg, 'barbarism'. (1989, 37)

Marx perceives historical progress, in Callinicos's view, as 'a contradictory and not a unilinear process' in which he explores 'the contradiction between the expansion of human productive powers which capitalism makes possible and the "limited bourgeois form" in which this takes place' (1989, 38).

However, although Callinicos's qualifications do provide a less overtly teleological reading of Marx, they do not resolve a number of difficulties that still persist in Marx's account. In spite of the fact that Marx saw progress under capitalism as a 'contradictory process', he did still see it as a *necessary* form of progress for the possibility of a future communist society, 'both because it immeasurably developed human powers and because it created the class which would achieve "its blessed end"' (Callinicos, 1989, 104). In spite of what he saw to be its disastrous social effects, Marx openly praised capitalism for its constant and expansive 'revolutionizing [of] the instruments of production' (Marx and Engels, 1982 (6), 487). In the *Grundrisse* Marx reiterates this praise, stressing 'the great civilizing influence of capital' and the way 'capital drives beyond natural barriers and prejudices' (1973, 409, 410), while in *The Communist Manifesto* Marx and Engels emphasize the productive dynamism of capitalism for its accomplishments of 'wonders far surpassing Egyptian pyramids, Roman aqueducts and Gothic cathedrals' (in Callinicos, 1989, 36).

Given that capitalism involves, Marx insists 'a complete emptying out of the . . . human content' (1973, 162) and has fundamentally alienated humans from their essential powers of praxis (the realization of which communist society is dependent on), it is hard to see why he sees it as a necessary historical phase of development for the possibility of communism. The answer to this lies either with Elster's teleological reading of Marx (in which 'full unity could not be achieved in any other way than by a temporary loss of unity') or with a reading of Marx that annexes him to a position where progress is viewed in simple linear terms and equated with the growth of productive forces. Either way, the Marxist view of the historical necessity of capitalism is fraught with difficulties.

5. Although Foucault rejected the label 'Marxist', stating in interview that 'I am a Nietzschean . . . [but] I have never been a Freudian . . . Marxist . . . [or] Structuralist' (in Callinicos, 1989, 86), and, like Lyotard, identifies Marxism as a 'coercive, global theory', he does contend that it can provide 'useful tools for local research' (1980, 81) and, in general terms, acknowledges a clear debt to Marx in his own work:

> It is impossible at the present time to write history without using a whole range of concepts directly or indirectly linked to Marxist thought and situating oneself within a horizon of thought which has been defined and described by Marx. (1980, 53)

In a similar vein, Derrida argues in *Spectres of Marx* that Marxism 'remains both indispensable and structurally insufficient'. Although he goes on to affirm that he 'is not a Marxist', he acknowledges that deconstruction is faithful to 'a certain spirit of Marxism' and would have been impossible without Marxism (1994, 101, 143, 127, 151).

One can also discern a reverence for 'a certain spirit of Marxism' in the co-authored texts of Deleuze and Guattari, particularly in *Anti-Oedipus*, where Marx is frequently cited as an authoritative source.

6. See Kellner (1988, 244).

7. See Best and Kellner (1991, 121).

8. In an article entitled 'The Year 2000 has Already Happened' published in 1988, Baudrillard offers three different interpretations (based on the models of astrophysics, the natural sciences and technology) to explain how history has come to an end. See Best and Kellner (1991, 134–5).

9. See Griffin (1988) for an excellent discussion of the theme of re-enchantment within postmodern science. Postmodern science is characterized by Lyotard as a perpetual search for instabilities which is concerned more with the generation of paradox than with logical proof:

> Postmodern science – by concerning itself with such things as undecidables, the limits of precise control, conflicts characterized by incomplete information, '*fracta*', catastrophes, and pragmatic paradoxes – is theorizing its own evolution as discontinuous, catastrophic, nonrectifiable, and paradoxical . . . It is producing not the known, but the unknown. (1984a, 60)

This form of science, Lyotard argues, is in contrast to modern science which is based on the general principle 'that physical systems, including the system of systems called the universe, follow regular patterns, with the result that their evolution traces a regular path and gives rise to "normal" continuous functions' (1984a, 55).

10. Following McBride's (1991, 131–2) suggestion that there is a nascent rationality of ecology in the *CDR*, it is possible to view Sartre's concept of the practico-inert as a warning against the disastrous effects of modern scientific technology and industrialization. His description of the practico-inert as a site of 'violence, darkness and witchcraft' (*CDR*, 318) is best viewed, I think, not as a neutral statement of fact and inevitability, but as a prescription to dissolve or keep to a minimum the size and power of its role in human affairs. Massive practico-inert constructions (such as large-scale industry) appear in this sense to harbour unavoidable, inherent dangers for human freedom, both ecologically (of causing disastrous counter-finalities) and socially (of requiring a division of labour and serialized infrastructures to maintain them). Even if communist society deployed this technology for

material need instead of profit, it would not dissolve the forms of seriality that Sartre sees as so damaging to human freedom, nor would it restore humans to the close, symbiotic relation with nature that Marx himself argues for in his early writings.

André Gorz argues in a similar vein that modern capitalist technology is based on a rationality of domination, both of the worker and of nature. Thus the proletariat, shaped by capitalism, its technology of domination and its hierarchical division of labour is, according to Gorz, 'constitutionally incapable of becoming the holder of power. If its representatives seized the apparatus of domination put in place by Capital they will reproduce the same type of domination and become in their day a *bourgeoisie de fonction*' (see 1982, Chapters 3 and 4).

11. See Poster (1979, 64).

12. Against this interpretation, Dobson (1993, 186) focuses on Sartre's intention to produce a single, intelligible history in the *CDR* which, he argues, runs in direct opposition to the postmodern quest for multiplicity. In contrast, Howells emphasizes the (postmodern) element of detotalization in Sartre's methodology, identifying 'the detotalized quality of all alleged totalities' and 'the impossibility of an ultimate synthesis' in Sartre's analysis and concluding that 'Sartre's aim is certainly not reductive: his stress on the present multiplicity of meanings . . . is far stronger than that on the future totalization' (1988, 111, 194).

Although Howells is right, I think, to emphasize the importance of 'the detotalized quality of all alleged totalities' in Sartre's work, in general terms Sartre's vacillation between 'the future totalization' and 'the present multiplicity of meanings' illustrates well the dual influence of the modern and the postmodern in his work. His theoretical preference for (postmodern) detotalization is in this sense offset by his (modern) political project for meaning, unity and direction. Although Sartre, like Foucault, stresses the interdependence of knowledge and power – 'Tout savoir est pratique' (1977 (8), 456) – there is a sense in which the epistemological and the political separate in Sartre's work, the first inclining him towards a postmodern perspective and the second towards a modernist (Marxist) perspective which sees fragmentation and 'the present multiplicity of meanings' as a distinct problem for class unity and progressive political change.

13. This is well illustrated in *Nausea* where Roquentin tries to apprehend the objective, unmediated reality of the roots of a chestnut tree but ends up feeling nausea prompted by the recognition of the stark separation between the brute, viscous reality of the thing and the words and concepts we use to capture it. In this respect it is possible to view Sartre's epistemology in

Nausea as a (postmodern) reaction against the (modern) scientific idea of *representation* in which it is thought that we can authentically represent or 'picture' the true, essential nature of things.

14. This applies particularly to Baudrillard whose later work stresses discontinuity and generally takes a much more belligerent attitude towards Marxism than Foucault, Derrida, Lyotard, Deleuze and Guattari do, for instance.

    Although Lyotard concurs with Baudrillard in identifying postmodern society as one based on computers, scientific knowledge, media information and advanced technology, he does not sever the link with political economy completely, recognizing that the flow and development of technology and knowledge essentially follow 'the flow of money' in contemporary society (1984a, 6). Though keen to stress the importance of micro-contexts of power, Foucault, Derrida, Deleuze and Guattari do not deny the importance of political economy altogether and generally lean towards a dialectic of continuity and discontinuity between the (modern) past and the (postmodern) present. Derrida writes, for instance: 'I do not believe in decisive ruptures, in an unequivocal "epistemomological break" as it is called today. Breaks are always and fatally, reinscribed in an old cloth that must continually, interminably be done' (1981, 24).

    Elsewhere, Derrida reiterates this historical logic of continuity and discontinuity:

    > My own conviction is that we must maintain two contradictory affirmations at the same time. On the one hand we affirm the existence of ruptures in history, and on the other we affirm that these ruptures produce gaps or faults in which the most hidden and forgotten archives can emerge and constantly recur and work through history. One must surmount the categorical oppositions of philosophical logic out of fidelity to these conflicting positions of historical discontinuity (rupture) and continuity (repetition), which are neither pure break with the past nor a pure unfolding or explication of it. (in Bernstein, 1993, 215)

    In Foucault's case, of course, this meant revising his earlier 'archaeological' analysis of history which, like Baudrillard's postmodern analysis, emphasizes discontinuity and rupture between different historical epistemes.

15. For an analysis of this distinction, see Poster (1990, 20–5).

16. By emphasizing the biographical influence of the theorist, Sartre can be seen as more Nietzschean than Foucault who, in his early archaeology, withdraws from the text in anonymity, declaring that 'I am no doubt the only one who writes in order to have no face' (1972, 17). In his later work,

of course, Foucault amended this view somewhat, insisting on the rooted-ness of his thought in the historical present.

There also exists an interesting parallel between Sartre's classification of *The Family Idiot* as 'un roman vrai' and of *Words* as 'un roman auquel je crois' (1977 (10), 146), and Foucault's acknowledgement that his histories, though based on 'true documents', are nothing more than fictions and artful constructs: I 'am fully aware that I have never written anything other than fictions . . . my book is a fiction; it is a novel' (1979, 75).

17. In Catalano's view, Sartre's theorization of scarcity successfully incorporates *both* elements of necessity and contingency. Following Sartre's comment that scarcity is 'a fundamental relation of *our* history and a contingent deter-mination of our univocal relation to materiality' (*CDR*, 125), Catalano argues that it 'is contingent because the precise scarcity from which we suffer has been historically forged' and also necessary in that 'once forged, it becomes a historical a priori that sets the limits of our humanity'. In this sense, he concludes that scarcity can be overcome in Sartre's view 'but only by changing the basis on which our history is founded' (1996, 56–7).

18. Commenting on Sartre's (and Hegel's) dialectic of self and other as appropriation, Cixous and Clément argue that this reveals the phallocentric nature of his thought in *BN* since it 'is erected from a fear that, in fact, is typically masculine . . . the fear of expropriation, of separation, of losing the attribute' (1986, 80).

19. This is reflected in Sartre's tendency to premise a future socialist society on a state of material abundance. Although Sartre views the idea of 'productive progress' in the Third Volume of *The Family Idiot* as 'the directing principle of *all* bourgeois ideology' (1974c, 282), in *The Communists and Peace* Sartre clearly expresses himself in favour of increasing production to meet material needs – a position that places him at odds with postmodernist critiques of the ideology of production.

As Marx's list of general human needs outlined in *The German Ideology* and elsewhere is simply for other people, sexual relations, food, water, clothing, shelter and circumstances conducive to health, self-development and needs arising from the 'universal metabolism' between humans and nature, it is difficult to see why both Marx and Sartre propose increasing production through industrialization in order to provide for them, and why Sartre often stresses the necessity of material abundance as a prerequisite for the possibility of a socialist society.

20. In Simont's view, for instance, Sartre's failure to complete his outlined project in the second volume of the *Critique* stems from this individu-alist perspective where, having set himself the task of elucidating the

intelligibility of class conflict, he becomes obsessed by *individual praxis* in the incarnation of Stalin:

> while he should have applied himself to studying the relations of different practical multiplicities and to showing how they can be totalized to form *one* history, he focuses anew on individuality and studies the praxis of a dictator, Stalin, or how the *praxis* of a single individual can enslave an entire society and divert that common project, socialism. (1985, 109)

Simont thus poses the question: 'Why does Sartre, proposing to study common action, not begin from the right end, that is, the community?'. Had he done so, she adds, it 'would have spared him a good many setbacks' (1985, 110).

Chapter 3

1. See Contat (1996, 12).
2. For a general overview of intellectuals' responses to Sartre's work following May 1968 in France, see Atack (1999, 35, 46).
3. Poster (1990, 131–2).
4. *New York Times*, 1969, cited in Hayman (1986, 385). As Daniel Cohn-Bendit remarked at the time:

   > Some people have tried to force Marcuse on us as a mentor: that is a joke. None of us has read Marcuse. Some read Marx, of course, perhaps Bakunin, and of the moderns, Althusser, Mao, Guevara, Lefebvre. Nearly all the militants of the March 22nd movement have read Sartre. (1968, 58)

5. See Aronson (1995, 32–5) and Birchall (1998, 74–8).
6. In addition to his admiration for Jean Genet, Sartre (along with Daniel Guérin) was one of the few to defend the rights of homosexual men when homophobia was common on the French Left in the 1950s. Similarly, his consistent opposition to fascism and colonialism marks his political project as clearly 'anti-racist'.

   However, there is some debate as to whether Sartre's political project can be described as 'feminist' or 'ecological'. Despite the fact that Beauvoir employed existentialist ideas of 'Otherness' similar to those of Sartre to yield the feminism of *The Second Sex*, Sartre's work (unlike Foucault's, for example) is not usually viewed by feminists as a valuable reference point or resource for further research. Indeed, Cixous and Clément (1986) see Sartre's project in *BN* as resolutely phallocentric. As I argued in the last chapter, although there is a nascent ecological rationality in Sartre's work, this is not always consistently maintained or adequately elaborated by Sartre. His 'green credentials', if present at all, lie buried deep within his texts and do not issue in any explicit ecological discourse comparable to the work of Gorz or Guattari.

7. For a more detailed account of Hegel's narrative of master and slave, see Singer (1983, 58–62).

8. See Bauman (1997, 81), for instance, who criticizes postmodernism along these lines.

9. This is an important issue within feminist theory. Ransom (1993, 125), for example, questions whether postmodernist forms of feminism which emphasize difference are able to generate a theory that can articulate the commonalities in women's experiences and form a basis for feminist solidarity and unity. Added to this is what might be called the 'trap of essentialism' – when differences become reified they are liable to take on the character of intrinsic and essential determinations.

10. Even when we extend an ethic of care beyond the human realm to include animals and other life forms, this is usually predicated on our being able to *identify* with them in some way within a context of sameness. In this respect we usually prioritize the needs of animals over those of vegetables, for instance, as the needs of animals are more familiar and less 'other' to us than those of vegetables.

    This link between otherness and care is dramatically illustrated in Kafka's *Metamorphosis* where the grotesque otherness of Gregor's insect-form causes his family finally to remove their ethic of care towards him and leave him to die.

11. See Keat (1981, 149). As Sartre points out in the *CDR*, Marxist accounts that hypostasize the community as a fixed, organic totality are no less abstract than the isolated 'Robinsonade' individual of bourgeois ideology:

    > Thus we now know that the concrete dialectic is the one that unveils itself through the common *praxis* of a group; but we also know that the untranscendability ... of organic action as strictly individual model is the fundamental condition for historical rationality ... Without this rigorous and permanent limitation which refers back from the group to its foundation, the community *is no less abstract* than the isolated

individual: there are revolutionary pastorales about the group which are the exact counterpart of Robinsonades. (*CDR*, 677–8)

12. See Best and Kellner (1991, 189–90).

Chapter 4

1. Sartre, of course, makes much use of this analogy in the *Second Critique* where he uses the example of two boxers to analyse the class struggle.
2. See Raulet (1983) and Lyotard (1987).
3. See Scriven (1999, 7).
4. See Annie Cohen-Solal's biography of Sartre, *Sartre: A Life*, for an account of this incident (1987, 780–1).
5. This applies especially to Sartre's dress-sense – in solidarity with the student groups and the general anarchistic aims of the movement, Sartre swore after 1968 never to wear a tie or suit again.
6. Foucault even suggests at one point in an interview in the 1970s that he and Sartre are philosophical brothers and sons of Nietzsche when he expresses enthusiasm for the fact that Sartre's first paper written as a student was on Nietzsche:

> Did you know that Sartre's first text – written when he was a young student – was Nietzschean? 'The History of Truth', a little paper first published in a *Lycée* review around 1925. He began with the same problem and it is very odd that his approach should have shifted from the history of truth to phenomenology while for the next generation – ours – the reverse was true. (Raulet, 1983, 204)

Bibliography

[ ] denotes original year of publication.

Works by Sartre

(1956) *Being and Nothingness: An Essay in Phenomenological Ontology*, tran. H. Barnes, London: Philosophical Library [1943].

(1957) *The Transcendence of the Ego*, tran. F. Williams and R. Kirkpatrick, New York: Noonday Press [1936].

(1963) *Saint Genet: Actor and Martyr*, tran. B. Frechtman, New York: Braziller [1952].

(1964a) *The Words*, tran. B. Frechtman, New York [1963].

(1964b) 'The Rome Lecture' at the Gramsci Institute (available at the Bibliothèque Nationale, Paris).

(1965) *Anti-Semite and Jew*, tran. G. Becker, New York: Schocken Books [1946].

(1966a) *Nausea*, Harmondsworth: Penguin [1938].

(1966b) *Existentialism and Humanism*, London: Methuen [1965].

(1966c) 'Jean-Paul Sartre répond', in *L'Arc*, 30, pp. 87–96.

(1968a) *Search for a Method*, tran. H. Barnes, New York: Vintage Books [1957].

(1968b) *The Communists and Peace*, tran. M. Fletcher and P. Beak, New York: Braziller [1952].

(1969) 'Itinerary of a Thought', *New Left Review*, 58.

(1971) *L'idiot de la famille*, vol. 2, Paris: Gallimard.

(1974a) *Between Existentialism and Marxism*, tran. J. Mathews, New York: Pantheon.

(1974b) *On a raison de se révolter*, with P. Gavi and P. Victor, Paris: Gallimard.

(1974c) *L'idiot de la famille*, vol. 3, Paris: NRF/Gallimard.

(1976) *Critique of Dialectical Reason: Theory of Practical Ensembles*, vol. 1, tran. A. Sheridan-Smith, London: New Left Books [1960].

(1977) *Situations*, vols 1–10, Paris: Gallimard [1947–76].

(1978) *What is Literature?*, London: Methuen [1947].

(1979a) 'Jean-Paul Sartre et M. Sicard: Entretien', *Obliques*, 18–19.

(1979b) 'Man muss für sich selbst und für die anderen leben', *Merkur* (December).

(1980) *Sartre by Himself* (interviews with A. Astruc and M. Contat), New York: Urizen.

(1981a) *The Family Idiot*, vol.1, tran. C. Cosman, Chicago: University of Chicago Press [1971].

(1981b) 'An Interview with Jean-Paul Sartre', in *The Philosophy of Jean-Paul Sartre*, ed. P. Schlipp, Illinois: La Salle.

(1983) *Cahiers pour une morale*, Paris: Gallimard.

(1991a) *Critique of Dialectical Reason*, vol. 2: *The Intelligibility of History*, London: Verso [1985].

(1991b) 'I am no longer a Realist: an interview with Jean-Paul Sartre', P. Verstraeten in *Sartre Alive*, ed. R. Aronson and A. van den Hoven, Detroit: Wayne State University Press.

(1996) *Hope Now: The 1980 Interviews* (with B. H. Lévy), tran. A. van den Hoven, Chicago: University of Chicago Press.

Works by other authors

Adorno, T. and Horkheimer, M. (1973) *The Dialectic of Enlightenment*, New York: Seabury Press [1944].

Althusser, L. (1971) *Lenin and Philosophy and Other Essays*, tran. B. Brewster, London: New Left Books.

Althusser, L. and Balibar, E. (1970) *Reading Capital*, tran. B. Brewster, London: New Left Books [1965].

Anderson, P. (1983) *In the Tracks of Historical Materialism*, London: New Left Books.

Anderson, T. (1993) *Sartre's Two Ethics: From Authenticity to Integral Humanity*, Chicago: Open Court Press.

Archard, D. (1980) *Marxism and Existentialism*, Belfast: Black Staff Press.

Aronson, R. (1980) *Jean-Paul Sartre: Philosophy in the World*, London: New Left Books.

—— (1992) 'Sartre on Progress', in *The Cambridge Companion to Sartre*, ed. C. Howells, Cambridge: Cambridge University Press.

—— (1995) 'Sartre and Marxism', *Sartre Studies International*, vol. 1, no. 1/2, ed. M. Scriven, C. Howells, R. Aronson and A. Van Den Hoven, Oxford: Berghahn.

Atack, M. (1999) 'Sartre, May 68 and Literature', *Sartre Studies International*, vol. 5, no. 1, ed. M. Scriven *et al.*, Oxford: Berghahn.

Bannet, E. (1989) *Structuralism and the Logic of Dissent: Barthes, Derrida, Foucault, Lacan*, Basingstoke: Macmillan.

Baudrillard, J. (1975) *The Mirror of Production*, tran. M. Poster, St Louis: Telos Press [1973].

—— (1981) *For a Critique of the Political Economy of the Sign*, St Louis: Telos Press [1972].

—— (1983a) *In the Shadow of the Silent Majorities*, New York: Semiotext(e) [1978].

—— (1983b) *Simulations*, New York: Semiotext(e).

—— (1984) 'On Nihilism', in *On the Beach*, no. 6, pp. 38–9 [1980].

—— (1987) *Forget Foucault*, New York: Semiotext(e) [1977].

—— (1988) *The Ecstasy of Communication*, New York: Semiotext(e) [1987].

Baugh, B. (1999) ' "Hello, Goodbye": Derrida and Sartre's Legacy', *Sartre Studies International*, vol. 5, no. 2, ed. M. Scriven *et al.*, Oxford: Berghahn.

Bauman, Z. (1997) *Postmodernism and its Discontents*, Cambridge: Polity Press.

Beauvoir, S. de (1984) *Adieux: A Farewell to Sartre*, tran. P. O'Brian, New York: Pantheon [1981].

Bernstein, R. (1991) *The New Constellation: The Ethical–Political Horizons of Modernity/Postmodernity*, Cambridge: Polity Press.

—— (1993) 'An Allegory of Modernity/Postmodernity: Habermas and Derrida', in *Working Through Derrida*, ed. G. Madison, Evanston, IL: Northwestern University Press.

Best, S. and Kellner, D. (1991) *Postmodern Theory: Critical Interrogations*, Basingstoke: Macmillan.

—— (1997) *The Postmodern Turn*, New York: The Guilford Press.

Birchall, I. (1998) 'Socialism or Identity Politics?', *Sartre Studies International*, vol. 4, no. 2, ed. M. Scriven *et al.*, Oxford: Berghahn.

Boundas, C. (1991) 'Translator's Introduction', in *Empiricism and Subjectivity*, ed. G. Deleuze, New York: Columbia University Press.

—— (1997) 'Foreclosure of the Other: From Sartre to Deleuze', in *Sartre's French Contemporaries and Enduring Influences*, ed. W. McBride, New York: Garland Publishing.

Callinicos, A. (1983) *Marxism and Philosophy*, Oxford: Oxford University Press.

—— (1989) *Against Postmodernism: A Marxist Critique*, Cambridge: Polity Press.

Catalano, J. (1996) *Good Faith and Other Essays: Perspectives on a Sartrean Ethics*, Lanham, MD: Rowman & Littlefield.

Caws, P. (1992) 'Sartrean Structuralism?', in *The Cambridge Companion to Sartre*, ed. C. Howells, Cambridge: Cambridge University Press.

Chancel, J. (1976) 'Radioscopie: Roland Barthes', *Radioscopie*, vol. 4, pp. 255–6.

Charbonneau, M.-A. (1999) 'An Encounter between Sartre and Lacan', *Sartre Studies International*, vol. 5, no. 2, ed. M. Scriven *et al.*, Oxford: Berghahn.

Cixous, H. and Clément, C. (1986) *The Newly Born Woman*, tran. B. Wing, Minneapolis: University of Minnesota Press.

Cohen-Solal, A. (1987) *Sartre: A Life*, London: Heinemann.

Cohn-Bendit, D. (1968) *The French Student Revolt*, tran. B. Brewster, New York: Hill and Wang.

Connolly, W. (1991) *Identity/Difference: Democratic Negotiations of Political Paradox*, Ithaca, NY: Cornell University Press.

—— (1993) 'Beyond Good and Evil: The Ethical Sensibility of Michel Foucault', *Political Theory*, 21 (3), 365–89.

Contat, M. (1996) 'Was Sartre a Democrat?', *Sartre Studies International*, vol. 2, no. 1, ed. M. Scriven *et al.*, Oxford: Berghahn.

Contat, M. and Rybalka, M. (1970) *Les écrits de Sartre*, Paris: Gallimard.

Corlett, W. (1989) *Community Without Unity: A Politics of Derridean Extravagance*, Durham, NC: Duke University Press.

Culler, J. (1976) *Ferdinand de Saussure*, New York: Penguin.

Deleuze, G. (1964) 'Il a été mon maître', *Arts* (November), 1207–27.

—— (1975) 'Ecrivain non: un nouveau cartographe', *Critique*, 343.

—— (1987) *Dialogues*, tran. H. Tomlinson and B. Habbersam, London: Athlone Press [1977].

—— (1994) *Difference and Repetition*, tran. P. Patton, London: Athlone Press [1968].

—— (1995) *Negotiations, 1972–1990*, tran. M. Joughin, New York: Columbia University Press.

Deleuze, G. and Guattari, F. (1983) *Anti-Oedipus*, Minneapolis: University of Minnesota Press [1972].

—— (1987) *A Thousand Plateaus*, Minneapolis: University of Minnesota Press [1980].

—— (1994) *What is Philosophy?*, London: Verso [1991].

Derrida, J. (1973) *Speech and Phenomena*, tran. D. Allison, Evanston, IL: Northwestern University Press [1967].

—— (1976) *Of Grammatology*, tran. G. Spivak, Baltimore: Johns Hopkins University Press [1967].

—— (1978) *Writing and Difference*, tran. A. Bass, Chicago: University of Chicago Press [1967].

—— (1981) *Positions*, tran. A. Bass, Chicago: University of Chicago Press [1972].

—— (1982) *Margins of Philosophy*, tran. A. Bass, Chicago: University of Chicago Press [1972].

—— (1983) 'The Principle of Reason: The University in the Eyes of its Pupils', *Diacritics*, 13, 47–52.

—— (1986) *Glas*, tran. J. Leavey and R. Rand, London: University of Nebraska Press [1974].

—— (1988) *Limited Inc.*, ed. G. Graff, Evanston, IL: Northwestern University Press [1988].

—— (1989) *Of Spirit: Heidegger and the Question*, tran. G. Bennington and R. Bowlby, Chicago: University of Chicago Press [1987].

—— (1994) *Spectres of Marx: The State of the Debt, the Work of Mourning and the New International*, tran. P. Kamuf, London: Routledge [1993].

—— (1996) 'Il courait mort: Salut, salut, Notes pour un courrier aux Temps Modernes', *Les temps modernes*, 587, 61–74.

Desan, W. (1966) *The Marxism of Jean-Paul Sartre*, New York: Anchor Books.

Dews, P. (1987) *Logics of Disintegration: Post-Structuralist Thought and the Claims of Critical Theory*, London: Verso.

Dobson, A. (1993) *Jean-Paul Sartre and the Politics of Reason: A Theory of History*, Cambridge: Cambridge University Press.

—— (1997) 'Sartre and Stalin: Critique of Dialectical Reason, Volume 2' in *Sartre Studies International*, vol. 3, no. 1, ed. M. Scriven *et al.*, Oxford: Berghahn.

Eagleton, T. (1990) *The Ideology of the Aesthetic*, Oxford: Blackwell.

Elster, J. (1986) *An Introduction to Karl Marx*, Cambridge: Cambridge University Press.

Ferry, L. and Renaut, A. (1990) *French Philosophy of the Sixties: An Essay on Anti-Humanism*, tran. M. Cattani, Amherst, MA: University of Massachusetts Press [1985].

Flynn, T. (1984) *Sartre and Marxist Existentialism*, Chicago: University of Chicago Press.

—— (1992) 'Sartre and the Poetics of History', in *The Cambridge Companion to Sartre*, ed. C. Howells, Cambridge: Cambridge University Press.

Foucault, M. (1970) *The Order of Things: An Archaeology of the Human Sciences*, tran. A. Sheridan-Smith, New York: Pantheon [1966].

—— (1972) *The Archaeology of Knowledge and Discourse on Language*, tran. A. Sheridan-Smith, New York: Pantheon [1969].

—— (1977a) *Discipline and Punish: The Birth of the Prison*, tran. A. Sheridan, Harmondsworth: Penguin [1975].

—— (1977b) *Language, Counter-Memory, Practice: Selected Essays and Interviews*, ed. C. Gordon, Oxford: Blackwell.

—— (1978) *The History of Sexuality: An Introduction*, vol. 1, tran. R. Hurley, Harmondsworth: Penguin [1976].

—— (1979) *Michel Foucault: Power, Truth, Strategy*, ed. M. Morris and P. Patton, Sydney: Feral Publications.

—— (1980) *Power/Knowledge: Selected Interviews and Other Writings, 1972–77*, ed. C. Gordon, Brighton: Harvester Press.

—— (1981) 'Is it Useless to Revolt?', *Philosophy and Social Criticism*, 8, 5–9.

—— (1983) 'How We Behave', with H. Dreyfus and P. Rabinow, *Vanity Fair*, November.

—— (1984) *The Foucault Reader*, ed. P. Rabinow, New York: Pantheon.

—— (1988) *Politics, Philosophy, Culture: Interviews and Other Writings, 1977–84*, tran. A. Sheridan-Smith, New York: Routledge.

—— (1991) *Remarks on Marx: Conversations with Duccio Trombadori*, tran. R. Goldstein and J. Cascaito, New York: Semiotext(e).

Gane, M. (1991) *Baudrillard: Critical and Fatal Theory*, London: Routledge.

Glucksmann, A. (1977) *Les maîtres penseurs*, Paris: Grasset.

Goodchild, P. (1996) *Deleuze and Guattari: An Introduction to the Politics of Desire*, London: Sage.

Gorz, A. (1966) 'Sartre and Marx', *New Left Review*, 37.

—— (1982) *Farewell to the Working-Class: An Essay on Post-Industrial Socialism*, tran. M. Sonenescher, London: Pluto Press.

Griffin, D. (1988) *The Re-Enchantment of Science: Postmodern Proposals*, Albany, NY: State University of New York Press.

Grimshaw, J. (1993) 'Practices of Freedom', in *Up Against Foucault*, ed. C. Ramazanoglu, London: Routledge.

Guattari, F. (1984) *Molecular Revolution*, Harmondsworth: Penguin [1977].

—— (1986) 'The Postmodern Dead End', *Flash Art*, 128, 40–1.

—— (1989) *Cartographies schizoanalytiques*, Paris: Galilée.

Guattari, F. and Negri, T. (1990) *Communists Like Us*, New York: Semiotext(e).

Habermas, J. (1987) *The Philosophical Discourse of Modernity*, Cambridge, MA: MIT Press.

Harland, R. (1987) *Superstructuralism*, London: Methuen.

Harvey, D. (1989) *The Condition of Postmodernity*, London: Blackwell.

Hassan, I. (1982) *The Dismemberment of Orpheus: Toward a Postmodern Literature*, New York: Oxford University Press.

—— (1987) *The Postmodern Turn*, Columbus, OH: Ohio State University Press.

Hayim, G. (1980) *The Existential Sociology of Jean-Paul Sartre*, Amherst, MA: University of Massachusetts Press.

Hayman, R. (1986) *Writing Against: A Biography of Sartre*, London: Weidenfeld and Nicolson.

Hirsh, A. (1982) *The French Left: A History and Overview*, Montreal: Rose Books.

Howells, C. (1988) *Sartre: The Necessity of Freedom*, Cambridge: Cambridge University Press.

—— (1992) 'Introduction' and 'Sartre and the Deconstruction of the Subject', in *The Cambridge Companion to Sartre*, ed. C. Howells, Cambridge: Cambridge University Press.

Hoy, D. (1986) 'Power, Repression, Progress: Foucault, Lukes and the Frankfurt School', in *Foucault: A Critical Reader*, ed. D. Hoy, Oxford: Blackwell.

—— (1993) 'Splitting the Difference: Habermas's Critique of Derrida', in *Working Through Derrida*, ed. G. Madison, Evanston, IL: Northwestern University Press.

Jameson, F. (1981) *The Political Unconscious*, New York: Cornell University Press.

—— (1984) 'Postmodernism, Or the Cultural Logic of Late Capitalism', *New Left Review*, 146, 53–93.

—— (1988) 'Cognitive Mapping', in *Marxism and the Interpretation of Culture*, ed. C. Nelson and L. Grossberg, Chicago: University of Illinois Press.

—— (1995) 'The Sartrean Origin', in *Sartre Studies International*, vol. 1, no. 1/2, ed. M. Scriven *et al.*, Oxford: Berghahn.

Jopling, D. (1992) 'Sartre's Moral Psychology', in *The Cambridge Companion to Sartre*, ed. C. Howells, Cambridge: Cambridge University Press.

Keat, R. (1981) 'Individualism and Community in Socialist Thought', in *Issues in Marxist Philosophy*, vol. 4, ed. J. Mepham and D. Hillel-Ruben, Brighton: Harvester Press.

Kellner, D. (1988) 'Postmodernism as a Social Theory: Some Challenges and Problems', *Theory, Culture, Society*, 5, 2–3, 239–70.

Kirsner, D. (1985) 'Sartre and the Collective Neurosis of Our Time', in *Sartre After Sartre*, ed. F. Jameson, Yale French Studies, no. 68.

Kruks, S. (1990) *Situation and Human Existence*, London: Unwin Hyman.

Lacan, J. (1977) *Ecrits: A Selection*, tran. A. Sheridan, London: Tavistock.

Laclau, E. and Mouffe, C. (1985) *Hegemony and Socialist Strategy: Towards a Radical Democratic Politics*, London: Verso.

—— (1987) 'Post-Marxism Without Apologies', *New Left Review*, 166, 79–106.

Lash, S. (1988) 'Postmodernism as a "Regime of Signification"', *Theory, Culture, Society*, 5, 2–3, 311–36.

Lefebvre, H. (1961) 'Critique de la Critique non critique', *La Nouvelle Revue Marxiste*, 1.

Levi, A. (1967) 'Existentialism and the Alienation of Man', in *Phenomenology and Existentialism*, ed. E. Lee and M. Mandelbaum, Baltimore.

Lévi-Strauss, C. (1966) *The Savage Mind*, London: Weidenfeld and Nicolson.

Lévy, B.-H. (1977) *La Barbarie à visage Humain*, Paris: Grasset.

Lipovetsky, G. (1983) *L'Ere du vide: essais sur l'individualisme contemporain*, Paris: Gallimard.

Lyotard, J.-F. (1973) *Derive à partir de Marx à Freud*, Paris: Union Générale d'Editions.

—— (1974) *Economie libidinale*, Paris: Minuit.

—— (1984a) *The Postmodern Condition*, tran. G. Bennington and B. Massumi, Minneapolis: University of Minnesota Press [1979].

—— (1984b) *Driftworks*, New York: Semiotext(e).

—— (1987) 'Rewriting Modernity', *Substance*, 54.

—— (1988) *The Differend*, Minneapolis: University of Minnesota Press [1983].

Lyotard, J.-F. and Thebaud, J.-L. (1985) *Just Gaming*, tran. W. Godzich, Minneapolis: University of Minnesota Press [1979].

Majumdar, M. (1997) 'The Intransigence of the Intellectual: Autonomy and Ideology in Althusser and Sartre', in *Sartre Studies International*, vol. 3, no. 1, ed. M. Scriven *et al.*, Oxford: Berghahn.

Marcuse, H. (1955) *Eros and Civilization*, New York: Vintage Books.

—— (1983) *From Luther to Popper*, tran. J. de-Bres, London: Verso.

Marx, K. (1973) *Grundrisse*, Harmondsworth: Penguin [1857].

—— (1975) *Early Writings*, ed. Q. Hoare, New York: Random House.

Marx, K. and Engels, F. (1965) *The German Ideology*, London: Lawrence & Wishart [1945].

—— (1982) *Collected Works*, New York: International Publishers, 1975–82.

McBride, W. (1991) *Sartre's Political Theory*, Bloomington, IN: Indiana University Press.

—— (1997) 'Existential Marxism and Postmodernism at our Fin de Siècle', in *Sartre's French Contemporaries and Enduring Influences*, ed. W. McBride, New York: Garland Publishing.

Meerster, F. and Meerster, M. (2000) 'An Interview with Bernard-Henri Lévy: Grandeur and Misery of Commitment' in *Sartre Studies International*, vol. 6, no. 2, ed. A. Leak, C. Howells, S. Hendley and A. Van den Hoven, Oxford: Berghahn.

Megill, A. (1985) *Prophets of Extremity: Nietzsche, Heidegger, Foucault, Derrida*, Berkeley, CA: University of California Press.

Merquior, J. G. (1985) *Foucault*, Berkeley: University of California Press.

Murdoch, I. (1953) *Sartre, Romantic Rationalist*, Cambridge: Bowes and Bowes.

Nietzsche, F. (1966) *Beyond Good and Evil*, tran. W. Kaufmann, New York: Random House [1886].

—— (1967) *On the Genealogy of Morals*, tran. R. Hollingdale and W. Kaufmann, New York: Random House [1887].

Poster, M. (1975) *Existential Marxism in Post-War France*, Princeton, NJ: Princeton University Press.

—— (1979) *Sartre's Marxism*, London: Pluto Press.

—— (1984) *Foucault, Marxism and History: Mode of Production versus Mode of Information*, Cambridge: Polity Press.

—— (1990) *The Mode of Information: Poststructuralism and Social Context*, Cambridge: Polity Press.

Ransom, J. (1993) 'Feminism, Difference and Discourse: The Limits of Discourse Analysis for Feminism', in *Up Against Foucault*, ed. C. Ramazanoglu, London: Routledge.

Raulet, G. (1983) 'Structuralism and Post-Structuralism: An Interview with Michel Foucault', tran. J. Harding, *Telos*, 55 (Spring), 195–211.

Reader, K. (1987) *Intellectuals and the Left in France since 1968*, Basingstoke: Macmillan.

Reich, W. (1972) *Sexual-Political Essays*, New York: Vintage Books.

Rorty, R. (1984) 'Habermas and Lyotard on Post-modernity', *Praxis International*, 4, 1, 32–44.

Rosenau, P. (1992) *Postmodernism and the Social Sciences: Insights, Inroads and Intrusions*, Princeton, NJ: Princeton University Press.

Schrift, A. (1995) *Nietzsche's French Legacy: A Genealogy of Poststructuralism*, London: Routledge.

Scriven, M. (1999) *Jean-Paul Sartre: Politics and Culture in Postwar France*, Basingstoke: Macmillan.

Silverman, H. (1980) 'Sartre's Words on the Self' in *Jean-Paul Sartre: Contemporary Approaches to his Philosophy*, ed. H. Silverman and F. Elliston, Pittsburgh: Duquesne University Press.

Simons, J. (1995) *Foucault and the Political*, London: Routledge.

Simont, J. (1985) 'The Critique of Dialectical Reason: From Need to Need, Circularly', in *Sartre After Sartre*, ed. F. Jameson, Yale French Studies, no. 68.

Singer, P. (1983) *Hegel*, Oxford: Oxford University Press.

Soper, K. (1986) *Humanism and Anti-Humanism*, London: Hutchinson.

Thody, P. (1992) *Jean-Paul Sartre*, Basingstoke: Macmillan.

Tucker, A. (1990) 'Vaclev Havel's Heideggerianism', *Telos*, 85, 63–80.

Vattimo, G. (1988) *The End of Modernity: Nihilism and Hermeneutics in Post-Modern Culture*, London: Polity Press.

Walzer, M. (1979) *The Company of Critics*, London: Peter Haber.

Warnock, M. (1965) *The Philosophy of Sartre*, London: Hutchinson.

APPENDIX 1

Chronology of Texts

Original year of publication in France.

1936   *La transcendence de l'égo*
1938   *La nausée*
1943   *L'être et le néant*
1947   *L'existentialisme est un humanisme*
1949   *Qu'est-ce que la littérature?*
1957   *Mythologies* (Barthes)
1960   *Critique de la raison dialectique*, vol. 1
1962   *La pensée sauvage* (Lévi-Strauss)
1963   *Les mots*
1965   *Lire le capital* (Althusser and Balibar)
1966   *Ecrits* (Lacan)
        Les mots et les choses (Foucault)
1967   *De la grammatologie* (Derrida)
        L'écriture et la différence (Derrida)
1969   *L'archéologie du savoir* (Foucault)
1971   *L'idiot de la famillé*, vols. 1 and 2
1972   *L'anti-Œdipe* (Deleuze and Guattari)
        Marges de la philosophie (Derrida)
1973   *Le plaisir du texte* (Barthes)
        Le miroir de la production (Baudrillard)
1974   *Glas* (Derrida)
        Economie libidinale (Lyotard)
        L'idiot de la famille, vol. 3
1975   *Surveiller et punir* (Foucault)
1976   *Histoire de la sexualité*, vol. 1 (Foucault)
1977   *Oublier Foucault* (Baudrillard)
1979   *La condition postmoderne* (Lyotard)

1980   *Mille plateaux* (Deleuze and Guattari)
1983   *Le différend* (Lyotard)
        Cahiers pour une morale
1985   *Critique de la raison dialectique*, vol. 2
1993   *Spectres de Marx* (Derrida)

APPENDIX 2

Jean-Paul Sartre (1905–80): A Brief Chronology

1905, 21 June: born Jean-Paul-Baptiste-Eymard Sartre near Paris.

1915: after a period of private tuition, attends Lyceé Henri IV where he becomes classmates with Paul Nizan.

1924: starts at the Ecole Normale Supérieure where he later meets Simone de Beauvoir with whom he would share a famous intellectual and emotional partnership until his death.

1933–4: undertakes a year's study at the French Institute in Berlin where he becomes acquainted with the phenomenology of Edmund Husserl.

1938: *La nausée* published by Gallimard.

1940s: taken as prisoner-of-war by the German army. As he commented in his *War Diaries*, this experience precipitated a change in his philosophical perspective leading him to a more political outlook which, by the end of the 1940s, culminated in his involvement with the RDR (*Rassemblement Démocratique Révolutionnaire*).

1942: completes *L'être et le néant*, his most important and famous work of existentialist philosophy.

1944: along with Simone de Beauvoir and friend and fellow philosopher Maurice Merleau-Ponty forms editorial committee for the journal *Les temps modernes*.

1945: gives lecture at the Club Maintenant in Paris in which he explains the basis of existentialism. Contrary to popular characterizations of existentialism as 'an invitation to people to dwell in the quietism of despair', Sartre claims that it is at heart a 'humanist philosophy of action, of effort, of combat, of solidarity . . .'.

1950s: the 1950s marked the increasing politicization of Sartre, beginning with growing support for the PCF (Parti Communiste Français) in the early 1950s and ending with outspoken denunciations of Soviet oppression in Eastern Europe. Also during this time Sartre speaks out against French colonialism, participating in a press conference in 1958 about the violation of human rights in Algeria.

1961, July: bomb attack on Sartre's flat in the Rue Bonaparte. Months earlier, following his signature of the Manifesto of 121 supporting civil disobedience in Algeria, 5000 war veterans including members of the OAS (Organisation de l'Armée Secrète) had marched down the Champs-Elysées shouting 'Kill Sartre'.

1962: elected Vice-President of the Congrés de la Communauté Européene des Ecrivains (COMES).

1964: refuses the Nobel Prize for Literature.

1968: fervently supports the student movement and uprisings.

1970s: Following the events of 1968, Sartre involves himself with Maoist and gauchiste groups, condemning the PCF as 'the largest conservative party in France'.

1970: becomes the nominal editor of *La Cause du Peuple* (a Maoist newspaper banned by the French government) and is arrested for distributing it in the Grands Boulevards.

1971: publication of *L'idiot de la Famille*, vols 1 and 2, his lengthy biography of Gustave Flaubert.

1974: meets Andreas Baader in Stammheim prison before the Baader-Meinhof trial in West Germany.

1980, April 15: after a long period of ill health, Sartre dies.

April 19: a crowd of over 50,000 people gather at the cemetery Montparnasse for his funeral procession which is broadcast on French television.

Index